NORTH BY NORTHWEST

by Christopher Weicht

Creekside  Division of
Publications MCW Enterprises

NORTH BY NORTHWEST

By Christopher Weicht

Chris Weicht
846 Joe Road, R.R.# 26
Roberts Creek, B.C.
V0N 2W6
Canada

Printed in Victoria, Canada

Cover Design by Malcolm Arthur depicts a Canadian Airboard deHavilland DH 9 traversing Yoho National Park in 1920
Interior design by Kim Clark
This author gratefully acknowledges product support from Chevron Canada
Published by Creekside publications in association with Trafford Publishing

Note for Librarians: a cataloguing record for this book that includes Dewey Classification and US Library of Congress numbers is available from Library and Archives Canada. The complete cataloguing record can be obtained from the Library and Archives Canada online database at: www.nlc-bnc.ca/amicus/index-e.html

ISBN 1-4120-2456-0

Published by CREEKSIDE PUBLICATIONS 846 Joe Road, R.R.#26 Roberts Creek, B.C. V0N 2W6, CANADA
Phone 604-886-6877 Fax 604-886-6867
E- mail sales cweicht@uniserve.com

In association with:
TRAFFORD PUBLISHING Suite 6E, 2333 Government St, Victoria, B.C. CANADA

Trafford Catalogue #04-0284

Table of Contents

Preface

This presentation of aviation history in the northwest differs from others in that it offers an in-depth historical review of each community's aviation presence along a predefined route.

Prior to the advent of modern air transportation, pilots of land based aircraft en route to the Yukon and Alaska sought an inland route through the interior of British Columbia to avoid the generally poorer weather and lack of airfields along the coast. Aircraft originating in the United States frequently departed that country via Spokane, Washington then proceeding north via central British Columbia. Aviation within the interior of British Columbia quickly developed following the first flights through this area and civic officials were quick to see the possibilities that air travel could bring to their often isolated communities.

The author has selected an airfield format for each community airfield, similar to those depicted in early pilot route manuals. Each describes its location and elevation, an airfield description, and often is accompanied by an airfield diagram and or a photograph. Much confusion exists in the description of aircraft landing areas throughout aviation's brief history i.e. landing ground, alighting area, landing field, air harbour, airfield, airstrip, and airport. The author has chosen to use the term airfield in reference to all but modern international airports. The term air harbour was used in the 1920's to describe both land and water landing areas and Canadian Air Board licenses were issued using this term. The author has also chosen to identify certain sea plane landing areas as air harbours as that term is fully descriptive of their purpose.

Historically, aviation uses the mile and the foot as its units of measurement and this format continues in use to this day. Therefore, to conform to this concept, the author has chosen to use these measures throughout rather than the metric system.

Many men and women have contributed to the historical information given here. Without their photographs, mementoes, and anecdotal stories this undertaking would not have been possible.

While this series attempts to fully record the aviation history of all the communities covered, I have chosen to place special emphasis on the smaller locations, often previously neglected by other historical presentations. Many, in fact, have no airfield today.

The title of this series stems from my previous publication *JERICHO BEACH and the WEST COAST FLYING BOAT STATION*S. When the Canadian Air Board advertised for pilots to staff its Air Stations across the country in 1919, the job description was stated as *AIR PILOT NAVIGATOR*. So, in honour of these pioneer airmen, many of whom went on to become commercial aviation's trailblazers, the title *AIR PILOT NAVIGATOR* has been selected for this projected series of seven books.

Chris Weicht

Acknowledgments

Airport Directory Company 1936, Hackensack, New Jersey
Ashcroft Museum
Attwood, W.C., Estate, Salmon Arm, BC
Aviation Archeological Investigation and Research, Mesa, Arizona
Boeing Company Historical Archives, Seattle, Washington
Brown, Jim, Pender Island, BC
Bulkley Valley Archives and Museum
Burke, Brian, Estate
Campbell,Ron, Victoria, BC
Canadian Airlines International Archives
Canadian Aviation Historical Society, Ottawa
Canadian Museum of Flight and Transportation, Langley, BC
CFS Masset, Queen Charlotte Islands, BC
Clark, Kim, Sechelt, BC
Consolidated Aircraft Corporation
Cooper, Donald S., Terrace, BC
Crombie,Alex, Trail, BC
Crosson, Joe, Estate
Cruikshank, J.
D.N.D. via Air Command Heritage & History, Westwin, Manitoba
Department of National Defence, Ottawa
Directorate of History, DND, Ottawa
Dubé,Timothy, Ottawa
Ellis,via Frank H.
Gilbert, Walther E., Estate
Gowans, Bruce, Calgary, Alberta
Hampshire, Al
Harbottle,Jean, Vernon, BC
Hazleton Museum
Hewlett,Frank, Prince George, BC
Hood, Richard
Hunter, Jack, Estate

Jane's All the World'sAircraft, ('27,'31,'38,'40,'43,'45,'53,'58)
Jarmin, Lloyd, Estate
Jasper Yellowhead Archives
Kamloops Museum and Archives
Kelowna Archives
Luck,Sheldon, Oliver, BC
Macleod, Earl, Estate, Vancouver, BC
Madill, Lock, White Rock, BC
Maude,George, Sidney, BC
McBride Public Library
McIvor,Dan, Burkeville, BC
Milberry, Larry, Toronto, Ontario
Miles, E.L. Edmonton, Alberta
Morrow, Trelle,Prince George, BC
Museum of Flight, Seattle, Washington
National Archives of Canada, Ottawa, Ontario
National Museum of Science, Ottawa
Naval Historical Center, Aviation History Branch; U.S. Navy, Washington, D.C.
North Peace Museum & Archives, Fort StJohn, BC
Oliver Archives
Penticton Archives
Place,Hilary, formerly of Dog Creek, BC
Prest, Clarence Oliver, Estate
Prince Rupert City & Regional Archives
Provincial Archives of Alberta
Public Archives of Canada, Ottawa
Quesnel Archives
Rowe, G. A. Library, CFB Comox, BC
Royal Canadian Air Force, D.N.D.
Ruotsala, Jim, Juneau, Alaska
Schofield. Jack, Sidney, BC
Septer, Dirk
Spillsbury, Jim, Estate
Stangoe,Irene, Williams Lake, BC

Acknowledgments

Stevenson,Henry, Nelson, BC
Templeton,Chris and Rose, Penticton, BC
U.S. Forest Service
United States Air Force Archives
Vancouver Public Library, Vancouver, BC
Vanderhoof Archives
Vernon Archives
Vernon, Jerry, Burnaby, BC
Vincenzi, Tony, Kitwanga, BC

Washington State Division of Aeronautics
Western Canada Aviation Museum
White, Elwood, Shawnigan Lake, BC
Wien, Noel, Trust Collection
Williams Lake Historical Society
Williams Lake Museum
Williamson, George, Sidney, BC
Worthylake, Mary, Estate

Abbreviations

AACS (U.S.) Army Air Corps, Army Airways Communication System
ABC 22Joint Canadian-United States Defence Plan No 2,1941
AC Army Cooperation Squadron
a/c aircraft
AC1 Aircraftman First Class
AC2 Aircraftman Second Class
A/C Air Commodore
ACAS Assistant Chief of Air Staff
A/C/M Air Chief Marshall
ADC Aircraft Detection Core
ADJ ....adjutant
AFB Air Force Base
AFC Air Force Cross
AFHQ Air Force Headquarters (RCAF)
A/M Air Marshall
AOC air officer commanding
A/S anti-submarine
ASR Air Sea Rescue
ASW anti-submarine warfare
A/V/M Air Vice-Marshall
AWA Alaska Washington Airways
AWOL absent without leave
BCATP British Commonwealth Air Training Station
BR.Bomber Reconnaissance Squadron (anti-submarine)
BCRD British Columbia Reconnaissance Detachment
CAC Coast Artillery Squadron
CAF Canadian Air Force (1920-1924)
CAFA Canadian Air Force Association
CAS chief of the air staff
Cat "A" category aircraft accident: a write-off
Cat "B" category aircraft accident: major, repairable at depot
Cat "C" category aircraft accident: major, repairable at unit

Cat "D" category aircraft accident: major, repairable at unit
CBCA Central B.C. Airways
CFRC Canadian Forces Recruiting Centre
CFS Canadian Forces Station
CFTSD.Canadian Forces Technical Service Detachment
CG chief of the general staff (Canadian army)
CinC commander in chief
CMU Construction and Maintenance Unit
CNR Canadian National Railway
CO commanding officer
Col ...Colonel
Com communications
COMINCO Consolidated Mining & Smelting Company, Trail, B.C.
CPA Canadian Pacific Airlines
Cpl ...Corporal
CPR Canadian Pacific Railway
CV Canadian Vickers
CWAC Canadians Women's Army Corps
CWC Cabinet War Committee (Canada)
DAS Director of Air Staff
DCAS Deputy Chief of the Air Staff
DCGAO Directorate of Civil Government Air Operations
DET Detachment
DF direction finding
DFC Distinguished Flying Cross
DFM Distinguished Flying Medal
DM deputy minister
DND Department of National Defence
DOT Department of Transportation
DR dead reckoning
DRO Daily Routine Orders
DSO Distinguished Service Order
DWC Douglas World Cruisers
EAC Eastern Air Command
EFTS Elementary Flying Training School

Abbreviations

Eng ......engineer
ETA estimated time of arrival
F fighter squadron
FB Flying Boat Squadron
FE Flight Engineer
F/L Flight Lieutenant
F/O Flying Officer
F/Sgt Flight Sergeant
FTS Flying Training School
G/C Group Captain
GMT Greenwich Mean Time
GP General Purpose Squadron
GR General Reconnaissance Squadron
GVRD Greater Vancouver Regional District
HF high frequency
HF/DF high frequency direction finding
HMS His Majesty's Ship
HMCS His Majesty's Canadian Ship
HWE Home War Establishment
ICA International Civil Aviation Organization
IG inspector general
JAG judge advocate general
JCS Joint Chiefs of Staff (United States)
LAC Leading Aircraftman
LCol Lieutenant-Colonel
LFWA Land Force Western Area
Lt ..Lieutenant
Maj ....Major
MARPAC Maritime Pacific Command
MC Military Cross
MD Military District
MO medical officer
MED ..medical
MLA Member of the Legislative Assembly
MP Member of Parliament
MT motor transport
MTB motor torpedo boat
NAC National Archives of Canada
NCO Non-Commissioned Officer

NDHQ National Defence Headquarters, Ottawa
NDB non-directional beacon
NORAD North American Air Defence Command
NPF Non-Permanent Force (RCAF)
NRC National Research Council
NWAC North West Air Command
OBE Order of the British Empire
obs observer
OC officer commanding
OIC officer in charge
OTS Operational Training Squadron
OUT Operational Training UnitPAA Provincial Archives of Alberta
PAC Public Archives Canada
PanAm Pan American Airways
PC order-in-council
PDSIU Pacific Detachment Special Investigative Unit
PF Permanent Force
PJBD Canada-U.S. Permanent Joint Board on Defence
P/O Pilot Officer
PWA Pacific Western Airlines
QCA Queen Charlotte Airlines
QM Quarter Master
QMG Quarter Master General
RAF Royal Air Force
RCAF Royal Canadian Air Force
RCCS Royal Canadian Corps of Signals
RCMP Royal Canadian Mounted Police
RCN Royal Canadian Navy
RCNAS Royal Canadian Naval Air Service
RDF radar direction finding
RF radio frequency
RFC Royal Flying Corps
RN Royal Navy
RNAF Royal Norwegian Air Force

Abbreviations

RNAS Royal Naval Air Service
RNNAF Royal Norwegian Naval Air Force
RO radio operator or radio officer
SAO senior air officer
SAR Search and Rescue
SASO senior air staff officer
SFTS Service Flying Training School
Sgt Sergeant
Standard Pilot Pilot with incomplete training
      assigned to guard duty, etc.
S/L Squadron Leader
SOS struck off strength
Sqn Squadron
SSgt Staff Sergeant
STANAVO Standard Aviation Oil Company
TB Torpedo Bomber Squadron
TOS taken on strength
UAT United Air Transport
u/s unserviceable
u/s a/c unserviceable aircraft
USAAC United States Army Air Corps
USAF United States Air Force
USN United States Navy
USS United States Ship
USSR Union of Soviet Socialist Republics
VAN DET Vancouver Detachment Canadian
      Forces Base Chilliwack
VATCO Vancouver Aerial Transportation
      Company
WAC Western Air Command
WAG wireless air gunner/wireless operator
W/C Wing Commander
WCA Western Canada Airways
WCAM Western Canada Aviation Museum
W/D Women's Division
WO1 Warrant Officer First Class
WO2 Warrant Officer Second Class
W/T wireless telegraphy

YMCA Young Men's Christian Association
YSAT Yukon Southern Air Transport
Z Greenwich Mean Time (Zulu time)

Foreword

Aviation history is much more than collection of places and aircraft. It is a history of economic development, military actions, communities and people's lives. Western Canada's aviation history is rich and exciting, as the unique geography of the region was a natural fit for the movement of goods and people by air, developing remote regions of the country and facilitating commerce and trade.

There are a few of us who fly for the joy of flying itself. However, for most people, the actual flying is often over-shadowed by the reason for the flight itself. We have progressed tremendously from the days when people used to pay for exhibition flights to experience the thrill of flying. Technological advances and training have made flying a safe, affordable means to visit friends and family, conduct business, and ship goods. Chris' work spans the pioneering first mail flights to the present day jets of commercial flying.

For those who have flown these routes to the small and large communities profiled or recognize aircraft that have had the pleasure of your contact in the pages of Chris' series, the memories of your own experience will be revived with clarity. For those who read with a passionate interest in the aviation history that shaped Western Canada, a new world of understanding and appreciation will be elicited. In either case, on your next WestJet trip across the rugged terrain of Western Canada, Chris' work will surely bring your thoughts down some 30,000 feet and back several years as your mind traces the history of the communities, aircraft and lives chronicled in this series.

Clive Beddoe

Clive Beddoe
Chairman, President and CEO
WestJet

March 2003

Introduction

BRITISH COLUMBIA AVIATION COUNCIL
4360 - Agar Drive, Richmond, BC V7B 1A3
Tel (604) 278-9330 Fax (604) 278-8210
Web www.bcaviation.org Email bcac@telus.net

March 25, 2003

Dear Reader,

Those daring young men in their flying machines opened up this magnificent province called British Columbia. It was a formidable task to fly in this province with mountains towering around you, with few instruments to guide the pilot and often as not the instruments were unreliable. That was the plight of the first group of aviators who challenged the elements in British Columbia.

In 1912 a Curtis Pusher flew over Armstrong piloted by Billy Stark. Mr. Stark learned to fly in San Diego California. He was the first licensed pilot in British Columbia and the second in Canada. Can you imagine the sight of this Curtis Pusher, all wires and fabric whistling in the wind, with all the citizens of this small Okanagan community their heads turned up to see and hear this calliope of sound. It was an aeroplane! Flight born in the mythology of Icarus.

Chris Weicht an accomplished pilot himself has chronicled the history of aviation in British Columbia. He captures the exploits of daring and defeat, accomplishment and failure. Weicht flew with many of the men he writes about. The names, now history, still resonant the role call of those who led the way such as Bertalino, McGregor, McIvor, Hoy, Duddle, Seymour, Luck, Dunbar, Baker, Coote, Gilbert and McConachie.
The men and women of this era created aviation history day-by-day, mile-by-mile, and built an industry that now flourishes in our province and Canada.

This is Volume One of a series that aviation author Chris Weicht has researched: he not only interviewed aviators, he also searched out next of kin who opened up their photo albums and often related the exploits of flights. He tapped all the sources around the province to present this outstanding historical aviation book. It is yours to enjoy.

Yours truly,

G.N. (Jerry) Lloyd
President and Chief Executive Officer

Celebrating 100 Years of Powered Flight

Air Route Chart (RCAF)

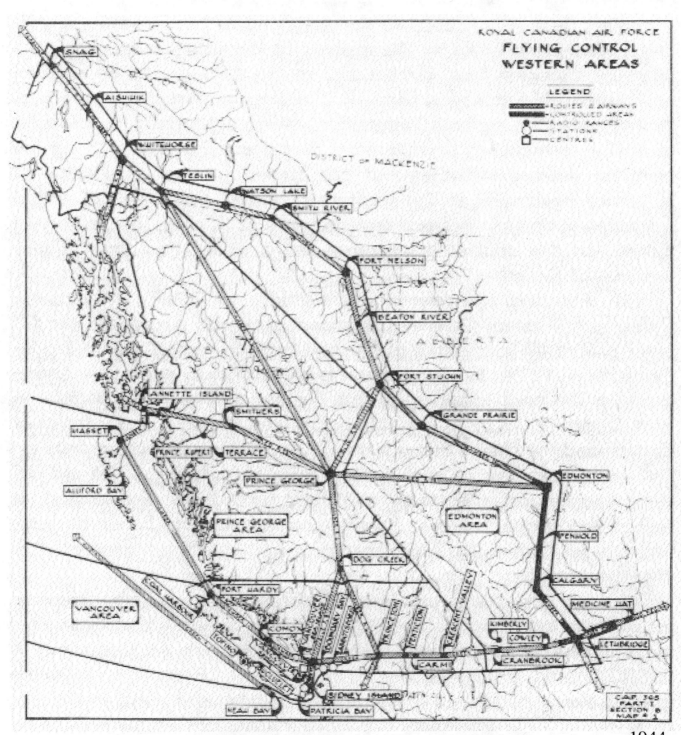

1944

13

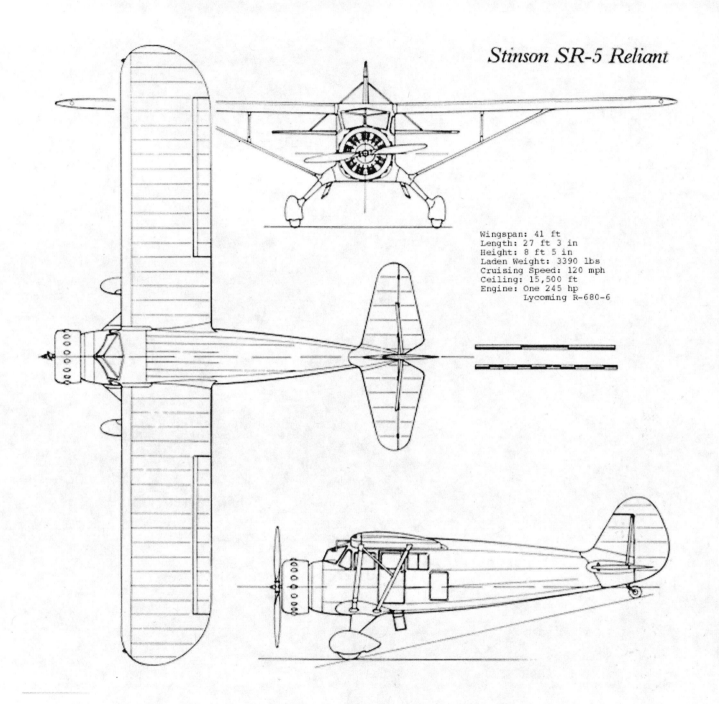

Stinson SR-5 Reliant

Wingspan: 41 ft
Length: 27 ft 3 in
Height: 8 ft 5 in
Laden Weight: 3390 lbs
Cruising Speed: 120 mph
Ceiling: 15,500 ft
Engine: One 245 hp
        Lycoming R-680-6

Spokane

The first ascent by man over Spokane reportedly occurred in 1906 when a balloon rose above the city. Four years later, the first flight by an airplane in Washington State happened at Seattle on March 11, 1910, which inspired a number of aviation enthusiasts in the northwest, including a man named Dishman who built and flew an aircraft of Bleriot design at Spokane.

Herb Munter was one of the first flyers to visit Spokane making a flight in 1920 from Seattle to Spokane in company with two passengers, in 2 hours and 50 minutes. Munter, at age 18, built the first aircraft constructed in Washington State, after which he became the first employee of Pacific Aero Products, later renamed the Boeing Airplane Company.

During 1920, aviator Foster Russell of the Russell Aviation School operated at Spokane offering flight training. One student of the school was a Canadian. Nelson, B.C., railroad engineer Clarence M. Lammedee had been inspired by an exhibition flight at Nelson on September 25, 1919. The following summer he journeyed to the Russell Aviation School at Spokane where he learned to fly and purchased plans and an engine for a homebuilt aircraft.

On June 21, 1922, Clarence Oliver "Ollie" Prest arrived over Spokane in his Standard J-1, the yellow-grey biplane christened the Polar Bear II. He had departed May 10 from Buffalo, New York, and had barnstormed his way across the country

C.O. "Ollie" Prest's Standard J-1 landed at the Foster Russell Field, June 21, 1922. Prest

en route to Seattle, from where he intended to continue by ship to Juneau, Alaska, and then fly on to Siberia. Prest landed in Spokane at the Foster Russell Field at 8:00 p.m. and remained overnight before departing westbound at 7:05 a.m. the following day.

In 1923, a de Havilland DH-4 bomber was loaned to the U.S. Forest Service by the U.S. Air Service. It was based in Spokane and was flown by Nick Mamer on fire patrols over the forests of eastern Washington State.

In 1924, Spokane's citizens raised $10,000 in order to finance the establishment of the first National Guard Air Corps Unit in Washington State, and the third in the nation. The 116th Observation Squadron, 116th Photo Section, and its Medical Detachment were soon established at Parkwater Field northeast of the city. These units were part of the 41st Division, Washington National Guard, initially equipped with Curtiss

JN-4 "Jenny" training biplanes, but later to receive de Havilland DH-4 and Douglas O-2 aircraft.

In 1927, Nick Mamer used a Buhl "Airster" in the Spokane National Air Race. Janes AWA

Spokane's Parkwater Field was located some five miles northeast of the city close to the Foster Russell Field. Eventually, Parkwater Field was enlarged and improved, and was renamed in 1927 as Felts Field in honour of National Guard Lieutenant Felts who had earlier been killed in a Curtiss JN-4 "Jenny".

The first Federal Air Regulations came into effect during 1926 and its regulations decreed the requirements for pilots, aircraft, and airfields. One of the first licensed airports in the nation was at Felts Field, Spokane.

Felts Field was built on 400 acres of land at an altitude of 2,000 feet above sea level. The irregular shaped field was 7,000 feet by 2,400 feet of sod and gravel. The Spokane River is on its north west side and railroad tracks and high power lines are on the southeast side.

On September 24, 1927, Spokane hosted the "Spokane National Air Race" in which 70 planes participated in two races culminating at Spokane, one originating in New York and the other in Los Angeles. $60,000 of prize money, raised by local businesses, resulted in hot competition. 100,000 spectators were on hand to witness the record breaking events which preceded each of the two day shows. Nicholas B. "Nick" Mamer of Spokane was an entrant in the race, flying a specially built Buhl "Airster" open cockpit biplane powered by a 200 hp Wright J-5 Whirlwind engine. Nick

Nick Mamer (L) and Art Walker (R). Museum of Flight

Mamer would finish third in the Class A event.

Mamer made aviation history on August 15, 1929, when he took off from Spokane's Felts Field on an endurance flight to New York and back without landing, a flight of 7,200 miles in 115 hours. Nick Mamer was a staunch advocate of Buhl airplanes ever since he participated in the Spokane National Air Race in 1927, and for his endurance flight selected a standard model Buhl CA-6 registered as N-962B and christened "Spokane Sun God". The aircraft was fitted with extra tanks for a total of 320

Mamer's Buhl CA-6 N-962B, the "Spokane Sun God", August 1929. Museum of Flight

Spokane

Modern air photo of Felts Field looking North.
Washington State Division of Aeronautics

FACILITIES

Hangars

Office Building

Telephone

Gasoline at Mamer Air Transport

Phone: Lakeview 1964

Standard Oil Phone Main 1191

ELEVATION - 1953'

POSITION
LAT. 47°38'N. LONG. 117°31'W.
4.5 miles E. of city

OPERATED BY
Municipal

REMARKS
Location of National Guard
Squadron #41

Open to all pilots

Old National Bank building near
city centre, marked **SPOKANE
AIRPORT** with arrow pointing to
field.

Spokane River on NW side R.R.
track and high power wires on SE
side.

Circle, "T" and field name on roof
of Army Hangar

Revolving beacon on hill NW 12
large flood lights mounted on
hangars. Boundary lights.

RUNWAYS
Gravel
NW - SW 7000'
NW - SE 2400'
(Irregular shape on 400 acres of
land)

OBSTRUCTIONS (ASL)
Pole line, buildings S and E
Grain elevator 2 miles W

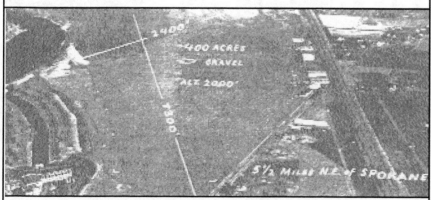

Early 1930's air photo of Felts Field looking East.
Airport Directory Company 1934

1929
Spokane

Felts Field, 1929. Museum of Flight

Alexander Eaglerock NC-3950, two biplanes and a Ford Trimotor at Felts Field, August 12, 1934. Henry Stevenson Collection via Nelson Museum

Two Spokane-based Swallow biplanes were used in the filming of the movie "Pyjamas", seen here at High River, Alberta, July 1927.
Bruce Gowans

Taylorcraft J-2 Cub at Felts Field, July 1937. H. Stevenson

Spokane

gallons capacity. En route, the "Sun God" was refueled in flight eleven times after a difficult takeoff from Felts Field due to the heavy fuel load.

The first refueling took place over San Francisco, where Mamer and co-pilot Art Walker maneuvered their craft under the refueling plane named the "Californian". Walker was able to safely grasp the whipping hose dangling below the flying fuel tanker. Their flight would take five days to complete, at an average speed of 65 mph. The most memorable refueling occurred at 10,000 feet over Wyoming, when turbulence and the altitude caused a few anxious moments.

Walter T. Varney of San Mateo, California, had been successfully operating an airmail contract for the U.S. Post Office since 1926 between Pasco, Washington, and Elko, Nevada, originally

National Guard Douglas O-38 at Felts Field, August 12, 1934. H. Stevenson

with a Swallow biplane capable of carrying five passengers or mail. During the summer of 1929, Varney won the airmail route from Portland to Seattle and Spokane to Pasco and a year later in 1930 provided passenger service between all these points.

Spokane's National Guard Air Corps Unit participated in international goodwill flights. At the grand opening of the Grand Forks, B.C. airfield on May 9, 1929, several Air Guard Douglas O-38

Varney Air Transport's Stinson SR-7 NC-295-W at Felts Field, 1936. H. Stevenson

aircraft, led by Lieutenant C.E. Forbes, were the first visiting aircraft to arrive.

By 1934, United Air Lines, which had previously been part of the Boeing conglomerate, was operating coast to coast with a direct link through

United Air Lines' Boeing 247D NC-19314 at Felts Field, August 13, 1934. H. Stevenson

Spokane from Seattle on a route through Salt Lake City. The route was flown with the new Boeing 247 airliners.

Nick Mamer and Mamer Air Transport became well known throughout the northwest, and the Mamer Trimotor Ford 4-AT-65, NC-8405, was a regular visitor across the border in B.C. at airfield opening celebrations and air meets.

Urban sprawl of the growing city, as well as noise of larger and more powerful aircraft, resulted in the need for a new and unrestricted airfield. Geiger Field was developed nine miles west of the city in the latter part of the 1930's period and in the post-World War II era was renamed Spokane International.

Felts Field would also become inadequate to the needs of the Army Air Corps, and in 1942 Fairchild Air Force Base was established west of the city of Spokane. The Air Corps established an engine overhaul facility at Fairchild A.F.B. which overhauled over 10,000 engines, as well as 1,250 B-17 Bombers for the war effort by 1945. In postwar years, Fairchild would become a USAF Strategic Air Command Base housing B-29 and B-36 Bomber Units. During the Cold War, Boeing B-52s were stationed there after 1957.

Ford TRI Motor N-9542 works on forest fire protection in Eastern Washington　　　　　U.S. Forest Service

SPOKANE
(Geiger Field) WASH.

POSITION
U.S. Sectional Chart:
SPOKANE
47°38' N. 117°31' W.
6 miles S.W. of city

| ALTITUDE | 2372' |
| VARIATION | 22°E. |

LANDING THRU OVERCAST			
DAY		NIGHT	
CEILING	VIS	CEILING	VIS
1000'	2	1000'	2
TAKE OFF THRU OVERCAST			
DAY		NIGHT	
CEILING	VIS	CEILING	VIS
1000'	2	1000'	2

RUNWAYS
(hard surfaced)
02 - 20	8200' x 150'
07 - 25	8200' x 150'
16 - 34	6960' x 150'

LIGHTING
Rotating beacon. Boundary lights. Contact lights. Obstruction lights. Flood lights.

OBSTRUCTIONS (A.S.L.)
E.–Water tank (2500') adjacent, lighted

RADIO DATA
	RECS	TRANS
RADIO RANGE:	3105	365
CLASS: SBRAZ - DT	3117.5	
(Call KGAS. W/T)	4495	
	6210	
CONTROL TOWER:	3105	396
	3117.5	(126.18
	4495	Mc/s)
	6210	
	(126.18	
	Mc/s)	

(Other frequencies on request)

Weather in the clear from range, time 29 M. No code.

RUNWAY ELEVATIONS
02 - 2368'	20 - 2320'
07 - 2372'	34 - 2372'
16 - 2324'	25 - 2368'

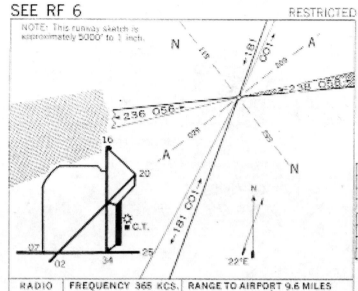

NOTE: This runway sketch is approximately 5000' to 1 inch.

| RADIO RANGE | FREQUENCY 365 KCS. IDENT. SM · · · | RANGE TO AIRPORT 9.6 MILES AT 232° MAGNETIC |

INSTRUMENT APPROACH PROCEDURE

("Z" Marker)

1. Twenty minutes before E.T.A. at range station call range requesting altimeter setting.
2. Initial approach 8000' a.s.l.
3. Shuttle—None.
4. Upon arrival at cone proceed out E. leg (final approach leg) for 3 minutes (6 miles) descending to 7000' a.s.l.
5. Make procedure turn left (to north of E. leg) for return to station (final approach). Altitude over range station 5500 a.s.l.
6. Passing cone, change heading 6° left to 232° Mag. and let down to minimum of 3350' a.s.l. following W. leg.
7. Ground contact not made at authorized minimum (see below) seconds after passing cone, Pull Up, full power to 8000' a.s.l. straight ahead.

MINIMUM SAFE ALTITUDES
For 1000 feet clearance
Orientation within 25 miles 7000' a.s.l.
Orientation LOST (within 100 miles)

8000
3 MIN. DESCENT TO 7000
DESCENT TO 5500
MINIMUM 3350' A.S.L.
W.   2372' A.S.L. (NO CONTOUR SKETCH AVAILABLE)   E.

PULL UP TIME RANGE TO AIRPORT 9.6 MILES
110 M.P.H.	120 M.P.H.	130 M.P.H.	140 M.P.H.	150 M.P.H.	160 M.P.H.
5 M. 14 S.	4 M. 48 S.	4 M. 26 S.	4 M. 06 S.	3 M. 50 S.	3 M. 36 S.

Spokane

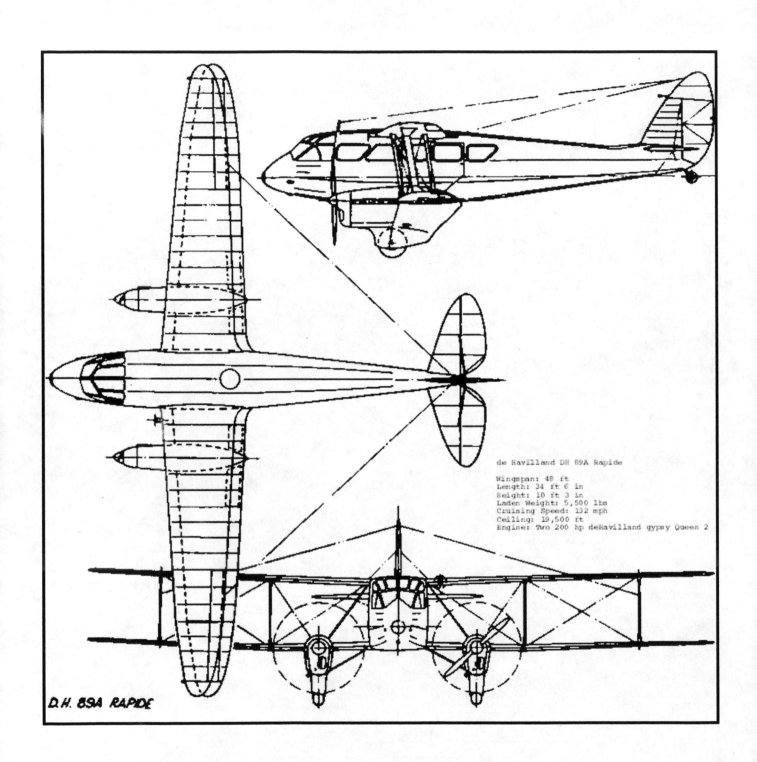

de Havilland DH 89A Rapide

Wingspan: 48 ft
Length: 34 ft 6 in
Height: 10 ft 3 in
Laden Weight: 5,500 lbs
Cruising Speed: 132 mph
Ceiling: 19,500 ft
Engine: Two 200 hp deHavilland gypsy Queen 2

D.H. 89A RAPIDE

Spokane

Aphotograph in the Vernon Archives shows what appears to be a Curtiss Pusher type biplane stated to be over Penticton in 1917 and further reports that it was possibly Billy Stark's aircraft.

Curtiss type Pusher claimed to be in flight over Penticton in 1917. Vernon Archives

Stark, a Vancouver shoe merchant, learned to fly in San Diego, California, at the Curtiss Aviation School where he received Aero Club of America licence number 110 on April 10, 1912. He was the first licenced pilot in British Columbia and the second in Canada.

Stark immediately purchased a Curtiss Exhibition Type biplane with a V8 Curtiss type engine and had it shipped to Vancouver where he began a series of exhibition flights. He was invited to the Okanagan town of Armstrong on July 1, 1912, and gave a performance to 4,000 people. Later that same month Stark journeyed to Portland, Oregon, and, while flying another

pilot's aircraft he had an engine failure and crashed in a parking lot but was not badly injured. However, his injuries prevented him from flying at Nelson in September. Instead, he passed the flight to an American aviator, Walter Edwards.

Stark resumed flying in 1914 and gave an exhibition at Chilliwack on July 4. He was later responsible for the organization of a training school for World War I pilots for the Royal Flying Corps. Stark later sold his Curtiss to the Aero Club of B.C. in 1915. By the end of that same year the aircraft was retired from service.

If the picture was of Stark flying over Penticton, it would have to be either in 1912 or 1914. The author can find no proof to substantiate his presence in the city in 1917. Stark was in the Okanagan in July 1912, and was also giving exhibitions in B.C. in 1914. Another possibility was that the aircraft belonged to an American pilot, either Walter Edwards who performed at Nelson September 24, 1912, or Weldon Cooke who also flew at Nelson in July 1914 and in Kelowna on August 4. Both these pilots flew Curtiss Pusher type aircraft.

If there are doubts as to the identity and timing of Stark's Curtiss Pusher at Penticton, there are no doubts as to the next aviator at Penticton who arrived in time to thrill an audience at the Domionion Day celebrations on July 1, 1919. Lieutenant Ernest 0. Hall and his mechanic

Spinning Nose Dives

Loop=the=Loops, Tail Spins,

Flying Upside Down

AND ALL THE OTHER AIR FEATS THAT OUR GALLANT
FLYERS HAVE MASTERED WILL BE GIVEN IN

PENTICTON

JULY 1 and 2

(TWO DAYS)

WHEN AN AEROPLANE FROM THE COAST WILL PER-
FORM AT THE TURF CLUB SPORTS, Recreation Grounds.

This is a great chance for the people of the Similkameen
and Lower Okanagan to witness the air stunts that we have
all read about. The machine and pilot are coming to Penticton
at an expense to the Turf Club of $800.00.

Other features of the two days of celebration include:

HORSE RACING; INDIAN and COWBOY RACES
A BASEBALL TOURNAMENT

Between Oroville, Keremeos, Kelowna and Penticton; and a
BIG SUPPER DANCE in King's Hall on the night of July 1.

SPECIAL BOAT FROM KELOWNA SOUTH.   SPECIAL RATES ON THE K. V. RAILWAY

Write J. S. HEALES, Secretary Penticton Turf Club, for
all information.

The Princeton Star   June 27, 1919

Lt. Ernest Hall landed this "Vatco" Curtiss JN-4 at Penticton's Turf Club; June 30, 1919. Vernon Archives

Dudley Smith had flown from Vancouver with stops at Chilliwack and Princeton for fuel. They arrived at Penticton at 9:30 p.m. Sunday, June 29. Hall was flying a Curtiss JN-4 Canuck belonging to the Vancouver Aerial Transportation Company, or VATCO.

The manager of VATCO, Mr. J.J. Simpson, had arrived earlier and made arrangements for the aircraft's arrival at the Turf Club recreation grounds on June 30. The Turf Club paid VATCO $800.00 for its sponsorship of the event. After the aerial exhibition and aeroplane rides were given on July 1 and 2, Hall and Smith flew to Oroville, Washington, for that city's Fourth of July celebration, later returning to Penticton. The two men then set out for Vancouver on July 5 with a fuel stop at Princeton.

The Vancouver branch of the Aerial League of Canada announced its plan to attempt the first crossing of the Rocky Mountains by air from Vancouver to Calgary. Newspapers in Vancouver, Lethbridge, and Calgary put up $950.00 in prize money for the successful completion of the flight under certain conditions. The league selected Captain E.C. Hoy, DFC, to make the flight, but Lieutenant Ernie Hall decided to try the feat himself. He set out in the attempt only to discover that one of the provisions for the prize was that the aircraft and its pilot both belong to the Aerial League.

Hall, therefore, was disqualified as his machine was owned by the Vancouver Aerial Transportation Company, which was a commercial venture. Hall determined that he would continue the flight to Calgary but would barnstorm along the way to help pay his expenses.

Hall arrived in Merritt on July 27 on a flight from Chilliwack. He gave an exhibition of aerobatics followed by 'cash for rides' to the town's people until August 1, when he flew to Kamloops where he arrived at 5:30 p.m., becoming the first aircraft to land at that city. He departed on Monday, August 4, for Vernon and arrived at Penticton August 6.

The Aerial League's official contender was Capt. E. Hoy who set out from Vancouver at 4:30 a.m. on August 7 and flew non-stop to Vernon. When Lt. Hall, in Penticton, learned that Capt. Hoy had taken off from Vernon for Grand Forks, Hall left Penticton and flew to Midway to refuel. Later, Lt. Hall flew to Creston, where he unfortunately was forced to crash into a parked car on takeoff to avoid hitting spectators on the field, which ended his attempt to be first across the Rockies. Hoy was successful however, and landed at Calgary's Bowness Park at 8:55 p.m. Lt. Ernie Hall, accompanied by his wife, arrived back in Penticton on August 11, 1919, having traveled by car. He later left for the coast by train.

On Hall's departure from Penticton, the Friday, August 15, 1919, edition of the Princeton Star stated that "it will probably be some time before Penticton is again visited by airplanes." The Star editor was accurate in his prediction, as no further reference has been documented of an aviation

Yukon Airways Alexander Eaglerock G-CAUZ arrived at Pentiction, September 1928. J. Harbottle

which took until December 1928. While at Penticton, Clyde Wann is quoted as saying that business was so brisk that in a one hour period they made 11 ten minute flights.

Another documented aircraft arrival at Penticton occurred between the summer of 1929 and 1931 when Humphery Madden and Joe Bertalino, who were operating a flying school at Kamloops, visited the towns in the area on weekends to drum up business for their school and to barnstorm or offer 'cash for rides' to eke out their meager existence. The pair flew in Madden's Fleet 2 CF-AKC. Whether Madden used the Penticton "Turf Club" field or some other location is unknown.

presence at Penticton for almost the entire 1920s. With the formation of the Air Board in 1919 to control the licencing of pilots, aircraft, and airfields, the practice of barnstorming out of fairgrounds in populated areas ceased and Penticton did not have a dedicated airfield.

In late September 1928, G-CAUX, a new Alexander Eaglerock christened "Northern Light", arrived in Penticton to barnstorm the city and offer 'cash for rides' and exhibition flights. Clyde Wann of the Yukon Airways and Exploration Company of Whitehorse had taken delivery of the aircraft at Denver, Colorado, and, after hiring pilot John Patterson, had flown to Vancouver where Canadian registration was assigned. The pair then proceeded to barnstorm their way to the Yukon,

On July 7, 1932 Penticton hosted the BC Air Tour organized by the Aero Club of B.C. out of Vancouver. As Penticton had no airfield, the air

This Fleet Model II CF-AKC flown by "Humph" Madden and Joe Bertalino arrived at Penticton 1929 Bertalino Collection

Aircrew of 1932 BC Air Tour pose at Penticton Aquatic Club. <u>Standing</u>: Maurice McGregor. Roy Drew, Bill Bolton, Jack Wright. <u>Front</u> <u>Row</u>: Betsy Flaherty, Hal Wilson, Joe Bertalino, Unknown, Dan Lawson, remainder unknown.

show took place in a meadow south of Queens Park. Penticton resident Hugh Cleland was a member of the organizing committee working with Reeve G.A.B. MacDonald, for the event. He recalls an impressive list of visiting aircraft in spite of the poor weather on the coast. A formation flying team named The Three Musketeers of the Aero Club of B.C. was flown by pilots A.H. Wilson, Maurice McGregor, and Don Lawson.

This group enjoyed the show at Penticton for more reasons than aviation. After a dinner and dance at the Aquatic Club, in the wee hours and after a little liquid courage, the trio decided that in view of their lack of swimsuits they should go skinny-dipping in the unattended pool. They were discovered and the group's name was unofficially changed to the Three Doukhobors.

Two Gipsy Moths (DH-60s) flown by L.L. Dunsmore of Vernon and Jack Wright of Vancouver and a 1932 Alexander D-2 Flyabout owned by J.E. (Ernest) Eve of Victoria were also present that day in July. In addition there was a Fairchild owned by T. Jones and flown by J.

Grubbstrom; an Aeronca C-3, CF-AQK, owned by Frank W. Gilbert of Vancouver; a WACO owned by Ed Bennett; C.S. Peen's Alexander Eaglerock, G-CATN; and from Chilliwack there was a Ryan B-1 Brougham CF-ATA owned by Ginger Coote and another Alexander Eaglerock, a 1929 model A-2 belonging to R.R. Brett.

The Penticton Herald reported that on July 7, 1932, Shell Oil's Lockheed Vega from San Francisco flew over but continued on to Vernon. The Vega, flown by company pilot W.G. Fletcher, returned the following day and landed at Penticton. Imperial Oil's famous pilot Pat Reid also arrived on July 8 in his company's DH-80A Puss Moth CF-IOL.

The BC Air Tour had departed Vancouver at 2:30 p.m. The first aircraft arrived over Penticton at 4:00 p.m. The stated aim of the tour was to promote the possibilities of aviation in the province. Before they departed for Vernon, the pilots told local authorities that the airfield provided by Penticton was far too short for regular flying requirements. The city then abandoned any ideas

Penticton

of utilizing this area south of Queens Park as an aircraft landing area.

During the next two years the municipal council purchased land south of the old Turf Club recreation grounds where Lt. Hall had first landed in June 1919. The Penticton Herald edition of March 21, 1935, reported the municipal council's debate on a proposal by the golf club to lease the airport property stating that very few airplanes had used the field and the community would be better served by an extension of the golf club to absorb the airfield lands.

Penticton Reeve, W. Oliver, observed that he had been looking forward to a real airfield in the city and lamented the fact that Penticton had been passed up by the federal government's development of an airway south of the city and the construction of an intermediate field at Oliver was taking place as part of the Unemployment Relief Scheme.

In 1936 the municipal council studied three new sites for an airfield. An airways inspector of the Civil Aviation Branch Department of Defence, in the company of the engineer in charge working on the Oliver airfield, inspected the sites during 1937 and recommended that the location on the Indian Band Reserve, west of the Okanagan River and north of Skaha Lake, be developed.

A detailed survey was made in January 1938 and a lease was agreed upon by municipal council and the Department of Indian Affairs for a site of 38 acres. Council paid the first year's rent and formally applied to Ottawa for an assistance loan to construct the airport.

Ottawa approved the plan after the original site was moved slightly further to the north, and, later yet, was enlarged to accommodate a radio range station. The entire airport would lie on Penticton Indian Reserve Number 1, a decision that much later would cause the city of Penticton much concern.

The original route of the trans-Canada airway had been via Princeton, Oliver, Grand Forks and then Cranbrook. But after this section of airway came into regular use, the Grand Forks range station gave navigational problems which were in part solved by the construction of two new range stations, one at Crescent Valley and a second at Carmi. The Penticton Herald edition of September 15, 1938, told of the estimated completion of the Carmi station by the end of that month, and subsequent to this Green 1 airway was moved northward to pass over Carmi, which in turn placed Green 1 airway just eight miles south of Penticton instead of overhead of Oliver. The smaller community of Oliver, south of Penticton, had initially upstaged the larger city, but this changed with the rerouting of the airway and Federal government assistance to build the Penticton airfield was forthcoming.

The Penticton Herald editorialized, on October 27, 1938, that "Quite possibly the government will be prepared to give some assistance with the construction of a field at south Penticton near Skaha Lake now that it learns that Penticton is directly under the line of trans-Canada flight and is ideally situated for landing field purposes."

In 1938, at the well-attended annual general meeting of the Penticton Board of Trade held at the Incola Hotel, Reeve Wilkins reported on the airport progress. A letter was read from Ginger Coote regarding his plans for the development of an airline route through the Okanagan, with service to Penticton and a possible feeder route to connect with the new Yukon Southern Air Transport service to Prince George and Fort Saint

John from Vancouver, which Coote and Grant McConachie were developing.

In the late spring of 1939, Ginger Coote's vision of a feeder line through the Okanagan became a reality. Coote, now associated with Grant McConachie's Yukon Southern Air Transport, started a scheduled service in January 1938 from Ashcroft to Prince George, with stops in the Cariboo and then on to Fort St John to connect with the airline's Whitehorse-Edmonton service. By the summer of 1938 the service started in Vancouver, and by the spring of 1939 the airline was flying twin engine Barclay Grows along the route which also came to include Kamloops.

YSAT based a WACO ZQC-6 five passenger biplane at Oliver, CF-BDM, and operated a weekly service to Oliver from Vancouver with the Barclay Grow. The WACO then operated to airfields up the Okanagan Valley to feed the service to Oliver and later to Kamloops from Vancouver. Penticton, however, was bypassed because of its inadequate facilities.

With the coming of World War II in September 1939, airfield construction received increased priority from the Federal government. In October 1940, the radio range navigational station at Grand Forks, that had been shut down because of the relocation of Green 1 airway, was moved to Penticton to create an instrument approach to that city's new airport.

On February 10, 1941, at 11:00 a.m., Trans Canada Airlines closed its company communications station at Oliver and the staff and equipment were moved to Penticton, where Mr. J.A. English served as station manager.

By March 1941 airfield lighting was installed and operational, and on May 2, 1941, the first

T.C.A. Radio Communications Office at Penticton after move from Oliver, February 1941. Oliver Archives

Air photo of RCAF Station Penticton looking South, October 11, 1942. RCAF PB-4868

official landing took place when the Department of Transport Lockheed 12A CF-CCT touched down on the field.

The Penticton Gyro Club began to make plans for a gala grand opening of the airport to coincide with July 1, 1941, Dominion Day celebrations. However, this plan was squelched by the Federal government officials in Ottawa who believed the celebration might interfere with the war effort.

The Department of Transport operated the

Penticton airfield throughout the war largely for use by RCAF and other military flights. Number 124 Ferry Squadron established a detachment at Penticton to service and administer to itinerant air force flights. The detachment, under its headquarters in Winnipeg, was commanded initially by S/L H. (Hump) 0. Madden who had barnstormed in Penticton in the early 1930s in his Fleet 2 biplane CF-AKC. Madden was replaced on April 30, 1943, by S/L E. (Ernie) Hall who previously, as Lt. Ernie Hall, was the first pilot ever to land his Curtiss JN-4 Canuck at the Turf Club recreation grounds at Penticton on June 30, 1919.

The Department of National Defence approved expansion of the airport to meet air force needs as an emergency field with the extension of the runway to 5,300 feet by 200 feet, plus a small taxiway, all of which was to be paved. The contract was given to Storms Contracting Limited and was finished by August 2, 1943. There was some question as to where the contractor obtained the landfill required. A large number of rattlesnakes ended up on the airport, which kept airport staff members busy for some time killing them.

The municipality of Penticton had also wisely obtained the foreshore adjacent to the airport for the development of a seaplane landing dock, which was developed by the outbreak of war.

During 1941 the RCAF moved a large number of Supermarine Stranraer twin engine flying boats from the east coast to Jericho Beach and the five other west coast flying boat stations as anti-submarine patrol aircraft. The majority of these aircraft passed through Penticton, often refuelling or holding for improvement of weather on the coast. The aircraft crossed the prairies landing at Waterton Lake, Alberta, Nelson, and Penticton, was the last facility available then until Vancouver at Jericho Beach.

A sad occurrence took place on November 4, 1941, when Stranraer 946 of 5 Bomber Reconnaissance Squadron stopped at Penticton to wait for improving weather to the west. The flight departed later that day under command of Sergeant E.T. Cox with four crew on board. The last radio report told of 946 being lost in cloud and attempting a descent - nothing further was heard from the aircraft and an extensive search was made without success. The Stranraer was not located until 1947, ten miles southwest of Squamish where the plane had crashed high in the coastal mountains at the 4,400 foot level. There was no evidence to suggest that there had been any survivors.

On October 10, 1942, RCAF Norseman on floats #2480, flown by F/Sgt. George Williamson with photographer WO2 L.B. Hackett, arrived from Lac La Hache on a photographic assignment taking vertical and oblique photographs of Princeton and Penticton airfield. Hackett recorded in his log that #2480 made a forced landing at Summerland, before returning to RCAF Patricia Bay at Victoria on October 13.

On September 17, 1942, an RCAF photographic aircraft was temporarily based at airports from Princeton to Cranbrook and its itinerary included a series of photographs of the Penticton airport itself. Bolingborke #9032 was flown by P/0 Moncrioff with RCAF veteran photographer W02 Hackett who had been in the air force since 1925. The group concluded their survey on September 23, departing for RCAF Station Sea Island at Vancouver at 10:30 a.m. The following day, September 24, Bollingbroke #9040 arrived and continued the photographic exercise, this time flown by F/0 George Williamson.

With the coming of the end of the war, the Penticton Board of Trade sought assurances that

RCAF Station Penticton with radio range and rotating beacon tower, 1943 D.McIvor

Aerial view of Penticton looking North, September 13, 1943. RCAF PB-7617

airlines would service the city. Trans Canada Airlines operated a flight direct from Lethbridge to Vancouver, and use of the airport at Penticton was not contemplated saving except in an emergency.

Grant McConachie of Canadian Pacific Airlines was approached as to the possibility of the city being included in CPA's route from Vancouver to Prince George. McConachie visited Penticton's airport on April 9, 1944, and advised that it was 150 miles out of the way of the Prince George route, but further stated that the service his earlier company (YSAT) had provided in 1939 proved

the necessity of an interior linkage of Okanagan communities by air.

During the summer of 1945, a large American four engine aircraft arrived at Penticton. It appears to have been a Consolidated PB4Y-2 Privateer. This aircraft would be powered by four 1,350 horsepowered Pratt and Whitney Twin Wasp R-1830 engines, had a 110 foot wingspan, and a gross weight of 64,000 pounds. The aircraft crew number would be 11 to 13 men. This was undoubtedly the largest aircraft to have landed at Penticton and one wonders how the asphalt runway and taxi area stood up to its footprint.

On November 1, 1945, a temporary airport licence was issued showing the operator of the Penticton Airport as the Department of Transport for 24 hour operation.

Dan McIvor was a pilot with RCAF Number 124 Ferry Squadron and had landed at Penticton many times during the war. McIvor settled in Penticton and attempted to become a fruit farmer. Another fruit farmer, Dave Smith, had aspirations in aviation and formed Filby and Smith Airways in 1946 at the Penticton airport, offering flight instruction and charter flights. Smith induced McIvor to come and fly for him using a Piper J-3 Cub, CF-DCM, a Piper Cub Cruiser J-5, CF-DNW, and a Taylorcraft BC-12D, CF-DBP. McIvor flew for Smith until 1947, when he left for greener pastures. Late in 1948 Smith was killed and the air service ended.

The communications equipment installed at Penticton for company use in 1941 was no longer required, and TCA closed the station on February 15, 1949.

In 1948, L&M Air Services Limited of Vernon got approval to operate a Class 2 scheduled serv-

1965 Air photo of Penticton looking Northwest. C.W.

ice linking Penticton, Kelowna, Vernon, and Kamloops using a Beech 18 on floats which docked at the north foot of Main Street on Okanagan Lake.

The Penticton Airport received a permanent licence on May 10, 1954, and later was served by Canadian Pacific Airlines after a terminal building was opened in 1963. The radio range had previously been upgraded with equipment bought from Dog Creek after the decommissioning of that radio range in the early 1950s.

In 1968, CPA serviced the community using Douglas DC-6B pressurized aircraft with two flights daily. Pacific Western Airlines took over this service in April 1969 with Boeing 737 jet aircraft. A further service was provided by Northern Thunderbird Air of Prince George.

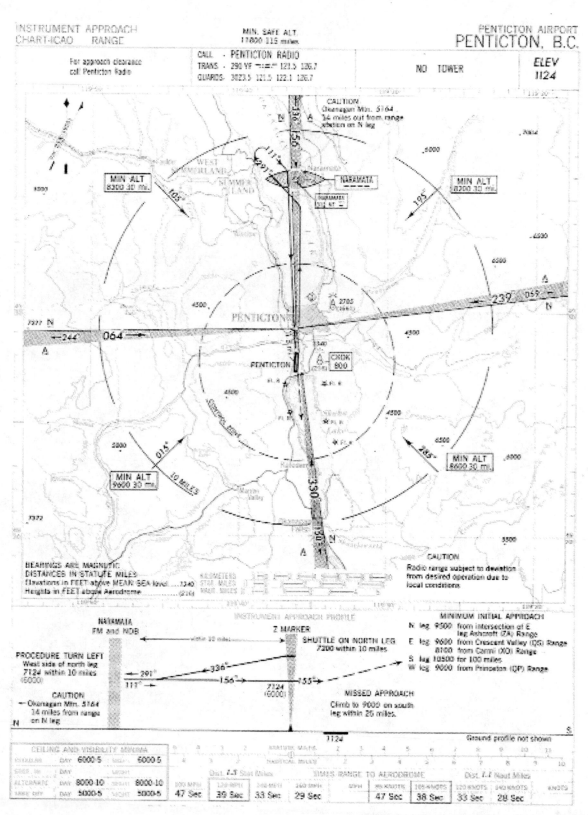

November 18, 1955

Penticton

33

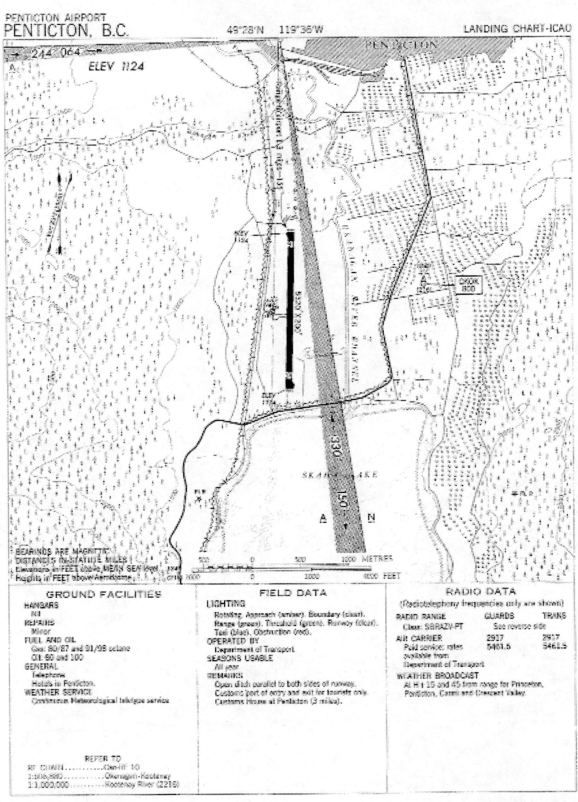

ELEV 1124

BEARINGS ARE MAGNETIC
DISTANCES IN STATUTE MILES
Elevations in FEET above MEAN SEA level
Heights in FEET above Aerodrome

GROUND FACILITIES

HANGARS
Nil
REPAIRS
Minor
FUEL AND OIL
Gas: 80/87 and 91/98 octane
Oil: 80 and 100
GENERAL
Telephone
Hotels in Penticton.
WEATHER SERVICE
Continuous Meteorological teletype service

REFER TO
RF CHART............Oxt-RF 10
1:506,880............Okanagan-Kootenay
1:1,000,000..........Kootenay River (2216)

FIELD DATA

LIGHTING
Rotating. Approach (amber). Boundary (clear).
Range (green). Threshold (green). Runway (clear).
Taxi (blue). Obstruction (red).
OPERATED BY
Department of Transport
SEASONS USABLE
All year
REMARKS
Open ditch parallel to both sides of runway.
Customs port of entry and exit for tourists only.
Customs House at Penticton (3 miles).

RADIO DATA

(Radiotelephony frequencies only are shown)

	GUARDS	TRANS
RADIO RANGE Class: SBRAZV-PT	See reverse side	
AIR CARRIER Paid service: rates available from Department of Transport	2917 5461.5	2917 5461.5

WEATHER BROADCAST
At H + 15 and 45 from range for Princeton,
Penticton, Carmi and Crescent Valley.

November 18, 1955

Penticton

34

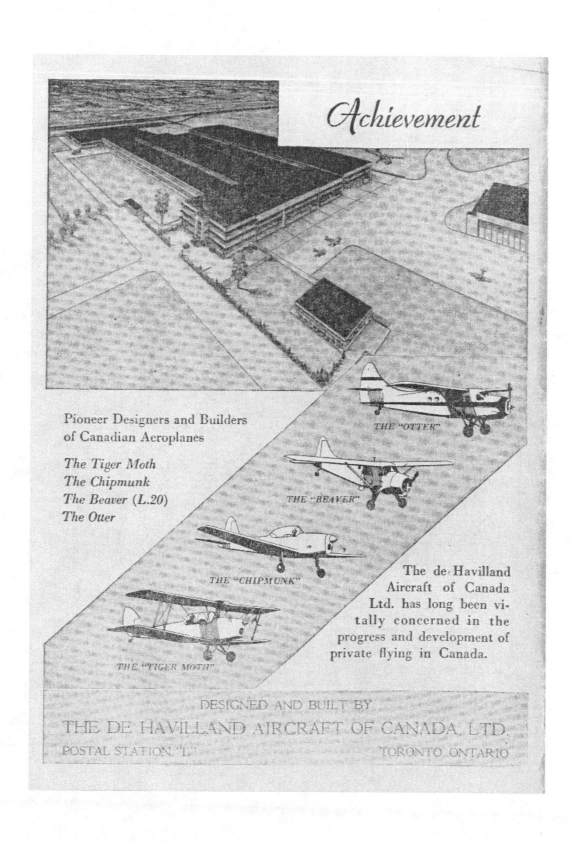

Achievement

Pioneer Designers and Builders
of Canadian Aeroplanes

The Tiger Moth
The Chipmunk
The Beaver (L.20)
The Otter

THE "OTTER"

THE "BEAVER"

THE "CHIPMUNK"

THE "TIGER MOTH"

The de Havilland
Aircraft of Canada
Ltd. has long been vitally concerned in the
progress and development of
private flying in Canada.

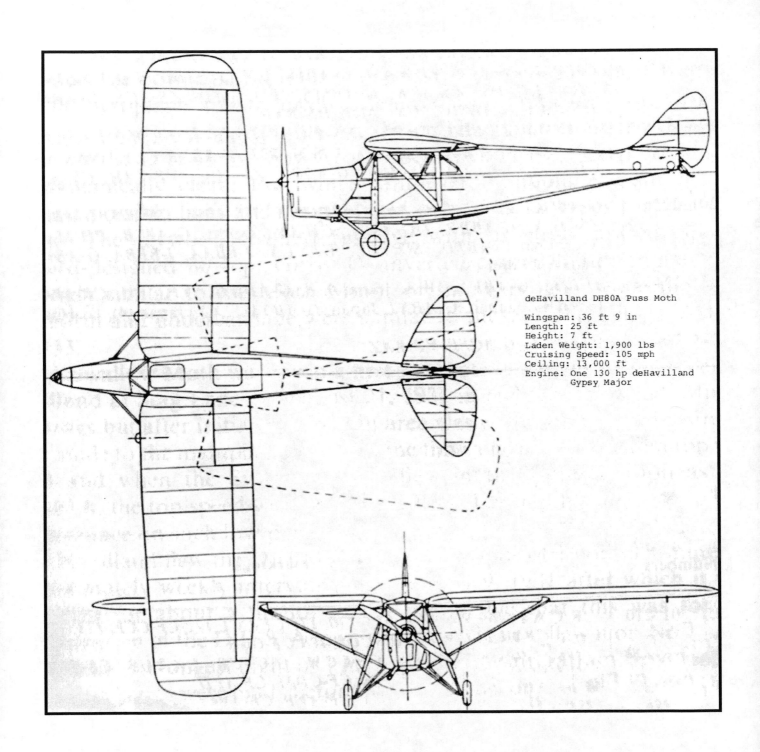

deHavilland DH80A Puss Moth

Wingspan: 36 ft 9 in
Length: 25 ft
Height: 7 ft
Laden Weight: 1,900 lbs
Cruising Speed: 105 mph
Ceiling: 13,000 ft
Engine: One 130 hp deHavilland
         Gypsy Major

The first flight at Kelowna took place at the city's annual Regatta on August 13, 1914. An American flyer from Oakland, California, Weldon B. Cooke, had obtained his pilot license number 95 from the Aero Club of America in January 1912. Cook owned a Curtiss type pusher powered by a six cylinder Roberts motor. Weldon Cook's "Hydro-Aeroplane" was a single float biplane. It arrived in Kelowna aboard the Canadian Pacific lake steamer "Sicamous" in several crates, and after assembly was flown only

Weldon B. Cook's "Hydro Aeroplane" flies by the Kelowna Regatta, August 13, 1914. Vernon Archives

once as Cooke experienced engine trouble. This would be the last exhibition flight in B.C. until the end of World War I.

Later, in August 1914, yet another flight occurred when Ralph Bulman and Stanley Silke built a biplane glider in the district of Ellison. Bulman was able to foot launch the craft (hang-glider) becoming airborne before crashing with some injury to himself. The glider was later displayed at the Kelowna Fall Fair in the city's exhibition building.

Weldon Cook's "Hydro Aeroplane" taxiing on Okanagan Lake at Kelowna Regatta, 1914. Vernon Archives

Lt. G.K.Trim flew the Vancouver Aerial League Curtiss JN-4 No.5 from the Polo Field during the Kelowna Regatta of 1919. H. Steveson

The second aircraft at Kelowna was scheduled as an exhibition flight at the Regatta of 1919. Lieutenant G.K Trim flew one of the Curtiss JN-4 Canucks of the Vancouver branch of the Aerial League of Canada to the city, which he then flew from the "polo field" east of the Gyro Park. After his exhibition,Trim was very successful in attracting passengers and remained in the city for some time.

That same month on August 7, the citizens of Kelowna witnessed Captain Ernest C. Hoy flying overhead on his way to Calgary from Vancouver via Vernon, Grand Forks, Cranbrook, and Lethbridge. Hoy was seen above the city just before 9 a.m. at a height of 4,500 feet. Hoy had lived in Kelowna since 1912, later enlisting in the Royal Flying Corps where he

was awarded the Distinguished Flying Cross in France.

During the 1920s Kelowna was visited occasionally by aircraft from the Jericho Beach Air Station, initially by a Curtiss HS-2L on detached duty based in Kamloops and Sicamous, and later by Vickers Vedettes and Fairchild FC-2Ws on photographic and forestry assignments.

The City of Kelowna began to appreciate the advantages of a community airfield and attempted to purchase land from Mr. Axel Autin, a Rutland fruit grower. Negotiations were unsuccessful, but local flyers persuaded Autin to allow the use of some of his land as an aviation field. It was to this field in late September 1928 that American entrepre-

RCAF Fairchild FC-2W2 G-CYXN and XQ were in the Okanagan on a photographic survey July 1930. DND

RUTLAND B. C.

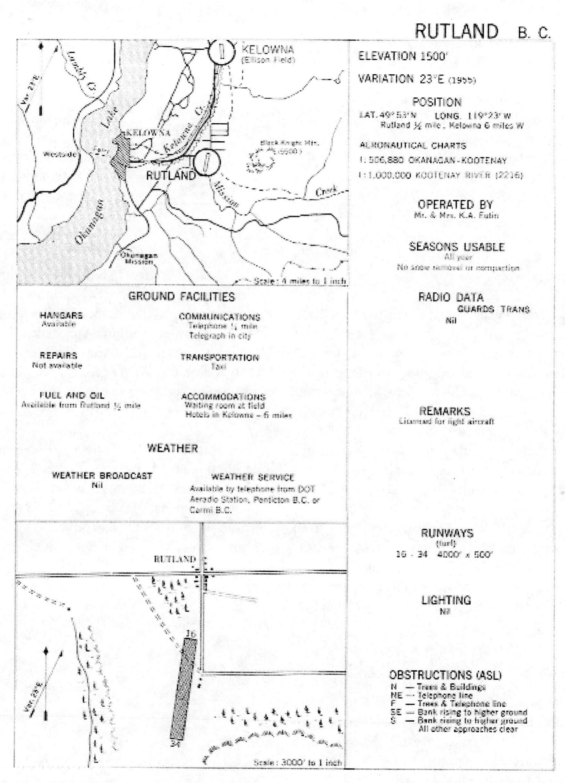

ELEVATION 1500'

VARIATION 23°E (1955)

POSITION
LAT. 49°53'N   LONG. 119°23' W
Rutland ½ mile , Kelowna 6 miles W

AERONAUTICAL CHARTS
1: 506,880 OKANAGAN - KOOTENAY
1:1,000,000 KOOTENAY RIVER (2216)

OPERATED BY
Mr. & Mrs. K.A. Futin

SEASONS USABLE
All year
No snow removal or compaction

RADIO DATA
GUARDS TRANS
Nil

REMARKS
Licensed for light aircraft

GROUND FACILITIES

HANGARS
Available

COMMUNICATIONS
Telephone ½ mile
Telegraph in city

REPAIRS
Not available

TRANSPORTATION
Taxi

FUEL AND OIL
Available from Rutland ½ mile

ACCOMMODATIONS
Waiting room at field
Hotels in Kelowna – 6 miles

WEATHER

WEATHER BROADCAST
Nil

WEATHER SERVICE
Available by telephone from DOT
Aeradio Station, Penticton B.C. or
Carmi B.C.

RUNWAYS
(turf)
16 - 34   4000' x 500'

LIGHTING
Nil

OBSTRUCTIONS (ASL)
N — Trees & Buildings
NE — Telephone line
E — Trees & Telephone line
SE — Bank rising to higher ground
S — Bank rising to higher ground
All other approaches clear

March 7, 1956

Kelowna

neur Clyde Wann brought his company's new Alexander Eaglerock A-2, registered a few days earlier G-CAUX in Vancouver. The three seat aircraft was flown by John M. Patterson of Denver, Colorado. The Eaglerock carried passengers for several days before heading to the Yukon, where Wann's airline, Yukon Airways and Exploration Company, would later operate it. AUX left Kelowna for Kamloops and arrived at Williams Lake September 13, 1928.

Yukon Airways Eaglerock G-CAUZ "Northern Light" barnstormed at Rutland, September 1928. CMFT

Apparently, Wann maximized the number of passengers he had pilot Patterson take up from the Rutland airfield. The front cockpit had two seats, but Wann crammed three people in if they were small enough. Cliff Renfrew, who would later become a pilot, recalled that on his first flight in the Eaglerock pilot Patterson did a stall turn, or hammerhead, and descended straight down toward the airfield. Renfrew was terrified, but later came back and did it again.

In February 1930, the Kelowna Board of Trade made representations to city council for the establishment of an airfield for the city and asked that the question be submitted to the ratepayers that $25,000 be allocated for acquisition of land and the construction of airport buildings.

On November 30, 1929, Radium Hot Springs Flying Service acquired a de Havilland DH-60M Gipsy Moth, CF-AGK, and owner John Blakely decided to base this aircraft at Kelowna's Rutland field and offer flying lessons. Blakely hired instructor Lowell Dunsmore to fly the Moth, and one of his first students was Cliff Renfrew who had caught the flying bug with Clyde Wann.

Blakely later relocated to Vernon as Rutland was unlicensed, but he continued to fly from Kelowna as needed.

Another aviation field at Kelowna was known as Boyce's field, on the property of Doctor Boyce, located between Ospray and Cedar Avenue and bounded on the east by Pandosy Street. This field was used by east Kelowna resident Barney Jones-Evans, a World War I RFC pilot who owned a Gipsy Moth. Jones-Evans was also a flying instructor at Dominion Airways in Vancouver and had helped teach Cominco's Trail mine manager William Archibald to fly in mid-1929. Barney Jones-Evans later flew in China for the Nationalist Air Force. He was killed in 1937 while flying from London, England, to Paris, France, when his aircraft crashed in dense fog.

In late 1929 the Civil Aviation Branch of the Department of National Defence authorized its Inspector of Western Airways, Dan McLean, to conduct an aerial survey for a proposed route from the prairies to Vancouver. While conducting this survey, McLean landed at Kelowna's Rutland

Radium Hot Springs Flying Service DH-60M "Gypsy Moth" CF-AGK at Rutland, Summer 1930. CMFT

de Havilland DH-60M CF-AGK at Rutland Field. Kelowna Archives

field. However, the eventual position of this airway would cross the southern Okanagan Valley near Penticton.

A group of enthusiasts attempted to introduce gliding to the Okanagan, bringing a Boeing-built single seat glider from Vancouver to Kelowna in 1930 which was launched from nearby Knox Mountain. An observer summed up the success of the attempt when he noted that the rudimentary craft "soared like a stone".

A newspaper clipping dated March 1931 records that a seaplane visited the city from Trail. The aircraft belonged to Cominco. Also during March a three seat Bird biplane arrived from Spokane, Washington, spending several days at Doctor Boyce's airfield.

The Vancouver Sun edition of June 16, 1931, proclaimed that a new aviation company, the All Canadian Enterprise Airways, was intending to start a main line scheduled service between Vancouver and Penticton, with a feeder service to Kelowna and Kamloops as well as Trail and Nelson, using a 23 passenger Ford. This service was slated to begin no later than August 1, 1931. However, this operation never got off the ground.

During October 1931, two RCAF Vickers Vedette flying boats landed on Okanagan Lake adjacent to the city. The aircraft had been flown from the Jericho Beach Air Station by Squadron Leader Earl McLeod and Flight Lieutenant A.D. Niverville.

On July 11, 1935, CF-ASJ was at Kelowna's Rutland field. The WACO A.T.0 Straight Wing was flown by Eric de Pencier, who later departed for Vernon. In the early fall, September 2, 1935, a Ford Trimotor 4-AT-A, G-CARC, of United Air Transport Limited owned by Grant McConachie, arrived at Rutland field. Six passengers were on board. One of the pilots was Len Waagen.

In 1939, YSAT's Waco 2QC-6, CF-BDM, began flights three times a week up the Okanagan Valley stopping at Kelowna. The service fed the company's Barklay-Grow service from Vancouver to Oliver, but due to lack of support it was cancelled after only six weeks of operation.

The field at Rutland saw some improvements during World War II and was used occasionally by military aircraft, but by 1945 this privately owned turf field was deemed too small to be further developed for future needs.

Kelowna

41

Kelowna Alderman Jack Horn was a long-standing advocate for a municipal airport for the community, and largely through his efforts a site was chosen at Dickson's Ranch, nine miles north of the city. The property belonged to Doctor Dickson. The 320 acres were eventually negotiated for $20,000, but first the city needed the ratifi-

First Terminal Building 1947. Kelowna Archives

cation of its ratepayers and needed 60% approval, which it surpassed by only six votes on December 13, 1945.

Ellison Field looking North, 1945. C.W.

The original field in the district of Ellison was known as Ellison Field and was 1,500 feet long in 1946. In 1948 this was extended to 3,000 feet by 300 feet and was seeded in grass. In 1947 a small terminal building was constructed at the north end of the field, followed in 1948 by a hangar. The field was licensed in the name of the City of

C.P.A.'s inaugural flight to Kelowna's Ellison Field, 1948. Avro Anson, DC-3, Cessna Crane. Kelowna Archives

Kelowna

42

KELOWNA (Ellison Field) B.C.

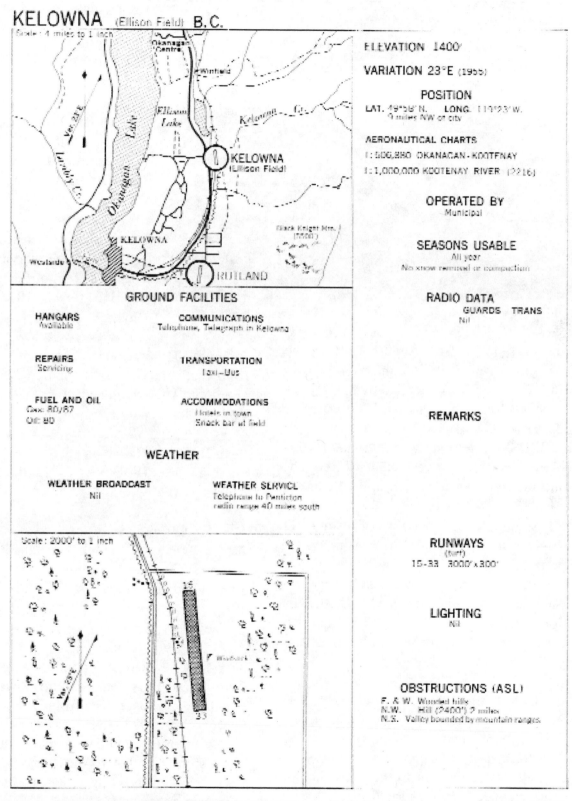

ELEVATION 1400'

VARIATION 23°E (1955)

POSITION
LAT. 49°58' N. LONG. 119°23' W.
9 miles NW of city

AERONAUTICAL CHARTS
1:506,880 OKANAGAN-KOOTENAY
1:1,000,000 KOOTENAY RIVER (2216)

OPERATED BY
Municipal

SEASONS USABLE
All year
No snow removal or compaction

RADIO DATA
GUARDS TRANS
Nil

REMARKS

RUNWAYS
(turf)
15-33 3000' x 300'

LIGHTING
Nil

OBSTRUCTIONS (ASL)
E. & W. Wooded hills
N.W. Hill (2400') 2 miles
N.S. Valley bounded by mountain ranges

GROUND FACILITIES

HANGARS
Available

COMMUNICATIONS
Telephone, Telegraph in Kelowna

REPAIRS
Servicing

TRANSPORTATION
Taxi—Bus

FUEL AND OIL
Gas: 80/87
Oil: 80

ACCOMMODATIONS
Hotels in town
Snack bar at field

WEATHER

WEATHER BROADCAST
Nil

WEATHER SERVICE
Telephone to Penticton
radio range 40 miles south

1955

Kelowna

L&M Air Service inaugural flight with a Beech 18 seaplane, flown by Dan McIvor who stands in doorway and greets Okanagan Mayors, 1948. D. McIvor

Kelowna in 1948, and on August 1, 1949, the official opening was held in conjunction with an air show. The event was attended by many visiting aircraft including a Canadian Pacific Airline Douglas DC-3, CF-CUD, and a Cessna T-50 Crane, CF-CSM. The first aircraft to land reportedly belonged to Kelowna resident Cliff Renfrew, who built the first private hangar at the field.

The first commercial operator at Ellison Field in 1946-47 was Filby and Smith Airways of Penticton. Pilot Dan McIvor and owner Dave Smith offered flight instruction and charter service in a Piper J-5 Cub Cruiser, CF-DBP. This operation was short lived as McIvor left for greener pastures and Smith was killed in a later crash.

The second operation at the field was Okanagan Air Services, who located there offering charter flights and instruction until 1951 when it reformed as Okanagan Helicopters. The company sold its equipment to the Aero Club of B.C., who operated at Ellison Field for about one year then moved back to its main base at Vancouver.

The field's first airport manager was ex -RCAF pilot Ralph Hermanson. Hermanson would later form his own company, Cariboo Air Charter Limited, in 1952, which offered instruction and charter flights.

In 1948, L & M Air Service started a licensed class two scheduled service from its base at Vernon using a twin engine Beech 18 aircraft on floats which initially docked at the foot of Kelowna's Bernard Avenue. This service connected Penticton, Kelowna, Vernon, and eventually Kamloops. This operation later switched to wheels using the Ellison Field.

In July 1958 Canadian Pacific Airlines inaugurated a daily DC-3 service to the field until August 1, 1959.

A 5,300 foot paved runway was completed in July 1960, and on July 1 Canadian Pacific Airlines reinstated service using Douglas DC-6B aircraft and later Convairs.

Pacific Western took over the service as of April 26, 1969, using Boeing 737 and Convair aircraft. A new terminal building was finished on October 26, 1968, and a control tower was constructed and operated from June 1971. On February 19, 1972, Ralph Hermanson's Cariboo Air Charter Limited initiated a protest against Abbotsford based Arrow Aviation Limited who were operating a flying school and charter base from Vernon.

Kelowna

Ralph Hermanson, the president of Cariboo Air Charter, was successful in securing a contract with the B.C. Forest Service to provide forest fire patrol aircraft from a number of bases throughout B.C. On May 11, 1972, Cariboo Air Charter Chief Pilot Bob Bluett hired the author as pilot and base manager on Cariboo's seasonal contract to the Forest Service. After receiving a proficiency check on the Super Cub float plane CF-LOU, I departed Kelowna in my Cessna 170A, N9264A, for Dawson Creek for the summer's patrol season.

Dan McIvor shakes hand of Kelowna Mayor D. McIvor.

The City of Kelowna still operates the airport today and over the years the terminal, runways, and aircraft parking areas have seen continual growth to accommodate the demands of air travel.

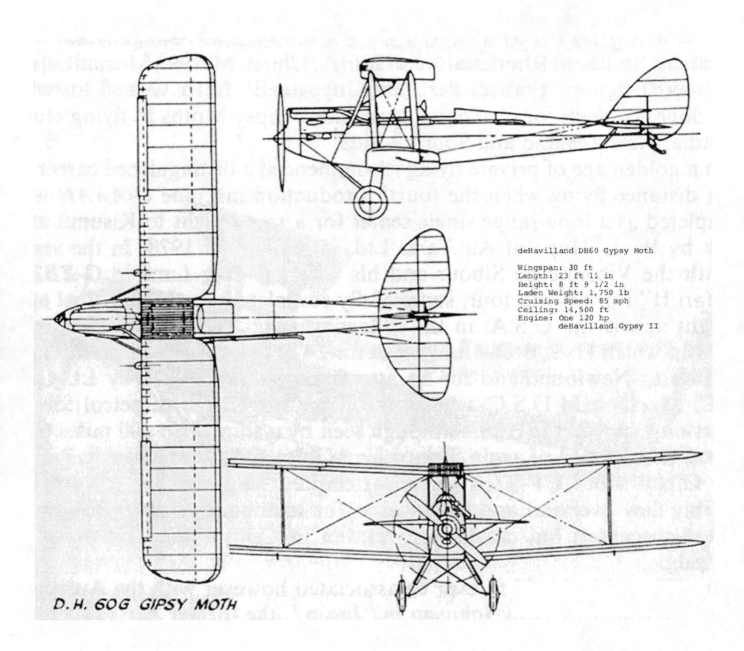

deHavilland DH60 Gypsy Moth

Wingspan: 30 ft
Length: 23 ft 11 in
Height: 8 ft 9 1/2 in
Laden Weight: 1,750 lb
Cruising Speed: 85 mph
Ceiling: 14,500 ft
Engine: One 120 hp
        deHavilland Gypsy II

D.H. 60G GIPSY MOTH

Kelowna

William "Billy" Stark made the first flight in BC Interior at Armstrong, July 1, 1915, in his Curtiss type Pusher.
Vernon Archives

The first flight to occur in the Okanagan Valley took place at Armstrong on Dominion Day, July 1, 1912, some fifteen miles north of Vernon, when Vancouver aviator William "Billy" Stark gave an exhibition flight to over 4,000 spectators.

Two years later on August 13, 1914, an American aviator Weldon Cooke flew his Curtiss Type Pusher Hydro-Aeroplane at the Kelowna Regatta, although most reports indicate that only a single flight was made from the lakefront because of engine trouble. A report by the Okanagan Museum and Archives Association, edited by Ian Pooley and Doctor Knox, states that Cooke's machine was equipped with a temporary float which detached after take off exposing a set of wheels, and that aviator Cook flew his Hydro-Aeroplane northward to "a rather bumpy landing at Vernon".

The first documented visit of a flying machine to Vernon was on August 4, 1919, when Lieutenant Ernie 0. Hall arrived in the late afternoon from Kamloops in a Curtiss JN-4 Canuck belonging to the Vancouver Aerial Transportation Company. Hall had agreed to the flight to participate in the Peace Day celebrations. Hall then departed Vernon after his exhibition and flew to Penticton.

Earlier that summer a Lieutenant G.K. Trim had traveled to Vernon by train to assist in the formation of a local branch of the Aerial League of Canada. Ex-Royal Flying Corps veterans at

Lt. Ernest O. Hall landed the Vatco Curtiss JN-4 at Vernon, August 4, 1919. Vernon Archives

Vernon included Billy McCluskey, Dick Monk, and Dolly Gray.

Just three days after Lieutenant Hall's first landing at Vernon, another Curtiss JN-4 Canuck arrived. On August 7 Captain Ernie Hoy, who had been selected to make a record breaking flight from Vancouver to Calgary and return by the Vancouver Branch of the Aerial League of Canada, arrived at Vernon's Mission Hill at 7:18 a.m. on the first stop on this previously unflown route.

After Captain Hoy was taken to breakfast by Mayor Shatford and his aircraft refueled, Hoy took off for Grand Forks at 8:19 a.m. Hoy was successful in reaching Calgary after twelve hours and thirty-four minutes of flying in the same day.

J. Scott Williams, owner of Curtiss JN-4 G-CAAG, arrived at Mission Hill Field June 1921. PAC

Trim remained in the Okanagan Valley for three or four weeks barnstorming, carrying passengers, and giving exhibition flights. He later did the same flying at Grand Forks and Nelson.

During June of 1921, Mr. Scott-Williams landed JN-4 Canuck, G-CAAG, at Mission Hill field. Scott-Williams reportedly made several public presentations regarding the future of aviation during his stay at Vernon.

For several years there were no further landings at Vernon although RCAF Vickers Veddettes and Fairchild FC-2W's from Jericho Beach Air Station were observed overhead, likely based at Kamloops or Sicamous on forestry or photographic assignments for the summer.

Capt. E. Hoy arrives at Mission Hill, August 7, 1919. Via J. Brown

However, his return from Calgary via Golden ended in disaster when his aircraft crashed on takeoff, luckily without injury to Hoy.

On August 21, 1919, two weeks after Captain Hoy passed through Vernon, another Aerial League pilot, Lieutenant G.K. Trim, arrived in yet another Curtiss JN-4 Canuck, number 5 of the Aerial League.

On September 6, 1928, a new Alexander Eaglerock biplane belonging to Yukon Airways and Exploration Company of Whitehorse, Yukon, arrived at Vernon's Mission Hill Field. G-CAUZ was flown by John M. Patterson with company official Clyde G. Wann. Wann had taken delivery of the Eaglerock, christened the "Northern

Vernon

Airphoto of Mission Hill Field, 1934.
1936 Established Landing Ground Directory.

FACILITIES

Hangars

Fuel and Oil - day only

Mission Hill Field under construction 1930. Vernon Archives

ELEVATION - 1485'

POSITION
LAT. 50°14'N.   LONG. 119°19'W.
On city limits to South

OPERATED BY
City of Vernon

REMARKS
At site of former military camp on 130 acres of land.

LANDING AREA
Rectangular shaped - sod and clay
E-W   2000' x 300'
N-S   2100' x 500'

OBSTRUCTIONS
Pole line - N.
Road and pole line - W.
Pole line - NW.
Slope and rolling hills adjacent to S. & SW.

1929

Light", in Denver, Colorado, on September 7, where Wann hired Patterson. After getting temporary Canadian registration at Vancouver, they were barnstorming their way to the Yukon. They did not reach Whitehorse until December 1928, by which time they had carried over 1,200 passengers. Wann later stated that the aircraft had cost fourteen thousand dollars but that it was paid for by the time it was delivered to the Yukon.

Starting in 1928, John A. Wilson, the Canadian Controller of Civil Aviation Department of National Defence, gave authorization for a preliminary survey for a trans-Canada airway from Vancouver to Halifax. The survey in British Columbia was undertaken by Squadron Leaders John H. (Tuddy) Tudhope, Superintendant of Airways, and A.D. (Dan) McLean, Inspector of Western Airways.

S/L Tudhope decided that Vernon's location and the Mission Hill field were ideally located as his base of operations during the survey in British Columbia. During his stay he did much to encourage and school the city's politicians in the development and promotion of their aviation field. Tuddy was able to convince city council as to the benefits of licensing the Mission Hill field and this would later result in John Blakely's flying school relocating to Vernon from Kelowna.

In the last part of 1929 Vernon City Council passed a bylaw resulting in the purchase of one hundred and thirty acres south of the town at Mission Hill funded by a four thousand dollar bond issue. Tuddy earlier arranged for S/L A.T. (Tom) Cowley to inspect the site and make recommendations on its site development.

On May 10, 1929, an RCAF photographic aircraft from Jericho Beach arrived at Salmon Arm and began an aerial survey of the northern Okanagan. The Fairchild FC-2W on floats, G-CYXQ, was flown by F/0 Windsor, with photographer mechanic William Cecil Attwood. XQ left the area on June 9.

On May 26, 1930, G-CYXQ returned to Salmon Arm on its photo survey, this time flown by F/0 C.R. Dunlap but again with photographer Attwood. On July 8 XQ landed at Vernon's nearby Okanagan Landing remaining until July 11, 1930. XQ was at Vernon to search for a missing aircraft flown by Alex Smith, which XQ located at Aberdeen Lake.

On April 21, 1930, Tuddy took delivery of a new Stearman 4C Junior Speedmail aircraft, CF-CCH, at Wichita, Kansas, and flew back to Vernon the same day.

On April 29, 1931, Dan McLean, District Inspector of Western Airways Civil Aviation Branch, flew into Vernon from Regina after an overnight stop at Trail. McLean landed his department's new Stearman 4C Junior Speedmail, CF-CCG, on the Mission Hill Field. He was at the city to meet with Vernon's airport committee headed by Alderman A.C. Wilde to work out the details of issuing an airport license. McLean stated he was satisfied with the field's location, but that the road going through it was undesirable.

In May 1930, Radium Flying Service operator John Blakely based a DH-60M Gipsy Moth, CF-AGK, at Mission Hill Field and his instructor pilot Lowell Dunsmore barnstormed, flew charters, and instructed area student pilots.

The Vernon Daily News edition of September 10, 1931, reported that the improvements necessary to license Mission Hill Field were well underway with two runways graded and leveled and runway markers in place. The Department of

Nick Mamer's Ford 4-AT NC-8403 from Spokane visits Mission Hill Field. Vernon Archives

Public Works had previously relocated the highway around the airfield.

On September 30 and October 1, 1931, Vernon hosted an Air Pageant which was rated a huge success in promoting aviation to the city. A temporary field license was issued for the occasion by the Civil Aviation Branch Department of National Defence. The Pageant was attended by fourteen machines, many from Washington State including Nick B. Mamer's Ford Tri-Motor and Aeromarine Klem NC-199M flown by Lana R. Kurtzer from Seattle, and many others. Also present were two RCAF Vickers Vedette MKV flying boats: number 116 flown by S/L Earl MacLeod, Commanding Officer of the Jericho Beach Air Station; and number 109 flown by F/L J.L.E.A. deNiverville, As well, as a large contingent from Vancouver attended.

On February 26, 1932, a letter was mailed to Alderman A.C. Wilde from the District Inspector, Western Airways Department of National Defence, advising of the issuance of permanent airport license number 155.

During July 1932 the Aero Club of B.C. organized the B.C. Air Tour which arrived at Mission Hill Field on July 8. Tour officials had limited the tour, with two exceptions, to aircraft owned by residents of British Columbia. The exceptions were Shell Oil's Lockheed "Vega" NC-657E from San Francisco and flown by Bill Fletcher, and Imperial Oil's DH-80A "Puss Moth" flown by Pat Reid from Winnipeg. A number of unofficial aircraft also arrived for the tour including six from Washington State.

On July 13, Shell Oil's Lockheed Vega returned to Vernon from Grand Forks. Company officials were on a tour of the Province organized by Charles Anstie, an employee of the company. Shortly after the completion of the tour, NC-657E crashed in Washington State and Pilot Bill Fletcher was killed after he flew for six hours trying to find a hole in the fog on the coast.

On July 12, 1932, CF-AMA, a Curtiss Robin belonging to Consolidated Mining and Smelting Company of Trail and flown by pilot Howard Anderson, arrived at Mission Hill on company business. AMA again arrived on July 13, also from Trail.

On July 14 a Brieze Monoplane NC-3817 arrived from Seattle flown by Ed Morris.

A 1923 Junkers F-13, CF-AMX, landed at nearby Okanagan Landing at 6:15 p.m. on September 10, 1932, flown from Burns Lake by Bill McCluskey. This was the same aircraft that was abandoned by Paddy Burke in October 1930 after it became frozen in on the upper reaches of the Liard River in the Yukon. Burke died of exposure while trying to walk out. AMX was later repaired and salvaged on February 11, 1931 by World War I German pilot Bill Joerss and R.I. Van der Byl, who were working for the aircraft owner, the Air-Land Manufacturing Company of Vancouver who still operated the machine.

A Ryan B-1 Brougham CF-ATA landed at Mission Hill at 10:45 a.m. October 1, 1932, flown

The Mission Hill Field aircraft register for the Vernon Air Pageant on September 30 and October 1, 1931, lists the following aircraft present:

FROM	AIRCRAFT	REGISTRA-	PILOT
Vancouver	RCAF Vickers Vedette	#116	S/L Earl MacLeod
Vancouver	RCAF Vickers Vedette	#109	F/L A. deNiverville
Vancouver	Fairchild 71 (floats)	CF-AJP	Gordon K. MacKenzie
Seattle	Travelair	NC-3824	Edward Morris
Seattle	Aeromarine Klemm	NC-199M	Lana R. Kurtzer
Vancouver	Fleet 2	CF-ANL	Haliburton Wilson
Vancouver	Waco 10	CF-AAQ	A.E. Bennett
Vancouver	DH-60M Moth	CF-ADY	William Bolton
Vancouver	Fleet 2	CF-ANN	J.A. Wright
Seattle	Stinson	NC-994W	J.F. Brod
Spokane	Buhl	NC-1732	Roy Shreck
Seattle	Great Lakes	NC-441Y	A.L. Lee
Spokane	Ford 4-AT-65	NC-8403	Nick Mamer
Radium Hot Springs	DH-60M	CF-AGK	L.L. Dunsmore

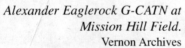
Alexander Eaglerock G-CATN at Mission Hill Field.
Vernon Archives

The Aero Club of BC Fleet 2's, CF-ANH, ANL and ANN at Mission Hill Field, October 1, 1931, for the Vernon Air Pageant. Vernon Archives

Aeromarine Klem NC-199M flown by Lana Kurtzer of Seattle at Vernon, September 30, 1931. Vernon Archives

Vernon

A Landing Gypsy Moth being watched by helmeted airman at Mission Hill.
Vernon Archives

A Fleet 2 at Mission Hill Field. Note blind flying hood in rear cockpit. Vernon Archives

Buhl CA-6 "Air Sedan" NC-1732 visits Mission Hill Field, October 1, 1931, from Spokane.

16 Planes Thrilled Vernon

VERNON, July 11.—A huge crowd thronged Vernon's civic airport Saturday afternoon to enjoy the program of thrills given by the pilots of the B. C. air tour contingent, and from the opening stunts of the three musketeers, A. H. Wilson, Maurice McGregor and Don Lawson, in their Aero Club fleet biplanes, to the final breathtaking parachute plunge of N. McKenzie, there was not an event that did not catch every eye.

Twelve planes were on the field for the opening and four machines from Seattle arrived shortly after lunch to augment the B. C. squad. The B. C. air tour planes will leave Tuesday morning for Kamloops, where they will give the show Wednesday afternoon.

The Kamloops Sentinel, Monday, July 11, 1932

Vernon

Vernon Air Pageant crowds September 30 and October 1, 1931.
Vernon Archives

by Ginger Coote of Cariboo Bridge River Airways. This aircraft was very similar to the Ryan used by Lindberg to fly to France.

During 1932 Vernon was designated as a Public Customs Point of Entry for aircraft.

At 12:30 p.m. June 10, 1933, a three engine Fokker, NC-565K, landed on a flight from

Fokker Tri Motor NC-565K lands at Mission Hill Field, June 10, 1933. Vernon Archives

Vancouver to Calgary flown by W.K. Scott. Five days later W.R. McClusky was back with Junkers F-13, CF-AMX, landing at Okanagan Landing.

Throughout the early 1930s Vernon became well known as a serviceable and reliable stop in southern British Columbia. Information and a

diagram of the field at Vernon's Mission Hill Field was published in a popular US pilots' manual entitled Airports and Established Landing Fields, published by the Airport Directory Company of Hackensack, New Jersey.

On January 27, 1934, W.J. Barrows arrived in a Consolidated Fleetster 17-A, NC-705Y. Barrows was en route to Alaska via Prince George. This aircraft was one of three built for Eastern Air Lines then sold to Pacific Alaska Airlines in June 1933. The other two Fleetsters, NC-703Y and 704Y, were sold by Pacific Alaska to Armtorg, the Soviet Trading Company, in March 1934 to be used in the rescue of the passengers and crew of the Russian vessel Chelyuskin that was crushed by ice in the Chuckchi Sea near Siberia.

On May 18, 1934, the District Inspector, Civil Aviation Branch, Carter Guest arrived from Grand Forks in CF-CCD, a 1930 DH-60M Gipsy Moth. This was Guest's second visit in CCD, the first being on June 6, 1933, when he flew in from Vancouver. He again landed at the Mission Hill Field on September 18, 1934 in CF-CCK, a DH-80A Puss Moth which he flew from Grand Forks.

Vernon's first home built aircraft, a Corben "JR Ace", CF-AOM. Vernon Archives

Vernon

CF-ARF, a Boeing A-213 Totem built by Canadian Boeing at Vancouver, landed on nearby Kalamalka Lake at 4:00 p.m. on August 14. ARF, operated by Canadian Airways, was flown by Bill Lawson from Vancouver.

On June 1, 1935, instructor Lowell L. Dunsmore made a flight test in a Corben Junior Ace, CF-AOM, powered by a Salmson Ad9 radial engine. The homebuilt aircraft, christened "City of Vernon", was constructed by Jack Taylor, Ernie Bulfum, Jim Duddle, and Eldon Seymour. Duddle later flew AOM to Edmonton, Alberta.

Vernon aircraft builders Eldon Seymour and Jimmy Duddle pose with Corben Jr. Ace CF-AOM in 1935. Vernon Archives

Kelowna resident Cliff Renfrew applied to rent a hangar on the Mission Hill Field for his 1934 de Havilland DH-80A Puss Moth, CF-AVA, becoming the second private aircraft based at Vernon.

During the later part of 1936 several experimental flights were carried out in conjunction with the future establishment of an airway from Lethbridge to Vancouver. Air Commodore Herbert "Bertie" Hollick-Kenyon of Canadian Airways based Lockheed 10A Electra, CF-BAF, at Mission Hill Field for nearly six weeks starting on November 23, 1936. This time he was accompanied by J.H. "Tuddy" Tudhope and three Department of Transport specialists in conjunction with the establishment of the Green 1 Radio Range airway to the coast.

Yukon Southern Air Transport inaugurated a weekly service between Vancouver and the Okanagan Valley in the spring of 1939 utilizing a Barkley-Grow T8P-1 twin engine aircraft, which would land at Oliver's new intermediate airfield on the trans Canada airway.

YSAT then based a WACO Model ZQC-6 Custom at Oliver. This aircraft would shuttle up the Okanagan to Penticton, Kelowna, and Vernon to feed passengers to the Barkley-Grow. The valiant attempt by YSAT however was not viable and lasted only six weeks and the WACO was withdrawn from the Okanagan.

The site of Vernon's Mission Hill Field had been a part of a military camp as well as a concentration camp during World

CF-AOM, a Corben Jr. Ace "City of Vernon" built at Vernon 1935 (shown here with cabin enclosed). Vernon Archives

Vernon

55

Vernon mural of Eldon Seymour and Jimmy Duddle with the "City of Vernon" homebuilt CF-AOM. C.W.

Cockpit of Electra "BAF". Vernon Archives

CF-BAF after snowfall at Vernon, December 1936.
Vernon Archives

*Lockheed 10A "Electra" CF-BAF at Mission Hill
November 1936, flown by Herbert Hollick-Kenyon.*
Vernon Archives

*Canadian Airways' Lockheed 10A "Electra" CF-BAF at
Mission Hill, November - December 1936.* Vernon Archives

Vernon

An RCAF Dakota Medivac flight was one of the last aircraft to use the Mission Hill Field. Vernon Archives

War I, and with the coming of World War II in 1939 the Department of National Defence advised the city that it would require the use of this land again. The city patriotically responded in favour of the request and the airfield changed hands for the sum of two hundred and forty-seven

dollars and fifty cents per year, which was the amount of interest payable on the bonds issued to originally fund the land purchase and the construction of the airport.

The Vernon News edition of January 4, 1940, advised that at the last council meeting held in December 1939, the city was trying to locate a site for a new airport and that Air Commodore Hollick-Kenyon was expected in Vernon the following week to assist in the selection of a suitable location.

Post War air photo of Vernon looking North. C.W.

Art Seller of Vancouver's U-Fly lands a Piper PA-16 "Clipper" at Mission Hill in 1946. Vernon Archives

Civil aviation ceased at Vernon for the duration of the war. The city and its advisors finally settled on a site two miles west of the city near Okanagan Landing on Okanagan Lake, east of the Indian Reserve and between Long Lake (Vernon) Creek and the roadway. The proposed airfield would have a single runway aligned 06-24 and be 1,950 feet by 500 feet.

The property, which was owned by a Mr. Paimar and Mr. Kulak, had been considered as

Vernon

VERNON B.C.

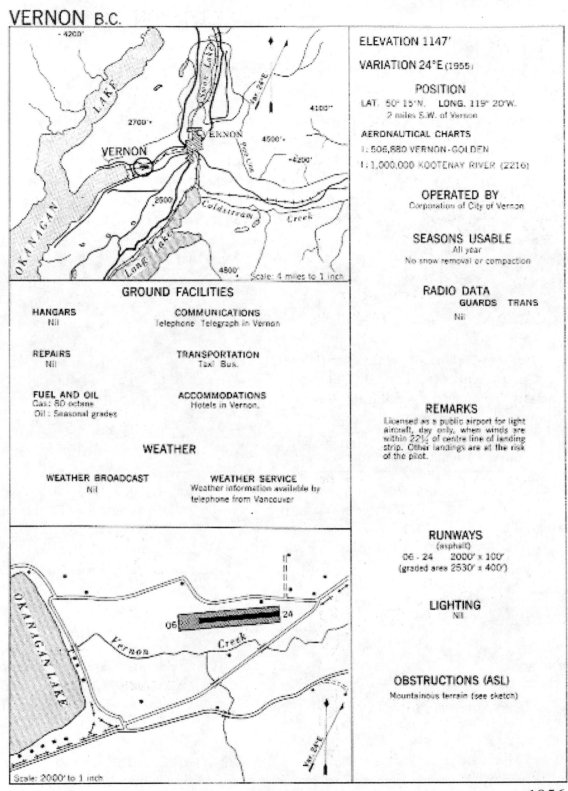

ELEVATION 1147'

VARIATION 24°E (1955)

POSITION
LAT. 50° 15'N.   LONG. 119° 20'W.
2 miles S.W. of Vernon

AERONAUTICAL CHARTS
1: 506,880 VERNON-GOLDEN
1: 1,000,000 KOOTENAY RIVER (2216)

OPERATED BY
Corporation of City of Vernon

SEASONS USABLE
All year
No snow removal or compaction

RADIO DATA
GUARDS   TRANS
Nil

GROUND FACILITIES

HANGARS
Nil

COMMUNICATIONS
Telephone Telegraph in Vernon

REPAIRS
Nil

TRANSPORTATION
Taxi Bus.

FUEL AND OIL
Gas: 80 octane
Oil: Seasonal grades

ACCOMMODATIONS
Hotels in Vernon.

WEATHER

WEATHER BROADCAST
Nil

WEATHER SERVICE
Weather information available by
telephone from Vancouver

REMARKS
Licensed as a public airport for light
aircraft, day only, when winds are
within 22½ of centre line of landing
strip. Other landings are at the risk
of the pilot.

RUNWAYS
(asphalt)
06 - 24   2000' x 100'
(graded area 2530' x 400')

LIGHTING
Nil

OBSTRUCTIONS (ASL)
Mountainous terrain (see sketch)

1956

Vernon

an airfield site in 1936 during the survey for a trans Canada airway, but was deemed unsuitable because it was on a C.P.R. right-of-way; however, this line was subsequently abandoned.

In a brief made in June 1946 by Mayor David Howrie, who had been on the airfield committee seven years before, stated "it is our intention to provide a small strip for light airplanes. The purchase of land from Palmer and Kulak would provide a strip 1,950 feet long and 700 feet wide. This purchase would leave a certain amount of land which would be negotiable for other purposes."

On Friday, June 28, 1946, Vernon's ratepayers were asked to vote on an eighteen thousand dollar bylaw for the purchase of fifty-two acres. The vote was positive and the City developed the land as previously stated and in 1947 applied to the Department of Transport for a license.

Just nine days after the approval of the airport bylaw the first aircraft landed at the site. Bob Filtness of Vancouver flew his Fleet Canuck into Vernon from Yakima, Washington. Filtness advised a local reporter that he intended to apply for a license to operate a charter service at Vernon.

An inspection was made by Department of Transport officials, and in due course the City was advised by the District Inspector of Airways, Bill Lawson, that the application was denied because his department felt the runway was too short and that it must be at least 2,500 feet long and clear of obstructions. The city had spent $18,000 on construction of the airfield and no further funding was available. The land to the east of the airfield was orchard land and was at the time too expensive. The City and airport committee

approached the Indian Band and were turned down. The development was stalemated.

R.H. Dick Laidman had grown up in the area and left in 1938 to work in eastern and northern Canada for several airline companies, first as an engineer and later as a pilot. At the war's end Laidman was in Yellowknife and applied for, and received, a license to operate a flying school and charter air service at Vernon. He owned a de Havilland DH-87, CF-BBE, a Hornet Moth and a DH-82C Tiger Moth and had returned to the city in September 1946 locating his aircraft on the new airfield. Laidman and his L&M Air Services were in a quandary - he had a license to operate, but the airfield had been refused a license.

Air photo of Post WWII Vernon Airfield. Vernon Archives

Laidman wasn't the kind of man to wring his hands and gnash his teeth. He decided to take the bull by the horns and went to see the local chief of the Indian Band, Pierre Jack. It took four months of negotiations but he got the city a lease on 600 feet by 400 feet of land. The city set about the development of the airfield so that it would meet the license requirements. By July 1, 1947 the license was approved and L&M Air Services was in full operation. By this time Laidman had

Vernon

two partners, ex-RCAF pilot Peter Dyck and Jimmy Inglis. Hugh Mann later joined the team and Manville Pepper was hired as a pilot.

When Okanagan Air Service moved from Penticton to Kelowna they were a Cessna dealer and operated new aircraft. Laidman realized that his Hornet Moth was fine in bush flying but the newer Cessnas were more economical and had more appeal. L&M soon purchased its first Cessna 140, CF-GII, and a Stinson 108 followed by an Avro Anson MKV, CF-FVA. In 1948 L&M purchased a Beech 18, CF-BQH, for use on the scheduled class 2 airline service that began on floats from Okanagan Landing to the foot of Barnard Street at Kelowna and to the north foot of Penticton's Main Street, as well as on the river in front of Kamloops. However, the service was poorly supported and, much like Yukon Southern's attempt to offer scheduled service in the Okanagan ten years earlier, soon came to an end. L&M was able to keep going largely because of the 1948 flood relief program to the Fraser Valley, but by the early 1950s they decided to close their doors.

Many private aircraft owners and aviation companies have based at Vernon since the 1950s. The original runway was considered by many to be difficult to approach and too confining. On

L&M Air Services Cessna 140 CF-GII at Vernon 1946.
Vernon Archives

September 5, 1955, CF-CIP, a de Havilland DH-82C Tiger Moth from Vancouver, stalled on its approach to the Vernon airfield and spun to the ground destroying the aircraft.

This author first landed at Vernon on May 13, 1969, after a flight from Bellingham, Washington, via Oroville in my 1939 Luscombe 8A, N-25109 (later CF-QRU). My first twin engine landing occurred June 22, 1976, in CF-SNC, an Aero Commander 680E operated by Futura Aviation Limited of Vancouver on courier operations.

August 7, 1969, was the 50th anniversary of the first flight across the Canadian Rockies from Vancouver to Calgary, and at 7:18 a.m. Captain Ernest Hoy of the Vancouver Aerial League had landed his Curtiss JN-4 Canuck at Vernon's Mission Hill Field on the first leg of his flight. A long-time Vernon resident, pilot, and chairman of the Vernon Flying Club, Douglas Kermode, suggested to his membership that the Club should host Hoy in honour of the 50th anniversary of the flight and fly him from Calgary to Vancouver with stops at Golden and Vernon. Air Canada agreed to fly Hoy from his home in Georgia, USA, to Calgary and the Vernon Flying Club arranged for a Piper PA-23 Apache to fly him from there.

The Vernon airport, when originally licensed, was only barely long enough to qualify, and its approaches from the east, especially, introduced an element of "pucker factor" particularly on a hot day in a high performance airplane. Rumors abounded about re-aligning the runway to make it safer and more usable to the community, however not much was accomplished until the City of Vernon decided to transfer its operation to the North Okanagan Regional District who arranged for a Federal Government grant of $450,000. The

Vernon

On August 7, 1969, Vernon Flying Club Chairman Doug Kermode (L) welcomes Ernest Hoy (C), with C.O.P.A. Director (R) on the 50th anniversary of Capt. Hoy's first flight over Rocky Mountains in 1919. Vernon Archives

new runway was built aligned 05-23 and was paved for 3,120 feet by 75 feet. A pilot operated lighting and approach aid system was also installed. The official dedication ceremony took place on Sunday July 6, 1986.

Okanagan North Member of Parliament Vince Dantzer officially opened the North Okanagan Regional Airport and many officials and dignitaries said the usual things, but one of the oldest Vernon pilots present probably summed up the occasion best. A pilot for over fifty-five years, Eldon Seymour was one of the three teenagers who in 1934 constructed the homebuilt Corben Junior Ace, CF-AOM, City of Vernon. Seymour was interviewed at the 1986 opening and he remarked that the new Regional Airport is "one of the better ones in the British Columbia interior, but not so long ago it was one of the worst."

On September 12, 1988, the author landed Mitsubishi MU-2F, CF-AMP, on the new runway. The MU-2 is considered by some to be difficult to fly. I experienced no trouble operating it at Vernon.

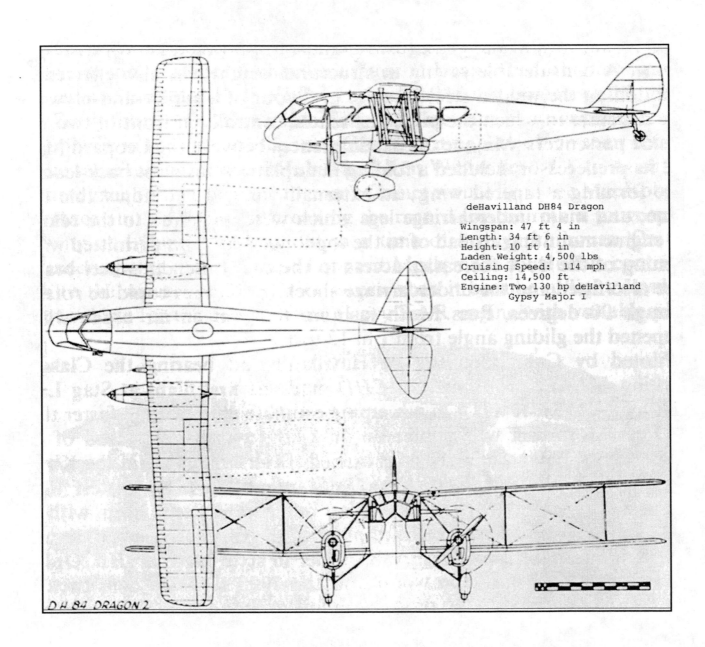

deHavilland DH84 Dragon

Wingspan: 47 ft 4 in
Length: 34 ft 6 in
Height: 10 ft 1 in
Laden Weight: 4,500 lbs
Cruising Speed: 114 mph
Ceiling: 14,500 ft
Engine: Two 130 hp deHavilland
        Gypsy Major I

D H 84 DRAGON 2

Vernon

Kamloops

At 5:30 p.m. on Friday, August 1, 1919, Captain Ernest 0. Hall arrived over the city of Kamloops in a Curtiss JN-4 Canuck owned by the Vancouver Aerial Transportation Company.

Hall flew into the city from Merritt where he had given exhibition flights for several days. After giving a demonstration of his stunting prowess, Hall landed at the Kamloops exhibition grounds at Fruitlands but later flew to the old polo grounds on the east side of the city. On August 2, Hall gave many of the citizens a flight around the city at a cost of fifteen dollars each. One of his flights was given to Chief Eli LaRue of the Saint Paul Reserve, who would be the first Native to fly in British Columbia. Hall left Kamloops on the afternoon of August 4 and flew to Vernon.

Kamloops received its next aircraft visit beginning in late October 1920. On October 28, 1920, Major Clarence

Curtiss JN-4 "Canuck" of Vatco" flown by Lt. Ernest Hall is the first aircraft at Kamloops in 1919. Kamloops Museum

Lt. Ernie Hall arrives over Kamloops in "Vatco" Curtiss JN-4, August 1, 1919. Kamloops Museum

Curtiss HS-2L G-CYBA at Kamloops October 1920. Major McLaurin stands on front of aircraft. Kamloops Museum

over an area of one hundred miles each side of the valleys between Kamloops and Sicamous.

In the summer of 1921, Major MacLaurin flew an HS-2L from Jericho Beach to Kamloops to assist in forest fire protection and other forestry surveys. MacLaurin's flight from the coast took two hours and forty-five minutes and was the first time a flying boat had been flown over the coast mountains.

MacLaurin, Superintendent of the newly created Canadian Air Board, Jericho Beach Air Station at Vancouver, shipped a Curtiss HS-2L, G-CYBA, to Carneys Landing near Sicamous to conduct an aerial survey of the Kamloops Forest District.

For fourteen days MacLaurin, in company with Roy Cameron, a Dominion Government Forester, photographer C.J. Duncan, and air mechanic A.C. Hartridge, flew the Curtiss HS-2L, G-CYBA,

Lieutenant Earl McLeod was stationed at Kamloops throughout much of the summer, until he was replaced by Lieutenant Harry Brown as Chief Pilot at the Kamloops Air Board Detachment.

In 1922, the Jericho Beach Air Station detached two aircraft to Kamloops for forestry patrols. For the remainder of the 1920s RCAF aircraft from Jericho Beach would continue to serve the Kamloops and Shuswap area from Kamloops, providing both topographic surveys and forestry patrols. Dominion Surveyor C.H. Taggart was based in Kamloops and he produced a series of topographical maps from data gathered by aircraft based at Kamloops.

As of 1927 the city still lacked an airfield. In the past, aircraft landed on the city's exhibition grounds and polo

RCAF Fairchild FC-2W G-CYXN at Kamloops, 1928. Kamloops Museum

RCAF Fairchild FC-2W G-CYXQ under tow to wharf at Salmon Arm, 1928.
Kamloops Museum

field, as well as the Saint Paul Indian Reserve. The Kamloops Board of Trade began a search for a site in 1927, initially choosing the Indian Reserve, but these negotiations collapsed largely due to financial reasons.

On Thursday, August 23, 1928, Flying Officer E.J.A.(Paddy) Burke of the RCAF station at Jericho Beach, who was temporarily stationed at Salmon Arm, attended an organizational meeting at Kamloops to assist in the formation of a light aeroplane club in the city.

Around September 10, 1928, a new biplane landed at the Saint Paul Indian Reserve at Kamloops. The Alexander Eaglerock A-2, with registration G-CAUZ, had flown from Vancouver where its temporary Canadian registration had been processed after its delivery flight from the factory in Colorado, USA. Pilot John Patterson and Clyde Wann

departed Kamloops September 13 for Whitehorse, Y.T.

In June 1929, the Indian Band agreed to allow the Kamloops Air Club to use the reserve subject to an annual lease.

Late in 1930, Humphrey Madden arrived in Kamloops and set up a flying school on the Indian Reserve, unofficially known as Rattlesnake Field, and on weekends he and Joe Bertalino, his air engineer, flew CF-AKC, a 1929 Fleet Model 2, throughout the area giving stunts and rides.

Earlier that same year Kamloops City Council had decided to establish its airfield at the Saint Paul Indian Reserve and, after the City advised the Directorate of Civil Air Operations, Department of National Defence, that Federal

G-CAUZ, a Yukon Airways Eaglerock barnstormed at Kamloops September 10, 1928. Kamloops Museum

Kamloops

RCAF F/O E.J.A. "Paddy" Burke and crew at Kamloops while on photographic survey, August 23, 1928. Kamloops Museum

"Humph" Madden's Fleet 2 CF-AKC at St. Paul Indian Reserve, Kamloops, April 1931. Kamloops Museum

Pilot Engineer Joe Bertalino poses with CF-AKC in front of their tent at the St. Paul Indian Reserve. Kamloops Museum

Air crew of the B.C. Air Tour at Kamloops, Summer 1932. Kamloops Museum

organization sent Major John H. Tudhope RCAF to inspect the site. Tudhope declared the site suitable, but when the City attempted to close the land deal with Reserve Elders they found that the Depression had pushed the price out of their reach.

In February 1931, Hump Madden received a telegram from DND Ottawa advising him that his Kamloops Air Service was to cease operations until such a time that an airport was licenced at Kamloops. Madden and Bertalino moved their flying school to the Columbia Gardens airfield near Trail.

The Kamloops Sentinel edition of Friday, June 5, 1931, advised that the City had selected a new airport site of 80 acres

near Brocklehurst five miles northwest of the city on property owned by B.C. Fruitlands.

On Tuesday July 11, 1932 the BC Air Tour arrived in Kamloops from Vernon. The aerial

Aero Club of BC Fleet 7B CF-CEM with parachutist Cecil McKenzie "Batman" in rear cockpit. Kamloops Museum

Kamloops

Fly-In to Kamloops 1938. L. to R.: CF-AVA, DH80 Puss Moth from Vernon; CF-CEM Fleet 7B from Vancouver; CF-ANN Fleet 2 from Vancouver.
Kamloops Museum

pageant was operated by members of the Aero Club of B.C. to promote aviation in the province and emulate the Trans-Canada Air Pageant held in 1931. The Air Tour used the new Kamloops airfield west of Brocklehurst.

Kamloops City Council announced on June 27, 1933, that the Dominion Government had made a proposal to the City that the Dominion

Government would extend its relief scheme to Kamloops if the City were to purchase the 80 acre airfield property and would utilize unemployed single men to develop and improve the airfield site. This was now the height of the Depression, and the City found itself financially unable to justify the expense of purchasing airfield lands.

In 1937, the Kamloops Sentinel ran a series of editorials scathing the City's lack of a licenced airfield when most other centres in the province had by this time opened their civic airfields. In the spring of 1938, the City finalized an agreement with B.C. Fruitlands to purchase 45 acres and obtained a temporary operating licence from the DOT.

During December 1938, G.C. Upson, Assistant Inspector Civil Aviation Department of Transport, Vancouver, examined the field and declared it satisfactory. On December 12, City Council was advised that C.D. Howe, Minister of Transport, Ottawa, had advised that his government would provide a grant of $6,000 to upgrade the airport and pave its runway.

On January 18, 1939, the Kamloops Flying Club was organized and on April 13 the first official landing was made when Cyril Jackson landed his Aeronca.

Stinson SR Reliant visits the Kamloops Air Show of 1939. Kamloops Museum

The airport was designated an official Customs Port of Entry on August 1, 1939, and on August 5 the airport held its official grand opening with many aircraft in attendance in spite of the inclement weather.

On November 1, 1939, the first official airmail flight from Kamloops to Prince George and Whitehorse was flown by a Yukon Southern Air Transport Barclay-Grow aircraft, CF-BLV, under the command of Sheldon Luck.

On April 16, 1942, the Gilbert's Flying School of Vancouver moved to Kamloops as all civil training west of the coast mountains was curtailed for the duration of the war. For a time the flying school was the only one in operation west of Winnipeg.

The Kamloops Flying Club ceased activity throughout the war years.

Between 1939 and 1945 the airport was developed by the RCAF as an alternate aerodrome and was used by the RCAF and United States Air Transport Command.

Kamloops Airport was designated by the RCAF as Number 16 Staging Unit on the Interior Staging Route to accommodate possible needs of the USAF in its Lend Lease Program of supply-

Dignitaries and aircrew at Kamloops Air Show 1939. Kamloops Museum

First official Air Mail flight at Kamloops November 1, 1939. Capt., Sheldon Luck stands 4th from left in front of Y.S.A.T. Barklay-Grow CF-BLV "Yukon Queen". Kamloops Museum

ing aircraft to Russia via Alaska. The airport was also considered as a possible "secondary line of defence" should the Japanese invade the west coast of Canada.

The Department of National Defence purchased an additional 861 acres of land and rebuilt runways to 5,200 feet. Taxiways were added and

Modern air photo looking North at Kamloops Airfield.
CW

twelve buildings were constructed starting in December 1942 and completed in June 1943. The RCAF staff complement at this period was over 100 strong.

At the end of hostilities, surplus land was sold to the City of Kamloops and the Department of Agriculture reduced the size of the airport to 570 acres.

On November 13, 1945, a flying club was again organized at Kamloops and was affiliated with the Aero Club of British Columbia.

In the late 1940s Harry Taylor and Pete Cornwell formed Taylor Cornwell Air Services, followed soon thereafter by Kamloops Air Services which was organized by Harry Bray. By the early 1950s Central B.C. Airways moved into Kamloops and in 1951 made the location its headquarters. Central

B.C. was formed by Russ Baker, later of Pacific Western Airlines, who had lobbied successfully and acquired a contract from the Provincial government to provide forestry protection services. This effectively eliminated all competition at Kamloops.

In August 1964, John Pickersgill officially opened the Kamloops Airport after extensive renovations. Some twenty years earlier the airport was named Fulton Field when the then Governor General, the Earl of Athlone, dedicated it to Wing Commander John Fulton, DSO, as well as to the airmen who lost their lives during the war.

Sheldon Luck at Kamloops 50th Anniversary of First Air Mail Flight,

KAMLOOPS B.C.

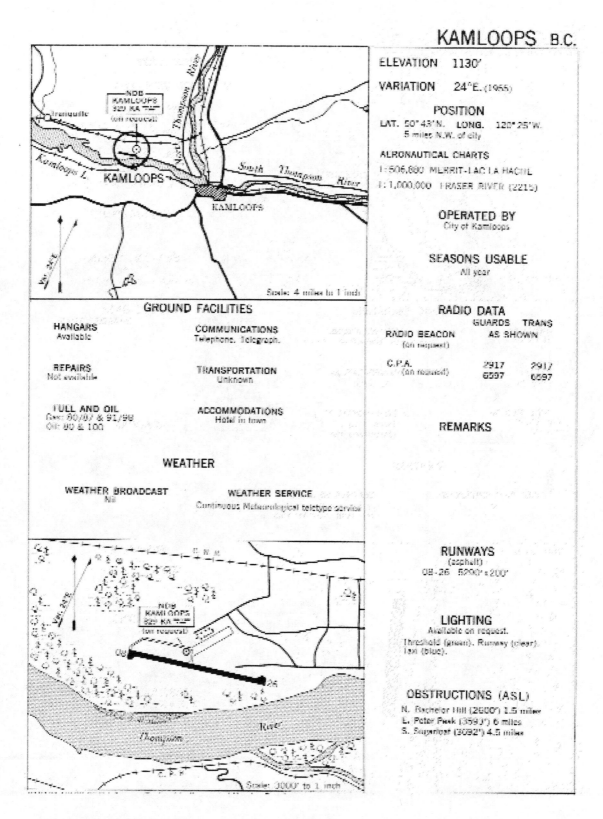

ELEVATION 1130'

VARIATION 24°E. (1955)

POSITION
LAT. 50°43'N. LONG. 120°25'W.
5 miles N.W. of city

ALRONAUTICAL CHARTS
1:506,880 MERRIT-LAC LA HACHE
1:1,000,000 FRASER RIVER (2215)

OPERATED BY
City of Kamloops

SEASONS USABLE
All year

RADIO DATA

RADIO BEACON (on request)	GUARDS	TRANS
	AS SHOWN	
C.P.A. (on request)	2917	2917
	6597	6597

REMARKS

GROUND FACILITIES

HANGARS
Available

COMMUNICATIONS
Telephone. Telegraph.

REPAIRS
Not available

TRANSPORTATION
Unknown

FULL AND OIL
Gas: 80/87 & 91/98
Oil: 80 & 100

ACCOMMODATIONS
Hotel in town

WEATHER

WEATHER BROADCAST
Nil

WEATHER SERVICE
Continuous Meteorological teletype service

RUNWAYS
(asphalt)
08-26   5290' x 200'

LIGHTING
Available on request.
Threshold (green). Runway (clear).
Taxi (blue).

OBSTRUCTIONS (ASL)
N. Bachelor Hill (2600') 1.5 miles
L. Peter Peak (3593') 6 miles
S. Sugarloaf (3092') 4.5 miles

November 16, 1955

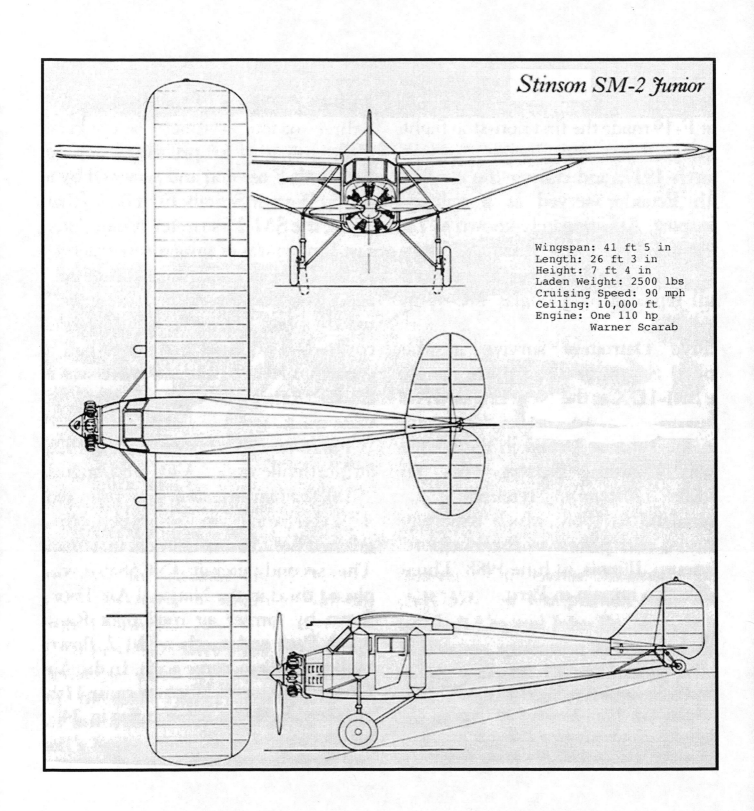

Stinson SM-2 Junior

Wingspan: 41 ft 5 in
Length: 26 ft 3 in
Height: 7 ft 4 in
Laden Weight: 2500 lbs
Cruising Speed: 90 mph
Ceiling: 10,000 ft
Engine: One 110 hp
        Warner Scarab

Kamloops

Ashcroft

The first aircraft to arrive at Ashcroft was on October 28, 1920, but did so on a CPR flat car en route from Vancouver to Kamloops. The Curtiss HS-2L, G-CYBA, was on a promotional venture for the fledgling Canada Air Board Dominion Air Station at Jericho Beach and would be flown by that station's Superintendent Major Claire MacLaurin in a survey for the B.C. Forest Service. It is likely that passing flights occurred during the first half of the 1920s by the Curtiss JN-4 Canucks of the Vancouver Branch of the Aerial League of Canada, or by the JN-4 belonging to VATCO, the Vancouver Aerial Transportation Company, with pilot Captain Ernest 0. Hall, who had flown to Kamloops from Vancouver via Merritt on August 1, 1919.

On September 15, 1928, Ashcroft citizens witnessed S/L Earl Godfrey (the Ashcroft Journal named him "Eagle" Godfrey) fly overhead at 4:00 p.m. on his across-Canada mail flight from Montreal to Vancouver, which he reached at 6:00 p.m. the same day.

Joe Bertalino poses with Fleet 2 CF-AKC. Kamloops Museum

Ashcroft

Ginger Coote landed CF-ATA Ryan B-1 Brougham at Ashcroft June 1, 1932.
Ashcroft Museum

It is uncertain when the first aircraft actually landed at Ashcroft, but certainly by the early 1930s it was becoming a port of call for itinerant aircraft. In the latter part of 1930, Humphrey O. Madden and Joe Bertalino established a flight training school on the Indian Reserve at Kamloops using a Fleet Model 2, CF-AKC.

When not instructing, the pair would fly to nearby communities and put on aerial exhibitions and offer rides for cash in order to eke out their meagre fortunes. They were known to have barnstormed Merritt, Princeton, Penticton, and quite likely performed in Ashcroft as well.

The first landing that this author has been able to identify was on December 19, 1932, when R.L. Ginger Coote arrived in Ashcroft from Barkerville with three mining officials on board who were planning on catching a CPR train to Vancouver. The flight was made in Ryan B-1 Brougham, CF-ATA, which Coote had purchased June 1, 1932, in

Eric de Pencier flew Waco ATO CF-ASJ to Ashcroft, January 30, 1933. CW

Ashcroft

Bellingham, Washington. Coote made the flight in three hours and forty minutes, in poor visibility in snow showers, so that the passengers could catch a southbound train to Vancouver.

On January 30, 1933, pilot A.E. Eric de Pencier and Tom Atchison landed at Ashcroft. The Waco Model ATO, CF-ASJ, was flown from Quesnel, where the aircraft had been holding for the weather to improve so that it could participate in a search for Ginger Coote, who was unaccounted for since January 18 on a flight to Findlay Forks. Fortunately, Coote showed up as soon as the weather cleared and he arrived back at Quesnel.

Waco CF-ASJ arrived at Ashcroft in mid-September, 1933 and remained until September 28 when pilot B.R. Ronald (who held Canadian commercial pilot licence #17) departed in ASJ for Vernon.

Pilot de Pencier returned to Ashcroft in October 1934, again flying Waco CF-ASJ, but this time accompanied by flying instructor Stan Auchland Sharp of Vancouver's Columbia Aviation School who was attempting to drum up business in the area. The pair later departed for Merritt.

Ginger Coote had entered into an arrangement with Grant McConachie whereby, in order to secure an air mail contract, Coote had applied in his name for the route Ashcroft to Fort Saint John and, in return, Coote was made District Manager of United Air Transport. After gaining the contract, the first flight occurred on Sunday, January 16, 1938.

Pilots Sheldon Luck and Ginger Coote took off from Barnes Lake, Ashcroft at 9:30 a.m. Sunday, January 16, 1938, on the inaugural flight of a

Inaugural flight of United Air Transport from Ashcroft's Barnes Lake to Fort St. John, departs at 9:00 am January 16, 1938. Ashcroft Musuem

U.A.T. Waco Custom CF-AZM refuels at Cornwall Field - Sheldon Luck right, January - March 1938. Sheldon Luck

U.A.T. Fokker Universal G-CAHE at Cornwall Field, flown by Len Waggen 1938. Sheldon Luck

Ashcroft

planned weekly air mail flight to Fort St. John, where it was planned to connect with the Edmonton-Yukon air mail flight. The inaugural flight was flown with CF-AZM, a Waco Custom Model ZQC-6 on skis. The flight was a historic event and was attended by dignitaries from throughout the province: George Miller, Mayor of Vancouver; Gray Turgson, Member of Parliament for Cariboo; T.G. O'Neal, Member of Parliament for Kamloops; George Murray, Member of the Legislative Assembly for Lillooet; as well as officials of the Provincial Police, County Court, Board of Trade, and local businesses.

The event at Barnes Lake became controversial when Margaret L. (Ma) Murray, wife of Lillooet MLA George Murray, wrote a letter published in the Vancouver Daily Province on May 26, 1938. She reported that during the inaugural ceremony the ice began to crack and George Murray supposedly got his feet wet, which she felt put the event in danger. The editor of the Ashcroft Journal took exception to the report in the Vancouver newspaper stating in his editorial of Thursday, June 2, 1938, that it was quite natural

for lake ice to crack and no one was in any danger. Ginger Coote had reportedly turned to Pilot Sheldon Luck during the event and whispered, "Cut this ceremony short and let's get away before the ice breaks under us."

The flight departed at 9:30 a.m. from Barnes Lake approximately five miles south of the village and was flown by Sheldon Luck with engineer Dick Green and Ginger Coote. AZM was flown to Williams Lake where, after formalities, it took off again for Quesnel, Prince George, and Fort St John with the MLA for Cariboo on board.

The first mail flights departed from Barnes Lake, but after the Ashcroft Board of Trade inspired local citizens to volunteer their labors to clear off sage brush and rocks, a strip north of Ashcroft Manor known as Cornwall Field came into use. The Ashcroft Journal reported in its February 11, 1938 edition that the construction party had begun on Sunday, February 6.

This service continued from Ashcroft until August 1, 1938, using a variety of aircraft. A Fairchild 51, CF-AUX; two more WACOs, CF-

Waco of Northern Airways, Carcross, Y.T. CF-BDZ at Cornwall Field, January 21, 1938. Sheldon Luck

Ashcroft

United Air Transport Ford Tri-Motor CF-BEP and a Bellanca at Ashcroft Manor early in 1938. Sheldon Luck

U.A.T. Ford CF-BEP in front of Ashcroft Manor, 1938. Ashcroft Museum

Ashcroft

BDL and AZM; occasionally the Tri-motor Ford 6ATS-Special, CF-BEP; and a Fokker Universal, G-CAFU. After August 1, the flight started from Vancouver.

In mid-February, United Air Transport pilot Len Waagen landed G-CAFU, a Fokker Universal, at Cornwall field. The Ashcroft Journal reported that Waagen had flown very low several times over the village prior to landing. AFU later departed for Edmonton on February 19 at 8:15 a.m.

Also at this time another WACO Custom ZQC-6, CF-BDZ, landed at Cornwall Field at Ashcroft Manor. This aircraft, flown by pilot Bill Holland with owner George Simmons of Northern Airways, was en route to Carcross, Yukon, where it would be based. BDZ had been purchased by

Northern Airways and registered in Canada at Vancouver on January 11, 1938, and commenced that airline's inaugural service to the Yukon on January 21, via Ashcroft.

Pilot Bill Holland again landed WACO BDZ at Ashcroft's Cornwall Field on March 12, 1938, southbound from the Yukon to Vancouver. Rivalry with Kamloops was reported by the Ashcroft Journal in June 1938, which took issuance with the Vancouver Daily Province of May 26 reporting that Northern Airways flight from Vancouver to Whitehorse routed via Kamloops. The Ashcroft edition stated all of that airline's flights had stopped at Ashcroft for the last five months, not at Kamloops. The writing was on the wall, however. In August, YSAT was flying from Vancouver to Ashcroft on the way north, but by November 1, 1939, that same com-

Ashcroft Board of Trade volunteers construct Cornwall Field, February 1938. Ashcroft Museum

Ashcroft

Canadian Airways Fairchild 71C refuels at Ashcroft Manor, 1938. Ashcroft Museum

U.A.T. Fokker Universal G-CAFU at Cornwall Field, 1938. Ashcroft Museum

Canadian Airways Bellanca CF-300 "Pacemaker" CF-BFB at Cornwall Field 1938 with damaged right wing and tail. Ashcroft Museum

Ashcroft

pany flew directly to Kamloops on their northern flight. Eventually Northern Airways discontinued their service to Vancouver from the Yukon.

Aircraft continued to use Cornwall Field, although to a lesser degree. NC-1246, a Stinson SM-8A (Special), belonging to J. Fairbanks, president of Paramount Studios of Sunset Boulevard, Hollywood, California, touched down there breaking one of the aircraft's landing struts and Fairbanks was delayed there while parts were obtained.

American owned Stinson SM-8A (Special) NC-1246 gets repairs to left landing gear strut. Ashcroft Museum

Cornwall Field is in close proximity to the Ashcroft Manor buildings and just north of the highway. In 1939 the Department of Transport erected a radio range station at the same site, with its antenna on the hill to the south. Department of Transport staff provided weather and communications to itinerant airmen from this facility until 1966, when these services were transferred to Kamloops. The radio range at Ashcroft was in integral part of AMBER 61 airway from Princeton to Prince George, and provided the primary approach aid for an instrument approach to Kamloops until 1975, when a localizer approach aid was installed at that city's airport.

By 1941 civil flight training and aviation activity had ceased on the coast. Gilbert's Flying

D.O.T. Radio Range buildings built during WWII, seen here October 2000. CW

Service at Vancouver had relocated for a time to Kamloops, but with the RCAF activity at Kamloops Gilbert had to move his aircraft elsewhere. Two trainers were moved to Cornwall Field at Ashcroft Manor and two were moved to Cranbrook for the duration of the hostilities.

F/L George Williamson recalls an emergency strip was constructed close to the station buildings at Ashcroft Manor alongside the Trans

Ashcroft

Aeronca 65 "Super Chief" CF-BTR, owned by F. W. Gilbert and L. Michaud, at Ashcroft Manor 1939. Ashcroft Museum

Another private airfield was established three and a half miles south of the village in postwar years by the Rafter (Bar Q) Ranch. It was a gravel strip 2,700 x 75 feet. Still later a new field was built on Indian land on the southeast side of the junction of the Trans Canada Highway and the Ashcroft access road. The field was 2,000 feet long and was eventually paved. The author landed there in 1976 with twin engine Aero Commander 680E, CF-FJR, on a charter from Vancouver. The field became a drag strip after the new airport was opened near Cache Creek.

The 1967 Fostair Pilots Guide lists an airfield, described as the Mesa Vista Airfield, one half mile east of the Ashcroft railway station, at an elevation of 1,430 feet. No other details are given.

The author visited the site of Cornwall Field in 1999 and 2000 and found no evidence of its aviation use over 60 years ago.

Air photo of 1970's airfield at Ashcroft at junction of Hwys #1 and 97C, looking toward North. CW

Canada Highway. However, the RCAF Airway Manual of 1945 lists it by name but gives no details.

FRIDAY, FEBRUARY 11, 1938

FUNDS TO BE
RAISED FOR AIRPORT

Last Sunday several enterprising citizens of Ashcroft turned out, at the request of the Board of Trade, to do certain improvement work to the airfield at Cornwall's, and although considerable work was done in the way of eliminating bad hazards, it was found, after the day's work, there was yet much more to do to bring the field up to Standard requirements. Realizing this, as also the urgent necessity of getting the field into first class shape as soon as possible, the airport committee met the Board of Trade Council on Monday evening, and as a result it was decided to call on the public for help in the way of subscriptions to enable the committee to complete this important work.

Interest has been aroused in neighboring towns and work is going ahead in several places, and it is in the ultimate interest of every public spirited citizen of Ashcroft and its vicinity, to put forth every effort to make our airport one to be proud of. No donation is too small, even if it is only a dime, of course no donation can be too big.

A list of donors will be published in this paper each week, and at the conclusion of a list a statement of expenditure will be shown. Act now before others who appreciate the importance of air travel jump ahead of us.

Leave your subscriptions at the Journal office or at the Bank of Montreal.

FOKKER PLANE 1938
LEAVES FOR NORTH

United Air Transport's Fokker plane left Cornwall airfield Sunday morning at 8:15 on its return trip to Edmonton. Pilot Les Wingen was at the controls and took along with him besides aircraft mechanic, Dick Greata, Mrs. Fred Pinchbeck, who received an urgent call to Carcross where her son is reported to be ill.

Sheldon Luck, piloting United Air Transport's four-passenger Waco plane came in from the north at noon Saturday. The plane was changed from skis to wheels at the Cornwall field here and continued on its way to Vancouver, which was Luck's first trip into Vancouver over this route. He returned Sunday noon with one passenger booked for Dawson. The plane was again changed to skis. The trip between here and Vancouver was made in an hour and a half both ways.

1938

Yas'm! We Still Insist!

Yowzah, folks! We read Margaret L. Murray's letter in the Vancouver Province re the ice cracking on Charlie Lake, January 16, during the inaugural ceremony of the Ashcroft-Fort St. John air service, and her insistence that it did crack and prevent a danger.

Well . . . we still insist the alight crack heard was a natural occurrence and for the sake of argument the original press report was not Margaret Murray's, but her husband's. How do we know? Right after the ceremony George told us he had covered the event for the Canadian Press. Therefore Margaret Murray is not the one "that causes the denial" which was sent to the Province by ourselves.

AND we still insist Pilot Coote did not start the motor of the plane. Pilot Locke and the others and was at the controls when the take-off was made. And Ginger must have whispered the words, "Cut this ceremony short and let's get away before the ice breaks under us," for we can't find anyone who attended the ceremony to say that he or she heard Ginger say this.

AND the water the Canadian Press reporter says he stepped in following the alleged crack, mystifies us. It might have been lake water seeping through the ice somewhere, or else . . . oh, well it's only natural for one to get a scare scare when ice beneath him emits a cracking sound, especially not knowing it should crack to be safe.

Article Untrue

According to an article in the Vancouver Daily Province under date of May 26, the air route Northern Airways have been trying to establish during the past winter and this spring touches Kamloops. Accompanying the story was a map showing the line followed by the Northern planes as from Vancouver to Kamloops and thence north. Both story and map are erroneous and evidently set out in this way for the sole purpose of misguiding, or otherwise was written by one totally ignorant of the Northern Airways operations during the past five months.

Not once, to our recollection, has a Northern Airways plane touched Kamloops on its way north. The statement that this company has been using that route for several months is untrue.

The Northern Airways started to pioneer a route from Vancouver to the Yukon on January 21, this year, and on every up and down flight changed from skis to wheels at Ashcroft until the end of February, when the change was made farther north on the route. United Air Transport planes did the same thing from January 16 until last part of February. The first through trip from Yukon to Vancouver was made on Saturday, March 12, by Northern Airways plane CF-BDX piloted by Bill Stafford, when a break was made at Ashcroft to refuel. Since then every plane going north or coming south has used the Ashcroft and Bonaparte valley route, and not Kamloops and over the Tranquille mountains some sixty miles east of here. The reason the pilots have been using this route to the north is because it is far safer than others, there being more places a plane can come down if forced to land. Hardly a week passes but an airman are seen overhead coming via this route, on their way north, proving this is the most logical and safest air road to follow.

Ashcroft has been advised by good authority that she is so located geographically it can handle planes at all times of the year and is the nearest place out of the far belt to Vancouver that a safe landing field can be made. It also has an alternate winter field at Barnes Lake which cannot be equalled in the interior should there not be sufficient snow at the Ashcroft Manny airport for planes to land on skis.

Planes took off and landed at Ashcroft airport last winter when all planes at the coast were grounded because of zero ceilings, a condition not experienced here.

Ashcroft is also in a direct line with Alaska from Spokane and nearly direct from Seattle, and is everything geographically it is in her favor there is little doubt when the time comes to permanently establish an air route to the north it will be via her doors.

Ashcroft Journal 1938

Cornwall Field and Ashcroft Manor from hill to South. Ashcroft Museum

ELEVATION - 1800' approx.

POSITION (approx.)
LAT. 50°42' N. LONG. 121°19' W.
adjacent to Ashcroft Manor to North.

OPERATED BY
Cornwall Ranch

REMARKS
Landing Area rough, use caution

FACILITIES

Standard Oil Products

LANDING AREA
DIRT & GRASS
All way landing
Field improved to 1800'

OBSTRUCTIONS (ASL)

Ashcroft Manor Roadhouse, October 2000. CW

1938

Ashcroft

Ashcroft

Noorduyn Norseman

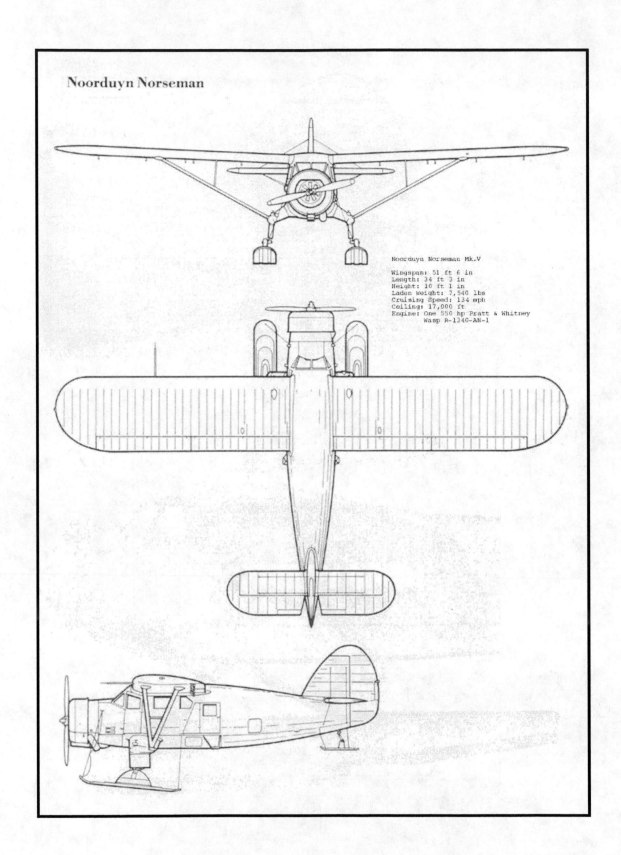

Noorduyn Norseman Mk.V

Wingspan: 51 ft 6 in
Length: 34 ft 3 in
Height: 10 ft 1 in
Laden Weight: 7,540 lbs
Cruising Speed: 134 mph
Ceiling: 17,000 ft
Engine: One 550 hp Pratt & Whitney
        Wasp R-1340-AN-1

Ashcroft

Dog Creek

Dog Creek is situated on the Cariboo Plateau 35 miles south of Williams Lake at an elevation of 3,382 feet above sea level. The airport sits on bench land close by, and to the east, of the Fraser River. Up until the Second World War this land was used primarily for cattle ranching and the property was known as the Diamond "S" Ranch owned by Colonel Victor Spencer of Vancouver. Spencer founded the Spencer stores of Vancouver, which later became Eatons.

RCAF Dog Creek looking West, August 1943. RCAF

In 1936, Pan American Airway's representatives arrived at the hamlet of Dog Creek to assess the possibility of building a single runway to land and service their aircraft while on an inland route to Alaska. Local rancher Charlie Place acted as their guide and they selected a site in Dog Creek Valley, east of the town and south of the position of the RCAF Station later built in 1942-43. However, longer range aircraft then coming into use precluded the need for a PanAm airport at Dog Creek.

After the Japanese fleet attacked Pearl Harbour December 7, 1941, British Columbia became concerned by Ottawa's lack of preparedness for an attack by Japan on Canada's West Coast.

Vancouver Sun correspondent Bruce Hutchison wrote scathingly, "The Canadian General Staff still had not grasped that the Axis powers were pursuing a strategy of global encirclement. British Columbia was in the front line and the government refused to send in reinforcements." It has been observed that the frightened citizens of B.C. forced the Ottawa government to take the defence of the Pacific Coast seriously.

In April 1942, the Joint Service Committee issued a new appreciation of the situation as a compromise between strategic priorities and the demands of the B.C. population. Several squadrons of RCAF aircraft were moved to the coast and a series of airfields were ordered con-

Dog Creek

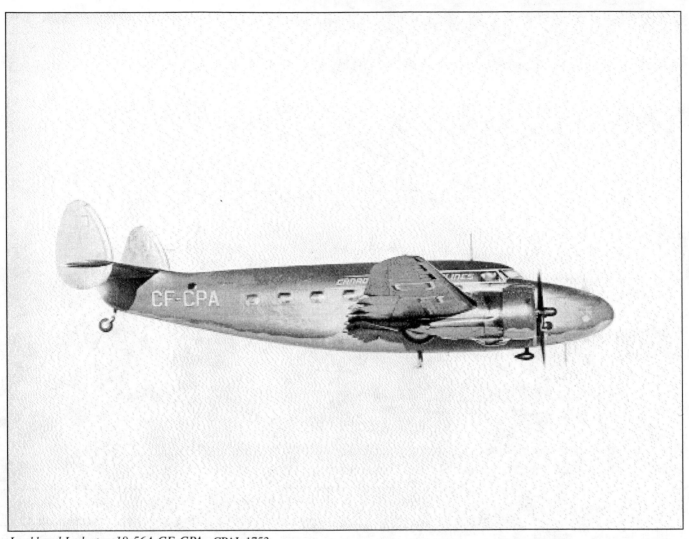

Lockheed Lodestar 18-56A CF-CPA. CPAL 1753

structed as protection for the coast. A further second line of defence called for the construction of airports in the interior of the province at Woodcock, Smithers, Vanderhoof, Prince George, Quesnel, Williams Lake, and at Dog Creek.

Colonel Spencer's Diamond "S" Ranch was expropriated and contractor Fred Mannix of Calgary, Alberta and sub-contractor Carter-Halse-Aldinger were appointed and preliminary preparations and clearing commenced. During the fall of 1942 the RCAF ordered a photographic reconnaissance of all the new airfield sites in the interior, and on October 9, 1942, RCAF Norseman on floats #2480, flown by F/Sgt George Williamson, with photographer W02 E.B. Hackett, began making a mosaic of the area at Dog Creek.

Secret Organization Order Number 126 of May 20, 1943, authorized the formation of No.11 Staging Unit at Dog Creek effective May 1, with F/0 L.S. Barlow as Officer Commanding the skeleton force of personnel on site. On August 24, 1943, RCAF Bolingbroke #9066 departed Sea Island Vancouver on a photographic assignment. Its first airport was RCAF Dog Creek. Pilot F/0 Williamson and his photographer remained

Dog Creek

overnight, departing August 25 for RCAF Williams Lake.

Throughout the summer the contractors continued the construction of buildings and runways, and by September 1 they were 60% complete. On December 4, 1943, a diesel power unit was installed providing power and electricity to the station. On December 18, the contractor handed over the finished station to the RCAF and at this time there was one officer and eighteen airmen on strength.

its nose when it touched down in soft gravel damaging its propeller and its pilot's (F/0 J.C.R. Dewar) pride. The pair were ordered by their squadrons to remain until repairs could be made and on April 8 a repair team arrived. Repairs were completed on April 22 and F/0 Dewar and R/O Marsden resumed their flight to Pat Bay in Hurricanes #5413 and #5414 after twenty two days temporary duty in the "boonies". The following day Lockheed #7650 arrived and picked up the repair party for Sea Island Vancouver.

On December 19, 1943, RCAF Station Dog Creek was visited by Air Vice Marshall A.B. Shearer and an inspection party who were traveling in RCAF Goose #940. At 2 p.m. on December 20, a Department of Transport Beechcraft 18, CF-CCA, arrived flown by Mr. Hillchie who calibrated the radio range station which had been installed earlier. RCAF Dog Creek now had almost daily aircraft movement:

January 4, 1944	Norseman 364 arrived 11:00 a.m.
January 5, 1944	Norseman 364 departed
January 6, 1944	Lodestar 568, No. 165 Squadron arrived and departed
January 7, 1944	Pan American Airway Lodestar NC33665 arrived and departed
January 10, 1944	Canadian Pacific Airlines Lodestar CF-CPF arrived via the Dog Creek radio range and later departed
January 16, 1944	RCAF Ventura 2225 and Goose 942 arrived. The latter was from Prince Rupert's No. 4 Group Headquarters. Both aircraft remained overnight
January 24, 1944	Department of Transport pilot J.D. Jack Hunter arrived in Lockheed 12 CF-CCT to complete the final calibration of the radio range station. Hunter remained overnight.

As of January 31, 1944, No. 11 Staging Unit at Dog Creek had one officer and thirty airmen on strength.

The station diarist reported on March 31 that two Hawker Hurricanes, #5413 and #5414, en route from Terrace to Patricia Bay (Victoria) landed at Dog Creek. Number 5414 went up on

May 11 saw the arrival of CPA Flights No. 21 and 22 en route to Prince George, which were redirected to Dog Creek due to weather at Prince George. A passenger was deplaned and driven to Williams Lake. Later the same day, Pan Am aircraft NC-65 landed due to weather and later departed for Prince George.

Dog Creek

May 20, RCAF Dakota #655 and two Canadian Pacific Airlines aircraft, CF-CPJ and CPB, all arrived and held for weather then later departed for Prince George.

On a rainy July 7, 1944, RCAF Goose #941 advised the station that it was on a medical flight to Vancouver and experiencing engine trouble and would be landing at Dog Creek. After landing the stretcher case was removed and later transferred to Lockheed 7650, which flew up from Vancouver to pick him up. The Goose remained until repairs could be made.

Earlier, on the 7th, RCAF Lodestar #560 and six Hurricanes, 5418, 5407, 5421, 5424, 5411, and 5428, made fuel stops at Dog Creek. (RCAF 5428 was restored in postwar years by the Reynolds's Aviation Museum at Wetaskiwan, Alberta.)

October 10, 1944, Major General G.R. Parkes and his party landed in RCAF Goose #384 and inspected the station. The following day Air Vice Marshall F.V. Heakes and his aides arrived in Goose #389 and also inspected the lands and buildings.

July 14	Department of Transport Anson CF-DTN arrived and departed.
August 7	Three RCAF Hurricanes, #5403, 5405, 5412, landed for fuel.
August 30	F/L J.B. Abraham arrived to take over the command of the station effective September 1. F/O L.S. Barlow was transferred to Western Air Command Headquarters.

Up until this time the station had been used in daylight hours only, but now a portable electric flare path was installed. On September 7 at 11:50 p.m. Pacific War Time (plus two hours), Canadian Pacific Airlines special flight number 6 arrived to test the approach and landing capabilities of Dog Creek's runways. This was the first night landing at the airport.

October 25, Wein Alaska Airways NC 13364 made a precautionary landing due to weather. The aircraft had ten Eskimo children on board and was en route from Barrow, Alaska, to Seattle, Washington, where the children were to be hospitalized.

Hillary Place, the son of Dog Creek rancher Charlie Place, was driving the Mack truck from

The Dog Creek station diary continued to see more and more American aircraft stopping for fuel and weather concerns.	
November 1, 1944	Pan American NC 63
November 5, 1944	US Navy Transport Service NC2245, a 1937 Waco custom cabin Model 2GC-7
November 8, 1944	A US Army Air Transport Command No. 32 arrived from Seattle after encountering extreme icing. They made an emergency landing to de-ice and refuel.

Dog Creek

November 11, 1944   Pan American NC 64

November 17, 1944   Pan American NC 65 and NC 63 refueled and departed. NC 65 returned to Dog Creek due to weather. Both Pan Am flights departed at 4:00 p.m. and returned to Seattle.

January 31, 1945   Hurricane #5579, flown by F/O K. Langell, arrived and stayed overnight and left the next day for Pat Bay.

February 1, 1945   RCAF Norseman #2470, flown by F/O J. Bell, departed Anaheim Lake for Prince George, but crashed on river ice on the west bank of the Fraser River 10 miles north of Dog Creek near the junction of the Chilcotin and Fraser Rivers. The six RCAF personnel on board were unhurt.

February 3, 1945   Four survivors of #2470 arrived at Dog Creek tired and hungry but otherwise okay.

February 4, 1945   Norseman #364 arrived and departed. Sergeant Sinclair, Station tractor operator, departed to crash scene of #2470 and assisted in the salvage operations. Sinclair and Corporal Ballard and LAC Park again drove to the crash scene on February 5, and returned to the station that night after burning the wreck.

February 6, 1945   Norseman #3236 arrived and departed. F/O Bell, pilot of the crashed Norseman #2470, arrived at Dog Creek, leaving on February 9 with other survivors on Norseman #364.

March 17, 1945   RCAF Harvard #3212 and #2618 arrived from Smithers en route to Vancouver and held overnight due to weather. They departed the next day.

March 20, 1945   A Japanese FU-GO fire balloon was found on the Airport road 12 miles from Williams Lake.

March 25, 1945   Corporal Arsens was hauling water to the station at 2:30 a.m. when he observed a brilliant white light in the sky when he was approximately ten miles north east of the Station. Department of Transport station operator G. Armstead also reported seeing a spectacular light - this could possibly have been a fire baloon, but no evidence exists. Many more positive sightings were reported by RCAF, Pacific Coast Militia Rangers, and other citizens in the area.

July 4, 1945   RCAF Goose #396, with G/C McNab and W/C Beardmore, visited the station.

Dog Creek

Williams Lake to Dog Creek in the early summer of 1945 when the truck was stopped on the airport road 15 miles south of Williams Lake by a group of B.C. Police and Pacific Coast Militia Rangers (PCMR) who advised Hilary that he could not proceed because of security reasons.

It seems that a Japanese FU-GO fire balloon was hung up in a cottonwood tree 50 yards from the road on property belonging to Sam Sorenson. Police and military officials had been ordered to ensure that knowledge of these balloons would not reach the general public; however "mail-man" Place stated to the police and militia that they were delaying the King's Mail. He was allowed to proceed, getting a close up view of the suspended Japanese weapon as he drove by.

Just after 10:00 p.m. one evening in the spring of 1946, a Canadian Pacific Airlines Lockheed 18-56A Loadstar departed Prince George with a full load of passengers en route to Vancouver. The flight's Captain was Sheldon Luck with co-pilot Stan Emery. The weather had been forecast as operational with marginal weather at Vancouver. Luck had selected Patricia Bay, Victoria, as an alternate and indicated to company dispatch that should Pat Bay worsen he would deviate to Dog Creek. After passing the Dog Creek radio range at 10,000 feet southbound, the flight began picking up ice and experiencing turbulence, and Luck requested a climb to 12,000 feet. At this point CPA dispatch directed Luck to turn around to Dog Creek and land there to await improved weather.

The Department of transport maintenance staff had taken over the operation of the Dog Creek

July 14, 1945	A US Navy Grumman F4F Wildcat crashed sixty miles west of Dog Creek near Alexis Creek in the Chilcotin. Sgt Sinclair and three airmen were dispatched to guard the aircraft until American military authorities could salvage it. No mention is made of the pilot.

Even though the war with Japan had not ended, more and more civil aviation activity seems to be reoccurring in spite of supposed restrictions.

July 19, 1945	A Luscombe 8A, NC28721, belonging to a Mr. and Mrs. Norris of Ann Arbor, Michigan stopped for fuel and departed
July 25, 1945	Interstate LC-6, NC49128, the personal aircraft of Colonel J. Nickell, US Army, arrived and later departed
August 30, 1945	No. 11 Staging Unit is now re-formed to Interior Staging Unit Dog Creek and the officer commanding is F/0 A.D. MacPherson who, on September 13, departed for Western Air Command Headquarters at Jericho Beach Vancouver pending his retirement. He is replaced by F/0 R.C. Brown
September 15, 1945	WAC sent a signal advising that Interior Staging Unit No 11 Dog Creek is to become inactive as of this date and will disband September 20, 1945. The Stations complement at this time was one officer, five sergeants, ten corporals, and twenty eight other ranks, for a total of forty four men.

Dog Creek

SIGNALS UNIT

DOG CREEK, B.C.

THE COMMANDING OFFICER
REQUESTS YOUR PRESENCE
AT THE . . .

REFRESHMENTS
·
FLOOR SHOW

Gala Pre Xmas Dance

NOVELTIES
·
DOOR PRIZES

TO BE HELD DEC. 1ST, 1945
SIGNALS UNIT, DOG CREEK

Invitation to 1945 Christmas Dance. Chris & Rose Templeton Collection

Dog Creek

Capt. Sheldon Luck (R) confers with Grant McConachie.
Sheldon Luck Collection

radio and airport after the RCAF station there was closed. The DOT radio operator at Dog Creek overheard the CPA directions for Luck to land at that station and called Luck by radio to advise that the runway was clear, but due to a large snowfall no clearing had been done to any accommodations and the buildings were not heated. Captain Luck had no intention of subjecting his passengers to these conditions so he returned to Prince George where full facilities were available. He later received a strong reprimand for this action which led to his resignation.

In July 1946, the property and station was transferred to the Department of Transport as an emergency airfield and maintained as a supplementary facility. The radio range continued to operate as part of the Blue Route 2 airway to Prince George.

Dog Creek

A temporary licence was issued on August 1, 1946, and an airport maintenance foreman, Mr. J.E. Ernie Eve, was appointed. A permanent licence was issued on July 19, 1947.

In April of 1950 the village of Williams Lake, thirty five air miles to the northeast of Dog Creek, made a proposal to the Department of Transport to move the radio range, the air radio, and weather reporting staff and equipment from Dog Creek to the Williams Lake municipal airport to better serve the needs of a much larger area - one that was being served by CPA. It further noted that Dog Creek was only being used as an emergency field. The Department of Transport agreed but would build a new airport at Williams Lake first.

On November 7, 1954, Aeronca 7AC, CF-HSR, was northbound from Boston Bar en route to Prince George following the Fraser River. The sky became sullen with mixed rain and snow showers, and visibility became challenging for the teenaged ninety-hour wonder at the controls. HSR was being flown by the author. I stopped at Dog Creek for a tank of 80/87 fuel obtained from the airport maintenance foreman Mr. Eve, who

The author, Christopher Weicht with Cessna 140 CF-GVM 1954

PB-33 DOG CREEK AIRPORT ALT 2000' Looking W 1222 HRS 25 AUG 43

Dog Creek Airport looking West August 25, 1943. RCAF PB-33

had obviously been around flying machines for some time. I checked with the Department of Transport air radio office and got a briefing for Quesnel and Prince George. It did not sound good but I pressed on, eventually turning back to Williams Lake to spend the night.

On November 14, 1954, I was now flying south bound from Prince George, this time in a Cessna 140, CF-GVM. The weather was again marginal with snow showers reducing visibility. After a brief stop for fuel at Dog Creek, I pressed on following the Fraser River until I was about ten miles north of Lillooet, when a narrowing river valley became choked with cloud and the contin-

uous snow reduced forward visibility to almost nil. I reluctantly turned back to Dog Creek where I landed in the declining light of the November afternoon and was met by the Maintenance Foreman Mr. Eve, who wisely advised me to stay the night. After helping me secure GVM, he showed me to a barracks building, a section of which was kept available for transients like myself. The spartan interior was at least warm and the grey blankets marked DND stacked on the dark brown metal-framed beds promised a reasonably comfortable night's sleep. Before leaving me, Mr. Eve invited me to their living quarters for dinner. I gladly accepted and over the course of the evening it became very apparent

Dog Creek

ERNIE EVE STRICKEN WHILE RIDING

Former Airport Manager Dies

J. Ernest Eve, noted horseman and pioneer airman, who was formerly manager of Dog Creek airport, died August 23 as he had lived most of his life—in the saddle.

Mr. Eve, who was 70 on his birthday, August 22, collapsed while riding in Victoria about 10:30 a.m.

His passing closed a colorful and adventurous career.

Ernie Eve had been an athlete, cowboy, test pilot, organizer of British Columbia's first scheduled air service, movie actor, provincial policeman and automobile distributor.

He is survived by his widow, Margaret, a daughter, Mrs. Jack Dangerfield, of Winnipeg, three grandchildren and a brother and sister in England.

Mr. Eve retired to Victoria after service as manager at Dog Creek airport. His retirement was hastened by a heart attack at that time.

He first came to Victoria in 1908, and in the early '20's operated Eve Motors, a new car agency, in partnership with his brother, Cecil H. Eve, who died two years ago.

Also with his brother, and backed by many Victoria businessmen, he formed B.C. Airways in 1928. After a few weeks of operating flights between Victoria and mainland points, the firm was broken up by the crash of one of its passenger planes and the loss of 10 lives.

Up to his retirement, Ernie took a prominent part in activities of the town and his own district. He was a member of the Kiwanis Club. Each year almost stopped the show when he rode down the street impeccably attired in a polo outfit.

that these two people, in the twilight of their years, had had a long and profound relationship with aviation in British Columbia going all the way back to the mid 1920s.

The weather on the following day was more promising and after thanking my hosts I departed to the south. I again ran into poor visibility and snow, but this time I headed to Kamloops.

That was the last time I saw Ernie Eve. Within a short time he suffered a heart attack and retired to Victoria. Ernie had a colorful life. He had been a cowboy, a Provincial policeman, a movie actor, an automobile dealer, and in 1928 he and his brother, Cecil, founded B.C. Airways Limited - the Province's first scheduled air service. Ernie

was also quite a showman. Irene Stangoe, the former editor of the Williams Lake Tribune, recalls that while Ernie lived at Dog Creek he always came down to the Williams Lake Stampede. Every year he almost stopped the show when he rode his horse through town impeccably attired in a polo outfit. Ernie Eve passed away on August 23, 1957, while out riding. It was the day after his 70th birthday.

In December 1960 the new airport opened at Williams Lake and, true to their promise, the Department of Transport relocated the staff and equipment for the air radio, weather, and communication facilities to Williams Lake, and as well realigned the airway Blue Route 22 between Ashcroft Radio Range Station and Quesnel Range Station.

Long time resident Hilary Place recalls grouse hunting on airport property in the fall of 1961 and coming upon the wreckage of a burning twin engine airplane. After making sure that no one was inside, he drove down the road toward his home and came upon the aircraft's pilot. Not much explanation was given and Place suspects the aircraft's demise was financial rather than mechanical.

The Dog Creek airport was not closed but remained as an emergency field. It saw little use and the property was eventually sold on May 16, 1962, to the Circle "S" Cattle Company. The outline of the three gravel runways remain visible to passing airmen to this day. Irene Stangoe, the Cariboo historian and former editor of the Williams Lake Tribune, wrote an article that tells of the history of the Dog Creek Airport:

Dog Creek

Dog Creek Airport - Looking Back
by Irene Stangoe

The opening of the Dog Creek airport during the Second World War brought a new excitement to the sleepy little village of Dog Creek four miles down the hill in the valley and many of the young Air force men found a "home away from home" in the warm hospitality offered by Mr. and Mrs. Charlie Place at their historic Dog Creek House.

Today there is little left of the once-busy airport which was equipped with thousands of dollars of radio equipment and "on duty" 24 hours a day, 365 days a year.

The airport was established in 1943 by the RCAF as a military base along with a civilian radio station. A home guard of Rocky Mountain Rangers was formed among the Dog Creek residents and old-timer Frank Armes of Williams Lake who lived at Dog Creek for 26 years was among those who kept watch for the fire-bombs sent over by the Japanese to British Columbia and Oregon.

"It was one of the best-kept secrets of the war," he says. Made cheaply of magnesium wrapped in newspapers, thousands of them were released on the Japanese air-currents to waft their way across the ocean. "We could see them coming," he says. "On impact they would flare up like balloons and could cause fires." But with the end of hostilities in 1945 the air force pulled out of the Dog Creek airport.

After that it operated with two distinct sections: first the civilian aviation department which kept the three 6,000 foot runways open for passing traffic (119 landings in July 1959) and second, a radio range or beacon which transmit-

Post war air photo of Dog Creek looking North. CW Col ted a signal in all directions and connected with a vast network of similar services all across Canada.

There was a lot of work for the ten men on staff. A big 5000-watt diesel power plant had to be operated and maintained, water was hauled four miles and dumped into a 20,000 gallon water tank, and then there was the refueling of aircraft and maintenance of machines and equipment as well as the upkeep of roads.

Burned out wreckage of Cessna Crane on Dog Creek Airfield, 1961. Irene Stangoe

Dog Creek

It was the only weather station in the Cariboo and staff had to make hourly weather observations day and night. The late Al Becker who was well known in Williams Lake was in charge of the radio and weather station for many years, and Clayton Dunlop was the airport maintenance manager. The Dog Creek airport was closed down in December 1960 when the new Williams Lake Airport opened. All the equipment was then moved into the lake town.

The old Dog Creek airport is now part of the huge Circle S Ranch owned by the James Cattle Company. Owner Lyle James tells me that remains of several of the old military buildings are still there although they cannot be seen from the road.

On Saturday June 28, 2003, this author returned to the former Dog Creek airfield after an absence of nearly forty-nine years. I had previously secured permission to enter the site of the long abandoned RCAF Station from the present owners, the James Cattle Company.

After opening the ranch gate, I began to drive along a very well built roadway,, now unused and overgrown. I passed several buildings in advanced disrepair, recognizing one as the site of the Radio Range Station, which had remained in use until 1960 when the the Department of Transport Air Radio facility was relocated to Williams Lake.

I selected a spot among the pines that surround the former station and set up camp with my Volkswagen Westphalia and sat to enjoy a cool one. While contemplating my past presence, here, and enjoying the view, I detected the sound of an engine and was soon astounded when a 1950's

Cessna 206 N-92523 parks next to remains of WWII buildings at Dog Creek in 1970's. CW

Dog Creek

vintage Cessna 140 took off from Runway 18 and passed in front of my vantage point before turning to the west. This was, indeed, déjà vu, as on the occasion of my last visit to Dog Creek on November 15, 1954, I, too, had flown a Cessna 140 "CF-GVM".

The following morning, I drove over all three runways which were now covered in grass and wildflowers. Occasionally, the remains of wooden runway boundary markers could be seen rotting in the sagebrush. On the north side of Runway 05, the frame of a wind indicator stands guard over the silent airfield, its canvas windsock having blown away long ago.

For many years I have flown over Dog Creek and, looking down from on high, promised myself one day I would return. Now in retirement after a fifty-one-year flying career, I indeed made the journey and felt the presence of pioneer aviator, Ernie Eve, who had counseled me to stay on the stormy night I last visited Dog Creek in 1954.

Aeronca Champion CF-HSR in Fraser Canyon near Dog Creek, 1954   CW Collection

Author stands next to aging wind indicator on Runway 18 at Dog Creek, June 2003   CWCollection

Remains of Dog Creek Airadio building, June 2003
CW Collection

Cessna 140 on departure from Runway 108 at Dog Creek, June 2003   CW Collection

Dog Creek

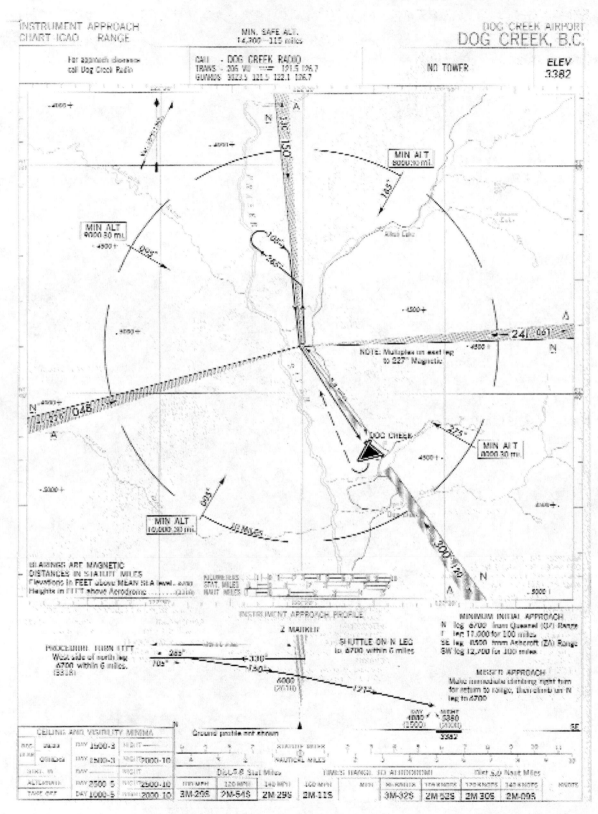

April 12, 1956

Dog Creek

100

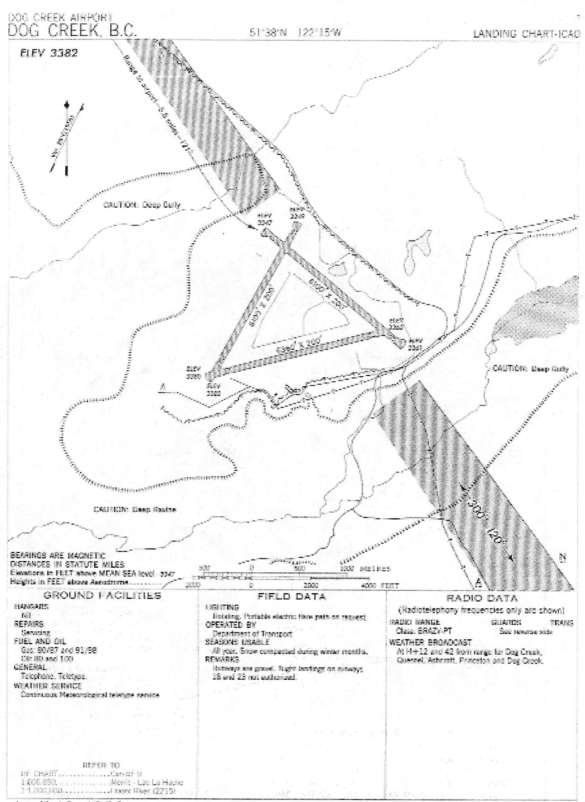

ELEV 3382

CAUTION: Deep Gully

CAUTION: Deep Gully

CAUTION: Deep Ravine

BEARINGS ARE MAGNETIC
DISTANCES IN STATUTE MILES
Elevations in FEET above MEAN SEA level - 3347
Heights in FEET above Aerodrome..........

GROUND FACILITIES

HANGARS
   Nil
REPAIRS
   Servicing
FUEL AND OIL
   Gas: 80/87 and 91/98
   Oil: 80 and 100
GENERAL
   Telephone. Teletype.
WEATHER SERVICE
   Continuous Meteorological teletype service

REFER TO
RF CHART..............Cat-RF 9
1:606,880...............Merritt - Lac La Hache
1:1,000,000............Fraser River (22125)

FIELD DATA

LIGHTING
   Rotating. Portable electric flare path on request.
OPERATED BY
   Department of Transport
SEASONS USABLE
   All year. Snow compacted during winter months.
REMARKS
   Runways are gravel. Night landings on runways
   16 and 23 not authorized.

RADIO DATA
(Radiotelephony frequencies only are shown)

RADIO RANGE
   Class: ERAZV-PT
GUARDS   TRANS
   See reverse side

WEATHER BROADCAST
   At H+12 and 42 from range for Dog Creek,
   Quesnel, Ashcroft, Princeton and Dog Creek.

April 12, 1956

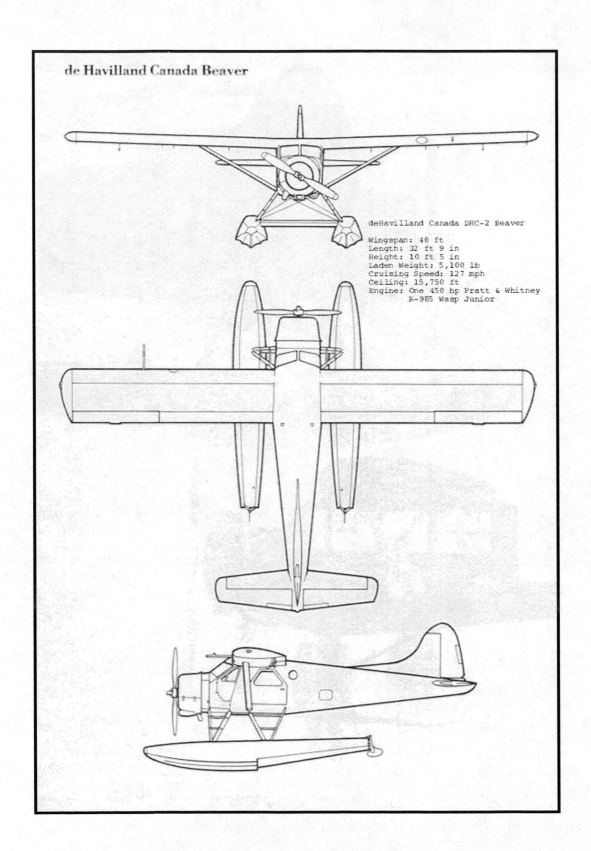

de Havilland Canada Beaver

deHavilland Canada DHC-2 Beaver

Wingspan: 48 ft
Length: 32 ft 9 in
Height: 10 ft 5 in
Laden Weight: 5,100 lb
Cruising Speed: 127 mph
Ceiling: 15,750 ft
Engine: One 450 hp Pratt & Whitney
R-985 Wasp Junior

Dog Creek

Anahim Lake

There was no airfield at Anahim Lake until well after the war period, but an event during Word War II is worthy of note.

During the winter of 1944-45, the Canadian Army at Prince George, in association with the RCAF, carried out the "Polar Bear Expedition" to train troops in winter operations and test equipment effectiveness. The expedition travelled overland from Prince George to Williams Lake then to Bella Coola, a total distance of some 450 miles. RCAF ground support personnel, along with No. 9 Construction and Maintenance Unit, travelled with the Army as far

RCAF Norseman MKIV #3536 with engine cover at Anahim Lake, Winter 1944-45.
Frank Hewlett Collection

as Anahim Lake, where its "Walter Snow Fighter", small bulldozers and a cat train, set up a temporary airfield on the ice of Anahim Lake itself. A camp was also set up on shore to accommodate maintenance and flight crews.

Aircraft from various units participated in the exercise: Norseman #3536 and #368 from No. 166 Communications Squadron from Western Air Command at Vancouver's Sea Island; No. 8 (BR) Squadron had four Lockheed Vega Venturas at Anahim Lake, including #2189.

Norseman MKIV #368 refuels at Anahim Lake.
Frank Hewlett Collection

Anahim Lake

A RCAF "Walter Snow Blower" from No. 9 Construction and Maintenance Unit clears landing strip on Anahim Lake. Frank Hewlett Collection

RCAF Lockheed-Vega Ventura G.R. MKV #2189 coded "Q" from No. 8 (BR) Squandron RCAF Station Port Hardy parked on ice at Anahim Lake early in1944. Frank Hewlett Collection

Anahim Lake

ELEVATION - 3600' approx.

POSITION
LAT. 52°30'N.   LONG. 125°20'W.
On Anahim Lake N. of the Village

OPERATED BY
Canadian Army and RCAF

REMARKS
Temporary ice runway in use only for operation "Polar Bear Expedition" winter 1944-45

LANDING AREA
LAKE ICE

OBSTRUCTIONS (ASL)

FACILITIES

RCAF only

Winter 1944-45

Anahim Lake

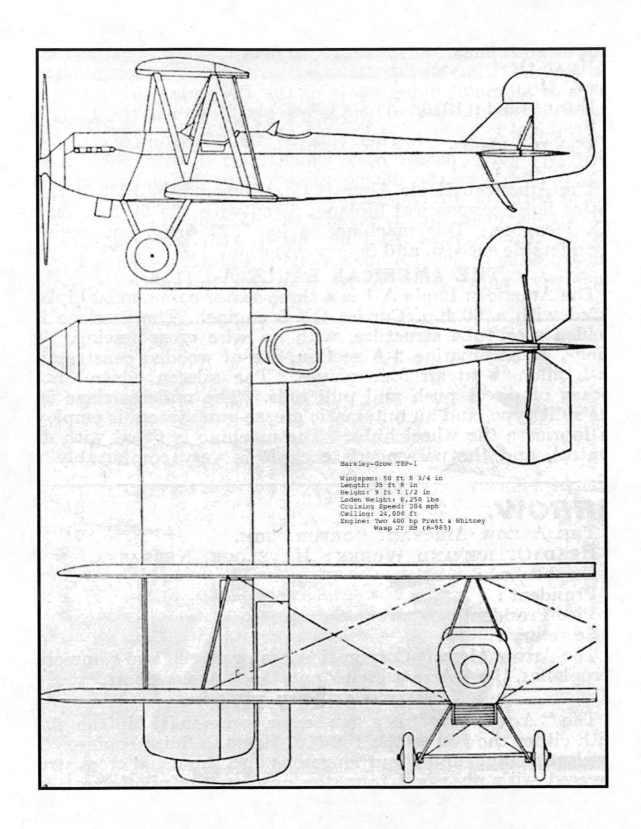

Barkley-Grow T8P-1

Wingspan: 50 ft 8 3/4 in
Length: 35 ft 8 in
Height: 9 ft 7 1/2 in
Laden Weight: 8,250 lbs
Cruising Speed: 204 mph
Ceiling: 24,000 ft
Engine: Two 400 hp Pratt & Whitney
Wasp Jr SB (R-985)

Anahim Lake

Williams Lake

The first recorded landing of an aircraft at Williams Lake was reported by Ben Clarke, and later by Irene Stangoe in the Williams Lake Tribune as September 13, 1927, But this is either a typo or an error as the reported aircraft was not built until 1928. G-CAUZ was an Alexander Eaglerock A-2 serial #647 built by the Alexander Aircraft Company at Colorado Springs, Colorado, in mid 1928. It was sold to Clyde Wann of Yukon Airways and Exploration Limited of Whitehorse, Yukon Territory, and imported into Canada at Vancouver, B.C., where it was assigned temporary registration in early September 1928. Wann and pilot John Patterson had earlier taken delivery of the aircraft in Colorado on September 7.

Wann and Patterson had planned a flight to the Yukon through the interior of B.C. and contacted settlements along the way advising of their intention of giving rides and exhibition

Williams Lake Airfield looking Northwest, September 30, 1943. RCAF PB-8726

Yukon Airways V.P. Clyde Wann left, and pilot John Patterson right, with friend, pose with "Northern Light", September 1928. Williams Lake Museum

Williams Lake

107

Williams Lake turns out to greet first aircraft, an Eaglerock G-CAUZ, September 13, 1928. Irene Stangoe

flights and barnstorming to finance the delivery flight home.

Keith Caverley was the contact person at Williams Lake who advised Wann of a potential landing area north of the village that at the time was used as a horse pasture and had previously been used as a race track. The area would later be known as the Airport subdivision at Williams Lake - 9th to 11th Avenue area. Caverley used old truck tires and marked the field's boundaries with white lime. He also stacked brush so that smoke from a fire could quickly indicate the wind direction.

The Eaglerock, christened "Northern Light", arrived later than expected on the morning of September 13, 1928, after a flight from Kamloops. Wann and Patterson remained in the Williams Lake area until October 23, when they flew to Quesnel with B.C. Police Sergeant Frank Gallagher on

board on official business. Sometime during their stay at Williams Lake, someone arranged to replace the brush pile wind indicators with a windsock, as one of the photos taken of the Northern Light clearly shows a professional looking windsock mounted on a pole on the uphill northern side of the airfield.

Float equipped aircraft and flying boats used Williams Lake itself for a landing area, using docks adjacent to the village proper..

The Willams Lake seaplane anchorage had been granted Public Permanent Licence No. 154 at a site on the north side of the lake, two miles east of town. The lake level was at 1,900 feet elevation, with an alighting area six miles long by one and three quarter miles wide, with service facili-

Joy riders and friends prepare for flight in Eaglerock G-CAUZ "Northern Light" September 1928. Irene Stangoe

Williams Lake

Two Western Canada Airways Boeing B-1E's at Williams Lake 1929-33, CF-ABB "Pintail" in foreground and CF-ABA "Petrel" at rear. Williams Lake Museum

ties available for day only. Williams Lake reportedly was frozen from December to April.

The Royal Canadian Air Force had been engaged in photographic survey work in the province for several years and on July 12, 1930, Fairchild FC-2W, G-CYXQ, landed at Williams Lake to conduct vertical photography of the area. XQ was flown by F/0 C.R. Dunlap, with Cecil Attwood as Photo Mechanic. The aircraft was on detached duty from the Dominion Air Station at Jericho Beach, Vancouver, spending the summer between Summit Lake and Salmon Arm.

Between 1929 and 1933, Western Canada Airways (later Canadian Airways) operated two Boeing B-1E aircraft at Williams Lake. The two flying boats, CF-ABA and CF-ABB, were likely on a mining contract in the area.

RCAF Fairchild FC-2W G-CYXQ at Williams Lake, July 12, 1930. Irene Stangoe

Williams Lake

109

de Havilland DH-80A "Puss Moth" CF-AGW at Williams Lake September 1935, flown by Sheldon Luck and Ron Campbell. Sheldon Luck

The airfield was inspected by the Civil Aviation Branch Department of National Defence (RCAF) from Jericho Beach Vancouver in late spring 1934, and an airport licence was issued on June 11, 1934, to the Village of Williams Lake for a site 2,700 feet long and 400 feet wide. Two local roads later crossed the airfield, but its biggest drawback was grazing cattle that would often obstruct the landing area.

Barney Boe was a well known pilot at Williams Lake. He bought a new Fleet Model 2 biplane on floats, CF-AOD, in Ontario September 15, 1930, and flew home to B.C. following the CNR railway via Jasper and the Yellowhead Pass. Boe had a mine at Likely and frequently showed up at Williams Lake in AOD, where he stayed at the Lakeview Hotel.

The first night crossing of the Canadian Rocky Mountains occurred on September 5, 1935. Pilot Sheldon Luck and Engineer Ron Campbell had been fruitlessly searching for charter work at Prince George and Williams Lake, B.C. The pair had earlier flown over from Calgary in Advance Air Services' de Havilland DH-80A "Puss Moth", CF-AGW, which was owned by Mrs. M. Muncaster of Calgary. On the night in question, Luck and Campbell found themselves broke and hungry, with only enough funds for gas to fly home. Ron Campbell tells the story.

When the village was incorporated in 1929, Chairman John Smedley began a campaign for the community to establish a licenced airfield. The local commission pursued this goal and with volunteer help an airfield was established at the site used by Wann and Patterson in 1928.

Williams Lake, B.C. to Calgary, Alberta - September 5, 1935

Keith Caverly, Tony Woodland and Bert Levens gave endlessly of their time. A small shed was built to serve as a terminal and a public works bulldozer leveled the strip.

Sheldon Luck and I worked for Advance Air Service based in Calgary, Alberta, where the company operated a de Havilland Puss Moth, CF-AGW. Business was slack at the time, so the manager decided to look further afield. He corresponded with the Mayor of Prince George, B.C. regarding providing an air service in that locality. He received some encouragement since Canadian Airways had closed their base at Summit Lake north of Prince George.

A formal request from Ottawa asked the village commissioners to prepare a detailed survey of the airport site during October 1932.

Williams Lake

In August 1935, Sheldon and I flew to Prince George via Jasper, Alberta. We scouted the area for a few days and concluded that the community would welcome a locally based air service. However, most of the flying would be to destinations requiring float equipped aircraft. The Puss Moth was only certified for use on wheels and skis, so we reluctantly abandoned the idea.

A relative of Sheldon had a placer mining operation on Keithly Creek not far from Williams Lake, so we decided to pay him a visit. On landing at Williams Lake the left shock strut collapsed. As a result, we had a prolonged visit awaiting a new shock strut from de Havilland in Toronto. No overnight Federal Express in those days - rail express only.

The replacement strut arrived about ten days later and we proceeded to install it. The job went without a hitch, but we were now down to our last dime. We pondered the situation another night with the stars for a roof or go home. Calgary was 300 miles as the crow flies from Williams Lake and we had ample fuel to make the flight. It was a beautiful September afternoon and without any knowledge of en route weather we took off for Calgary.

The first part of the flight was uneventful. We climbed to 15,000 feet and crossed the Cariboo Mountains. Soon after passing the Thompson River Valley we were cruising above scattered clouds that eventually became solid. Consequently, we were unable to observe any landmarks along our planned flight path. To compound the situation it was getting dark. We then realized that we hadn't taken the time differential between Williams Lake and Calgary into account. The Puss Moth wasn't equipped for night flying and we had no instrument lights. Fortunately, I had some matches (the old wood type about

two inches long) and at regular intervals I struck matches to give Sheldon some light to read the compass. After close to four hours in the air, the cloud cover started to break. Shortly thereafter, through a gap in the clouds, we spotted the lights of the Ghost River dam just west of Calgary. We were on track and began our descent, landing in Calgary four hours and ten minutes after takeoff.

RMC November 5,1997

Note: In the cold dawn of a new day, Sheldon and I didn't give ourselves very high marks for the flight, nor did the local aviation fraternity. Nevertheless, we lived it down and it was a lesson learned that served us well in the years ahead.

The November 21, 1935, edition of the Williams Lake Tribune reported that Ginger Coote's Bridge River and Cariboo Airways secured a contract from the Taylor Windfall Mining Camp at Taseko Lake and would be basing a float plane there for the season using the property of Mr. Smedley as his base of operations.

Ginger Coote's Fairchild 51A CF-AUX at Williams Lake April 1, 1937. Audrey Burke Coll., Williams Lake Museum

Williams Lake

Another aircraft operated by Ginger Coote arrived April 1, 1937, when CF-AUX, a wheel equipped Fairchild 51A, began using the Williams Lake airfield on the Taylor Windfall Mining operation. AUX had originally been built in 1927 as a Model FC-2 registered G-CAIH, but had been modified and rebuilt on January 18, 1934, and later purchased by Bridge River and Cariboo Airways.

After the Williams Lake Airfield was crossed by two roads, the Department of Transport lapsed the village's airport licence on September 28, 1937.

On Sunday, January 15, 1938, the inaugural air mail flight took off from Ashcroft at 9:30 a.m. with pilot Sheldon Luck at the controls and with Ginger Coote, United Air Transport's Vice-President and General Manager for B.C., as co-pilot and air engineer Dick Green. The WACO Custom CF-AZM's first landing was at Williams Lake where the chairman of the Village, Commissioner Sid Weston, made a presentation to Ginger Coote. Mr. Louis L. Bourdais, MLA for Cariboo, boarded the WACO when it left for Quesnel at 11:30 a.m. The flight later continued to Prince George and Fort St John where it connected with the Yukon Edmonton air mail flight. This weekly flight was continued from Ashcroft until May 1938, when the route originated in Vancouver.

Several months after the Y.S.A.T. inaugural air-mail flight, Sheldon Luck was south-bound in the WACO from Prince George to Williams Lake with one passenger, Joe Dwyer, a reporter with the Edmonton Bulletin. Five minutes out of Williams Lake, Luck began experiencing control problems with the WACO's ailerons. Glancing at the top right corner of the aircraft's cabin he saw the upholstery was tearing and that the wing root structure appeared to be moving.

The weather was clear, but gusty wind conditions made for a turbulent flight. The pilot knew something was terribly wrong and very gently began a descent to a successful landing at Williams Lake. On investigation Luck found the right wing's front spar had become detached from its mount on the fuselage. The pair were very lucky to have survived the flight. Both Luck and Dwyer checked into a hotel to wait for company pilot Ted Field who flew in the following day.

The April 6, 1939, edition of the Williams Lake Tribune reported the cancellation of Yukon Southern service to Williams Lake due to safety concerns, and the cancellation of the airport licence after

U.A.T. WACO ZQC-6 Custom CF-AZM arrives at Williams Lake January 15, 1938.
Sheldon Luck

Williams Lake

PC-216. WILLIAMS LAKE. 20 AUG 43. K10. 1500' SW.

Williams Lake Field looking Southwest, August 20, 1943. RCAF PC-216

Yukon Southern Air Transport (YSAT) had begun using its Barclay-Grow twin engine aircraft on the route. The Village commissioners immediately set to work to rectify the situation. Trees would have to be cut at both ends of the single runway. It would have to be fenced and the road crossing the airfield re-routed around the perimeter.

On October 30, 1939, a report states the Department of Transport had awarded a contract for the development of the airport to Thode Bros. of Saskatchewan who were to enlarge the airfield to 3,400 x 400 feet and level and seed the grass areas.

In 1940, on the completion of improvements, the licence was re-instated and YSAT resumed its service to the community.

During early 1941, a non-directional radio beacon was installed to aid aircraft landing or transitioning by Williams Lake. Yukon Southern Air Transport again suspended service to the community in mid July 1941, stating that the airport length was insufficient to accommodate its new larger aircraft on the route.

The airport was now under the administration of the Department of Transport who stated that no further money was available for improvements. After the attack on Pearl Harbour by the Japanese, the Department of National Defence assumed responsibility and the airport became RCAF Station Williams Lake.

Williams Lake

113

RCAF organization order No. 126 dated May 20, 1943, stated that Williams Lake would be designated as No.12 Staging Unit and would be improved so that in an extreme emergency, and should an enemy gain a foothold on coastal stations, fighter aircraft could quickly be located here to form a secondary line of defence.

On October 6, 1942, an RCAF Norseman #2480 on floats arrived at Williams Lake on a photographic survey of the Williams Lake airfield. #2480 was flown by F/Sgt George Williamson with photographer W02 E.B. Hackett. The men operated from Williams Lake itself until they departed for Kamloops on October 9. Williamson would again return to photograph Williams Lake airport with W02 Hackett on August 25 and 26, 1943, this time in Bolingbroke RCAF #9066. By this time Williamson had been commissioned and held the rank of Flying Officer. The pair again remained overnight departing for Sea Island at Vancouver.

By 1943, Canadian Pacific Airlines had assumed the YSAT airmail routes and a November 1943 schedule listed Williams Lake as a flag stop.

In September 1945, Williams Lake was handed back to the Department of Transport and a temporary airport licence issued to the Village on December 20, 1946. The Village approached the Department of Transport in April 1950 stating that the Department operated radio navigation facilities (radio range), and the air radio and weather reporting service at Dog Creek, should be relocated to Williams Lake to better serve the larger community.

On May 31, 1946, the Williams Lake Flying Club purchased a DH-82C Tiger Moth, CF-CIG, from the War Assets Corporation, later selling it July 17, 1946, to the Victoria Flying Club.

By June 1950 the airport was 5,200 feet long by 200 feet wide and, because of the terrain of the site, had been expanded to its maximum potential. In 1953 the Village requested that Ottawa develop a new airport, and in September 1956 the Department of Transport commenced construction of the present airport four and a half miles north east of the Village, which opened in September 1959 with a single 7,000 x 200 foot runway licenced for day use only.

In 1950 CPA expanded its northern service to include Williams Lake on a regular schedule, and almost half the village turned out to welcome the inaugural flight, which arrived in CPA's DC-3 #276, CF-CPW. The 500 wellwishers in attendance brought along the village "Rube Band" which

Brisbane Aviation Aeronca S15-AC CF-FNV at Williams Lake 1947.
Williams Lake Museum

Williams Lake

CPA DC-3 CFW arrives at Williams Lake in 1950. Irene Stangoe

Tribune Editor Irene Stangoe left, and her sister centre, greet CPA crew. BC Police Constable second from right.
Irene Stangoe

Williams Lake

Williams Lake "Rube Band" greets CPA flight in an earlier mode of transport.
Irene Stangoe

arrived by stagecoach. Dozens of local horsemen rode up and down the gravel runway and one cowpoke induced a CPA stewardess to gallop down the strip, to the glee of the crowd. Village chairman John Anderson officially welcomed the flight. Grant McConachie, CPA President, stated "I've never seen anything like it for a town this size."

In early November 1954, the author was engaged by Pacific Wings Limited of Vancouver to deliver a used Aeronca 7AC, CF-HSR, from Vancouver to Prince Rupert via the inland route. On the late afternoon of November 7, I landed HSR at Williams Lake village airfield. The field was deserted except for a pilot preparing an aircraft for flight. After securing the Aeronca for the night, I made my way to the Maple Leaf Hotel operated by Mrs. Charlie Moxon, which I had been told was the cheapest place in the village but had the best home cooking. Early next morning I returned to the airport and started to clear a light dusting of snow in preparation for my departure for Prince George. HSR had no electrical system and I endlessly swung the prop to no avail. About 9:00 a.m. a CPA DC-3 arrived and discharged its

passengers. Apparently it would not leave Williams Lake for some time and its two pilots wandered over to see what this 18 year old kid was doing with the Aeronca.

Both pilots in turn tried, without success, to get HSR started. A decision was made and both pilots shed their uniform jackets and hats, rolled up their sleeves, got a tool box from the DC-3, and the airline captain and his first officer pulled and cleaned sparkplugs, checked the wiring leads, reinstalled the cowlings and, after the usual cacophony of "switches on, throttle set, brakes set, contact", the First Officer gave HSR's prop a professional looking swing and the Continental's 65 horsepower all roared into life.

By this time the DC-3 passengers were showing up at the little hut that served as the airport terminal. The Captain and his First Officer wiped their greasy hands, put their hats and jackets back on, and headed back to the DC-3. At the time I was most appreciative of this crew of a mighty airliner stopping to help a greenhorn kid. Indeed a wonderful example of airmen helping airmen.

On June 7, 1955, the Williams Lake Flying Club purchased CF-BTR, an Aeronca 65-CA Super Chief, which was sold August 19, 1957.

During the summer of 1958 the Village and the Williams Lake Flying Club held its first, and very successful, air show and fly-in, with at least 20 aircraft in attendance. An aerial photograph, courtesy of Irene Stangoe, shows one hundred

Williams Lake

First Air Show at Williams Lake June 4-11, 1958, looking South. Air Cadets, centre, march on runway.
Williams Lake Historical Society

and ten cars and two buses at the field, and Royal Canadian Air Cadets parading down the runway.

community. A subdivision was later built on the site.

Canadian Pacific Airlines continued to use the village airfield, unless it was too soft due to heavy rain, in which case its DC-3s would land at the new airport.

On December 14, 1960, the landing and approach lighting at the new airport was completed and, on December 19, CPA began using the new airport exclusively in the Vancouver-Quesnel-Prince George service. Official opening of the new airport occurred July 5, 1961, and the village airfield was closed after 33 years of service to the

1958 Air Show looking West. Williams Lake Historical Society

Williams Lake

Williams Lake

WILLIAMS LAKE B. C.

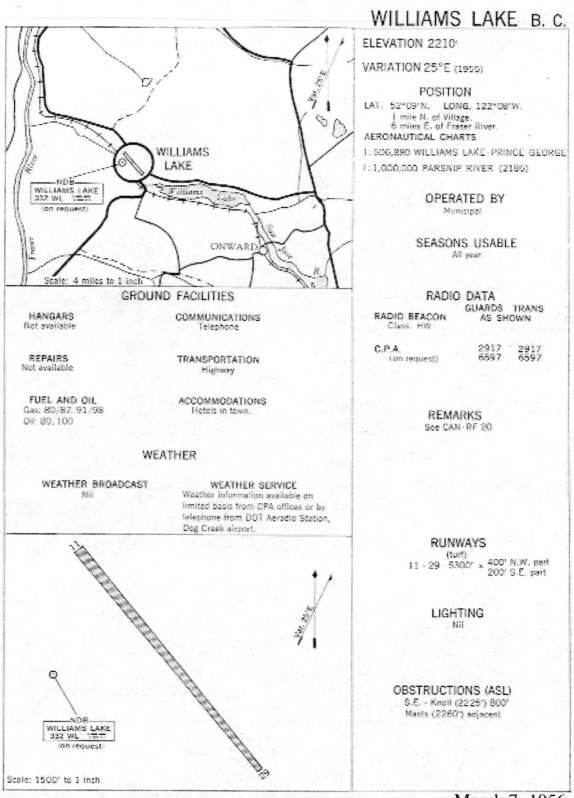

ELEVATION 2210'

VARIATION 25°E (1955)

POSITION
LAT. 52°09'N.   LONG. 122°08'W.
1 mile N. of Village.
6 miles E. of Fraser River.

AERONAUTICAL CHARTS
1:506,880 WILLIAMS LAKE-PRINCE GEORGE
1:1,000,000 PARSNIP RIVER (2180)

OPERATED BY
Municipal

SEASONS USABLE
All year

RADIO DATA

RADIO BEACON		GUARDS	TRANS
Class: HW		AS SHOWN	
C.P.A.	(on request)	2917 6597	2917 6597

REMARKS
See CAN-RF 20

GROUND FACILITIES

HANGARS
Not available

COMMUNICATIONS
Telephone

REPAIRS
Not available

TRANSPORTATION
Highway

FUEL AND OIL
Gas: 80/87, 91/96
Oil: 80, 100

ACCOMMODATIONS
Hotels in town.

WEATHER

WEATHER BROADCAST
Nil

WEATHER SERVICE
Weather information available on
limited basis from CPA offices or by
telephone from DOT Aeradio Station,
Dog Creek airport.

RUNWAYS
(turf)
11 - 29 5300' x 400' N.W. part
200' S.E. part

LIGHTING
Nil

OBSTRUCTIONS (ASL)
S.E. - Knoll (2225') 800'
Masts (2260') adjacent

NDB
WILLIAMS LAKE
332 WL
(on request)

Scale: 4 miles to 1 inch

Scale: 1500' to 1 inch

March 7, 1956

Williams Lake

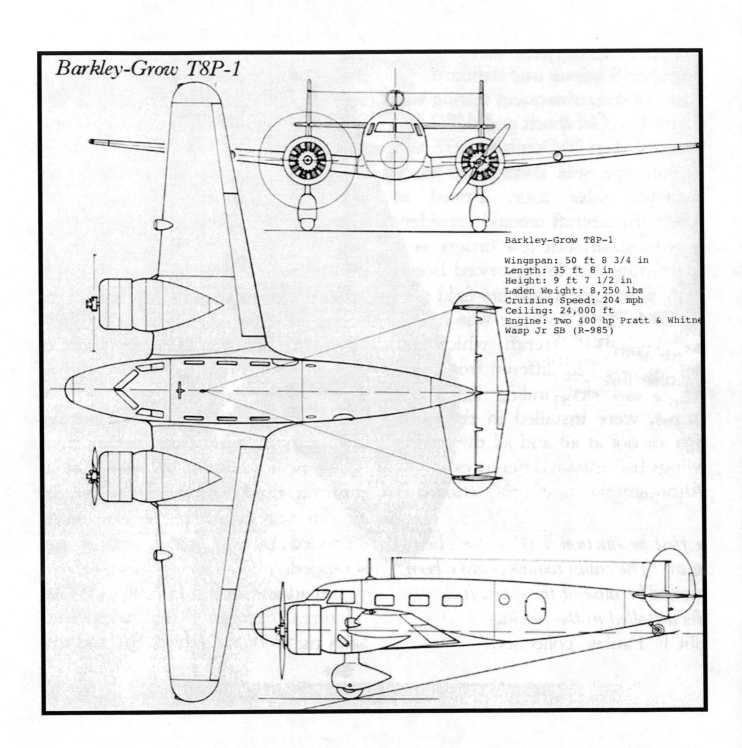

Barkley-Grow T8P-1

Barkley-Grow T8P-1

Wingspan: 50 ft 8 3/4 in
Length: 35 ft 8 in
Height: 9 ft 7 1/2 in
Laden Weight: 8,250 lbs
Cruising Speed: 204 mph
Ceiling: 24,000 ft
Engine: Two 400 hp Pratt & Whitne
Wasp Jr SB (R-985)

Williams Lake

Quesnel

Twelve years before the first recorded landing of an aircraft at Quesnel, two air-minded brothers decided that they both wished to become aviators. In October 1916, Clarence L. Hilborn and William C. Hilborn of Quesnel traveled by BX stage coach and train to Vancouver where on October 16 they both signed up for pilot training with the B.C. Aviation School. This was the first step necessary before joining the Royal Flying Corps and later serving over the front lines of Europe in the First World War.

Both brothers fought with distinction. William was awarded the D.F.C. and Clarence was twice mentioned in dispatches. Sadly, William was killed in the last days of the war in 1918. Clarence returned to British Columbia and died in 1978.

RFC Lieutenants William and Clarence Hilborn served with distinction in the war of 1914-18 and were Quesnel's first aviators. Quesnel Archives

It would be twelve years later when on October 23, 1928, G-CAUZ, a new Alexander Eagle Rock A-2 Christened the Northern Light, arrived from Williams Lake landing at Johnston's Field. The aircraft was flown by pilot John M. Patterson and was registered to Yukon Airways and Exploration Company. After leaving Vancouver in early September, it had barnstormed its way earning money for expenses by giving rides and exhibitions at towns along the way.

A B.C. Police Sergeant Frank Gallagher was also on board on police business, having chartered the aircraft from Williams Lake. The Eaglerock later departed Johnson's Field for Prince George.

On September 11, 1929, a Western Canada Airway Boeing B-1E Flying Boat, CF-ABB, landed on the Fraser River at Quesnel for fuel.

Yukon Airways Eaglerock G-CAUZ arrives at Quesnel October 23, 1928.
Quesnel Archives

The aircraft was flown by Walter Gilbert who had flown from Stewart B.C. on an emergency request from Cominco's Emerald Mine near Burns Lake. The mine superintendent had been badly mauled by a grizzly bear. After refueling the Boeing, Gilbert took off for Vancouver with a brief stop at Bridge River.

During the winter of 1929-30, a Consolidated Mining and Smeltering Company aircraft, Fairchild 71 CF-AHC, landed on the ice of the Fraser River next to the bridge at Quesnel.

CF-AHC, a Consolidated Mining and Smelting Co. Fairchild 71 landed on ice of Fraser River at the Quesnel Bridge, Winter 1929-30. Quesnel Archives

On March 9, 1931, pilot Tom S. Corless and air engineer Bill Jaquot made a forced landing due to weather at 3:00 p.m., six miles north of Quesnel at Nam Sing's field. The pair was en route from Vancouver to Prince George having left Vancouver at 10:15 a.m. and landing in a field at Alexandria at 2:00 p.m. where they refueled from cans carried on board.

The Stinson SM-8A Junior Detroiter, CF-ANE, was owned by Corless of Prince George who anticipated using the aircraft for prospecting. He had purchased the aircraft from Commercial Airways of Vancouver on February 12, 1931.

Sometime during the summer season 1930, CF-ALX, a Junkers F-13 operated by Air-Land Manufacturing Company of Vancouver, landed at the fork of the Quesnel and Fraser Rivers at the old sternwheeler riverboat landing. ALX was based at Prince George's six mile (Tabor) Lake and was flown by Wilhelm A. Joerss, a World War One German Ace who had flown throughout 1929 in another Junkers, G-CADP, which was flown without a licence.

On December 19, 1932, Ginger Coote flew from Quesnel to Barkerville where he picked up four officials of the Cariboo Gold Quartz Mine and flew them to Ashcroft. The 280 mile flight took three hours and forty minutes due to numerous snow showers, fog and

Quesnel

Junkers F-13 CF-ALX at Quesnel's old stern-wheeler landing, 1930. Quesnel Archives

Waco ATO CF-ASJ flown by Eric de Pencier held at Quesnel until January 30, 1933, to assist in search for Ginger Coote. CW Collection

head winds. When they landed the miners caught the CPR train to Vancouver.

On Friday, January 14, 1933, Ginger Coote and air engineer Cliffe Peene were summoned from Quesnel by Wilson Brothers Mine near Findlay Forks to pick up a seriously ill employee who died before the aircraft arrived. After Coote's landing on January 18, he was unable to leave because of the weather, and on a take off attempt later broke a ski which took three days to repair. At

Quesnel

Ginger Coote's Ryan B-1 "Brougham" CF-ATA was destroyed by fire at Quesnel March 1, 1933. Sheldon Luck

A Canadian Airways Loening Amphibian on skis, G-CARS, landed at Quesnel in mid March 1933, and on its take off on March 16 the aircraft hit an obstruction forcing it to land. When the pilot, W.J. Holland, attempted to restart the engine the Loening burst into flames destroying the aircraft.

this time the temperature dropped to minus 62 degrees (F).

In the meantime the government telegraph operator at Quesnel, Mr. Louis Labourdais, had alerted an itinerant aircraft to the possibility of a search. Pilot Eric de Pencier and Tom Attchison held until January 30 before departing in their WACO model ATO, CF-ASJ, for Ashcroft after Coote's safe return to Quesnel.

Russel L. "Ginger" Coote incorporated Bridge River and Cariboo Airways in October 1933, but had been operating in the area previously as an independent operator, what used to be known as a chisel charter. When a gold rush occurred near Quesnel in the early 1930s Cootes was quick to see the possibilities and for a time operated from Quesnel.

On March 10, 1933, CF-ATA, a Ryan B-1 Brougham belonging to Ginger Coote Airways, was preparing for its day's activities and its crew began to preheat the engine with a blow torch. This procedure set the aircraft on fire and quickly destroyed the machine before the fire could be put out. The 1928-built Ryan had been imported June 1, 1932, by Ginger Coote and was at this time the bread and butter aircraft in his business.

On May 21, 1934, pilots William M. Archibald and Page McPhee landed at Quesnel in a de Havilland DH-60M Gipsy Moth having flown there from Trail, B.C. on Cominco business.

Many wheel-equipped aircraft heading to Alaska preferred the inland route up the Fraser River to Prince George then west to Hazelton before entering Alaska. This preference was due to the complete lack of airfields on the coastal route between Vancouver and the Panhandle of Alaska.

During early May 1934, Frank Dorbandt had flown Ford 4-AT-65, NC-8403, newly acquired by Tom Marshall Kester and Edward H. Groenendyke of Pasadena, California. NC-8403 had previously been registered to Nick Mamer Flying Services at Spokane, Washington. On May 5, 1934. Dorbandt flew the Ford to Seattle, Washington, from California and was en route to Alaska.

Pioneer American aviator Frank Dorbandt was chief pilot for a newly organized airline that intended to provide scheduled service between Fairbanks, Cordova and Anchorage using the first Ford Trimotor in Alaska. He took off from Seattle's Boeing Field on May 21, 1934, and set out toward Prince George. Underestimating his time and fuel requirements, he found himself over Nazko, some 80 miles to the west of Quesnel, where he made a precautionary landing in a swamp-meadow belonging to Mike Ranger. Dorbandt, pilot Don Glass, and eight passengers spent the night in a haystack, as Ranger's cabin was too small for the party. Ranger however laid on a hearty meal of moose meat and fresh fish.

Pioneer American Aviator Frank Dorbandt landed Ford 4.AT Trimotor NC-8403 at Quesnel's Baker's Field May 22, 1934. J. Brown photo

At first light Dorbandt and Glass lifted off the swamp meadow with only the crew and 1800 pounds of freight aboard, intending to return after obtaining fuel. At 5:45 a.m. the Ford arrived over Quesnel and landed at Bakers Field where they were greeted by William Archibald, Mine Manager for Cominco at Trail B.C., who had arrived the previous day by air. After obtaining fuel, Dorbandt took off at 8:30 a.m. for Prince George where he arrived at 9:45 a.m. Here he unloaded the freight and left at 10:15 a.m. for Nazko.

Meanwhile, his eight passengers had been moved 12 miles east by wagon to a much larger and firmer field belonging to rancher Shorty Harrington. On landing the Ford, the passengers were quickly loaded and the flight departed for Prince George.

The inaugural airmail flight in the British Columbia central interior arrived at 11:31 a.m. on January 15, 1938. United Air Transport had succeeded in getting the post office to award

it the contract, which started at Ashcroft and proceeded via Williams Lake, Quesnel, Prince George, to Fort St John, where it connected with the company's flight from the Yukon and then on to Edmonton, Alberta.

The first flight was in a CF-AZM, a Waco model YKS-6 flown by Sheldon Luck with Ginger Coote, now an official with United Air Transport, and company air engineer Dick Green. It had departed Ashcroft at 9:30 a.m. It was the

U.A.T. inaugural airmail flight in Waco CF-AZM flown by Sheldon Luck at Quesnel January 15, 1938. Sheldon Luck

Quesnel

first weekly flight on this route that would use several different aircraft - the Waco, a Fairchild 71, and on occasion the Ford 6-ATS Special Trimotor CF-BEP. After May 1938 the flight was to start from Vancouver. On the first flight WACO AZM landed on skis at Dragon Lake south of Quesnel.

Aircraft landing at Quesnel over the years used a variety of fields, starting with the 1928 landing of the "Northern Light" at Johnston's Field. Tom Corless landed six miles north of the town at Nam Sing's Field in 1931, and by 1934 Frank Dorbandt used Baker's Field. Float equipped aircraft also used a number of landing areas nearby to Quesnel in the early 1930's. Junkers CF-ALX landed at the Quesnel Steam Boat Landing. During the winter of 1929-30, Cominco Fairchild 71, CF-AHC, landed on skis next to the Fraser River Bridge at Quesnel.

Still later, Dragon Lake became the preferred landing area for float aircraft. During the month

CPA Barklay-Grow CF-BQM taking off Fraser River at Quesnel, 1942.
Sheldon Luck Collection

of December 1940 the village of Quesnel made a formal inquiry to the Department of Transport in Ottawa respecting the establishment of an airport. The town stated that they had chosen a site four miles north of town. The location was within city limits and could accommodate a 6,000 foot runway. The Department of Transport agreed to the airport being established at this site but did not act on it.

In 1942 the Department of National Defence at Ottawa decided to develop the field as an intermediate airport between Williams Lake and Prince George. The airport was developed for use by the air force and was named RCAF Station Quesnel.

On May 20, 1943, RCAF Organization Order No. 126 established Quesnel as No. 13 Staging Unit being part of the

Quesnel Airfield looking South, September 30, 1943. RCAF PA-6730

Quesnel

126

Interior Staging Route. The RCAF established a Radio Range aircraft navigational facility nearby for use by military aircraft. Potentially the field, and others on the staging route, constituted a second line of defense to be used in extreme emergency should an enemy gain a foothold on the B.C. coast. On short notice fighter aircraft could be operated defensively from these stations.

RCAF Beech 18 "Expeditor" #1384 refuels at Quesnel. Quesnel Archives

At the end of hostilities in 1945 the airport became surplus to RCAF needs and was handed over to the Department of Transport in 1946 and an airport licence was issued on April 1, 1946. On April 30, Tom Corless, now a resident of Quesnel, purchased CF-BRE an Aeronca 7AC Champion from Brisbane Aviation of Vancouver. The aircraft had been manufactured in 1945, as serial #7AC-346, and was powered by a Continental A-65 engine. Corless sold the aircraft to Port Alberni Airways on September 21, 1950.

On December 23, 1953, R.F. McLeod and D.K. Styan of Quesnel bought a de Haviland DH-82C Tiger Moth, CF-CIK, from Skyway Air Services at Langley, B.C., which was later damaged beyond repair in a crash at Shalalth, B.C. while on a flight from Boston Bar to Dog Creek.

Quesnel airport's 5,500 x 200 foot runway No 13-31 was paved in 1958 and a new terminal building constructed in 1967. CPA began using Quesnel on its Vancouver to Prince George scheduled service using DC-3 aircraft on December 19, 1960. The airline had served the community previously but on a sporadic basis.

A D.O.T. Lockheed 12A CF-CCT visits Quesnel during WWII. Quesnel

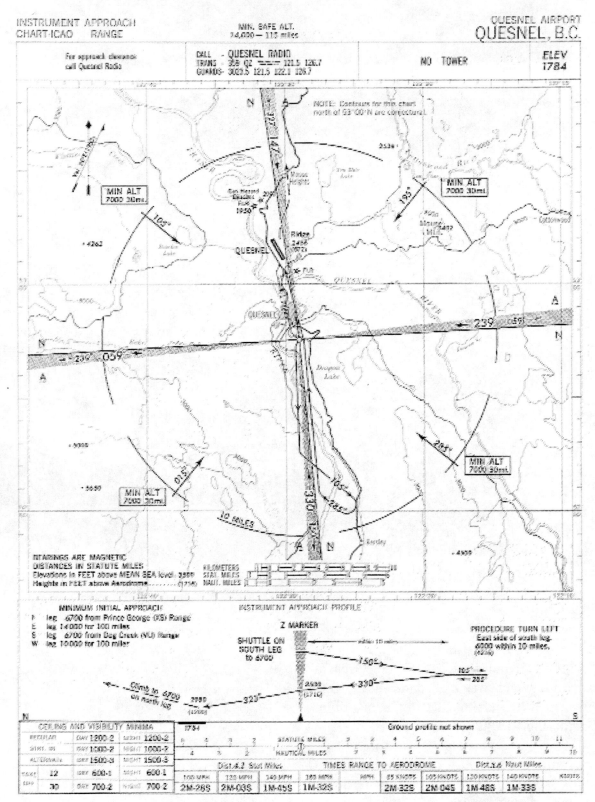

October 28, 1955

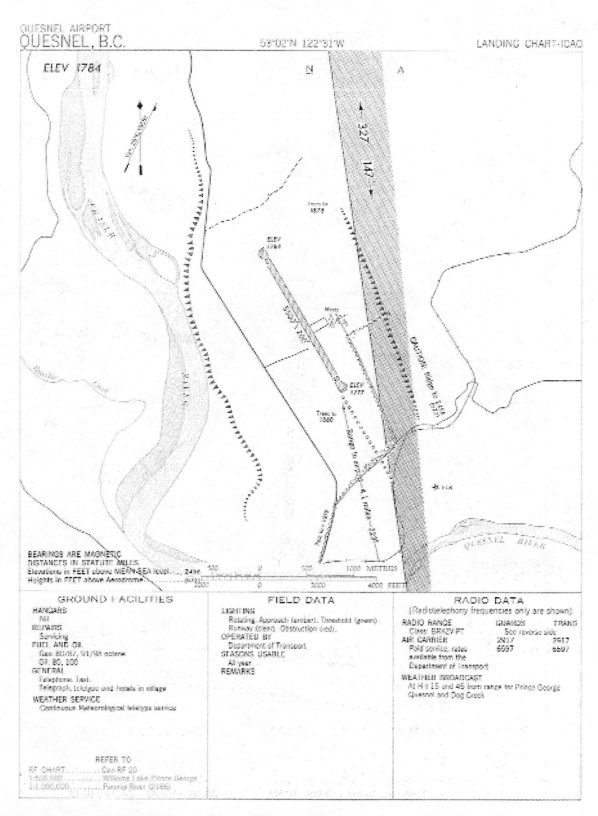

ELEV 1784

BEARINGS ARE MAGNETIC
DISTANCES IN STATUTE MILES
Elevations in FEET above MEAN SEA level ... 24x
Heights in FEET above Aerodrome

GROUND FACILITIES

HANGARS
Nil
REPAIRS
Servicing
FUEL AND OIL
Gas: 80/87, 91/98 octane
Oil: 80, 100
GENERAL
Telephone. Taxi.
Telegraph, teletype and hotels in village

WEATHER SERVICE
Continuous Meteorological teletype service

REFER TO
RF CHART ... Can-RF 20
1:506,880 ... Williams Lake-Prince George
1:1,000,000 ... Parsnip River (21:86)

FIELD DATA

LIGHTING
Rotating. Approach (amber). Threshold (green).
Runway (clear). Obstruction (red).
OPERATED BY
Department of Transport
SEASONS USABLE
All year
REMARKS

RADIO DATA
(Radiotelephony frequencies only are shown)

	GUARDS	TRANS
RADIO RANGE		
Class: BRAZV PT	See reverse side	
AIR CARRIER	2917	2917
Field service rates	6697	6697
available from the		
Department of Transport		

WEATHER BROADCAST
At H+15 and 45 from range for Prince George
Quesnel and Dog Creek

October 28, 1955

Quesnel

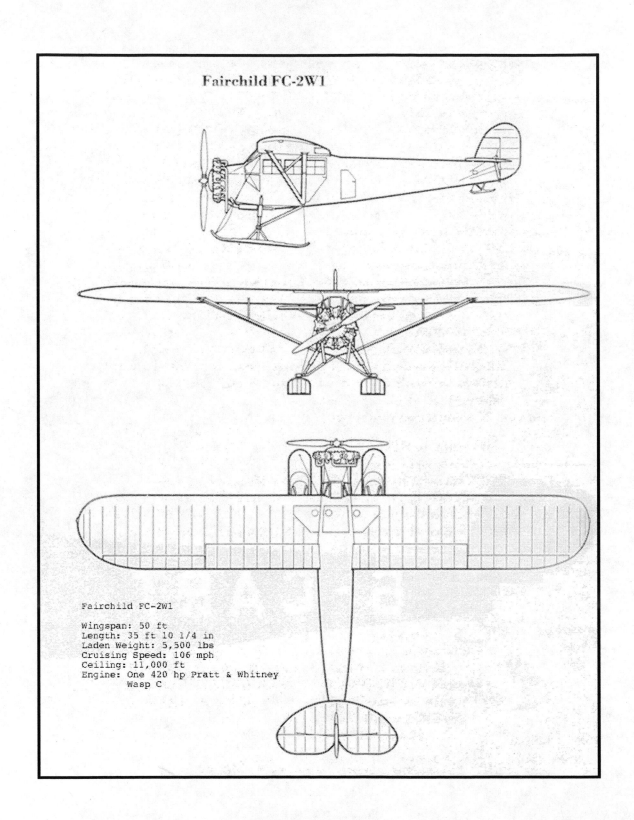

Fairchild FC-2W1

Fairchild FC-2W1

Wingspan: 50 ft
Length: 35 ft 10 1/4 in
Laden Weight: 5,500 lbs
Cruising Speed: 106 mph
Ceiling: 11,000 ft
Engine: One 420 hp Pratt & Whitney
        Wasp C

Quesnel

Late in 1919 the U.S. Air Service, under the authority of Brigadier General Billy Mitchell, set about planning a flight from Mitchell Field, New York to Nome, Alaska. As much of the proposed route would pass through the Dominion of Canada, as protocol demanded, an official request was made to Ottawa which was ultimately approved and passed to the newly formed "Air Board" for action.

Captain H.A. LeRoyer was assigned by the Air Board to liaise with the Planning Committee and in April 1920 he, in company with U.S. Air Service Captain Howard T. Douglas, began to assess the potential landing fields in Canada for the "Alaska Flying Expedition".

In late April, Captains LeRoyer and Douglas headed west on the Grand Trunk Pacific Railway

LEAKY GAS TANK CAUSES POSTPONEMENT AIR FLIGHT TO JASPER UNTIL FRIDAY

Every Precaution Being Taken to Guard Against Mishaps on Hazardous Journey Through Mountains; Landing Places Are Few and Far Between

Another day's delay in the New York to Nome, Alaska, flight being made by the four American army aeroplanes, has been caused by a leak in the gas tank of one of the machines, and some minor defects which were discovered in the overhauling given the planes Wednesday. Consequently the hop-off which was scheduled for this morning has been postponed until 9 o'clock Friday.

Capt. Street and his mechanic realize that the most difficult part of their hazardous journey lies immediately ahead of them. On the jump from Edmonton to Jasper they enter the Rocky mountains about sixty miles, and from Jasper to Prince George a landing place in case of trouble would be practically impossible to find, as here the mountain ranges are highest and all heavily wooded. There are very few clearings in the district, and with this in view every possible form of trouble must be guarded against.

The aviators plan to cross the mountains at a height of 2,000 feet above the highest peaks to avoid the dangerous wind pockets that are known to exist in mountain flying; a fact that was amply proven in the negotiation last year of the Kicking Horse pass from Vancouver to Calgary.

Edmonton Journal July 29, 1920

(CNR Route) from Edmonton to Jasper, Alberta, where they were met by Colonel Maynard Rogers, Superintendent of Jasper National Park. Rogers had previously been apprised of the needs of the expedition and escorted them to a site he had chosen 9 miles north of the Village of Jasper and half mile north of Henry House, on a flat plain at the mouth of the Snaring River where it empties into the Athabaska River. The site was bounded by jack pine and trembling aspen, and was often frequented in winter by large herds of elk that wintered (yarded up) in the area. The site was perfect, and with minimal preparation was ideal for the needs of the forthcoming flight.

On July 31, 1920, the expedition's four de Havilland DH-4B World War I bombers took off from May-Gormon Aerodrome at Edmonton for

Edmonton Journal, August 2, 1920

Jasper, following the Pembina River. After a flight of 69 miles they ran into fog and low cloud and returned to Edmonton.

The next day dawned clear and the four aircraft, headed by the expedition's leader, Captain St. Clair Streett, took off at 9:30 a.m. Streett noted the difficult terrain they were passing over and realized that his earlier decision to turn around had been the correct one. Streett later summed up his feelings in an article in National Geographic: *"Our motors hummed sturdily over this terrible landscape - terrible to the anxious pilot who is constantly straining his eyes to select the site for a forced landing should his motor fail."*

The New York to Nome flyers camp at Henry House near Jasper, August 1, 1920. Provincial Archives of Alberta

The entire area had been devastated by forest fires and presented an awesome sight as seen from their cruising altitude of 6,000 feet. Entering the Athabaska River Valley, they soon spotted the landing field prepared for them next to the junction of the Snaring River. After a flight of 200 miles, the aircraft started their landings at Jasper - plane #4 at 11:00 a.m., #3 at 11:02, #2 at 11:05, and Captain Streett in #1 at 11:07 a.m.

Lieutenant Clifford Nutt, the second in command on the flight, later noted "Here we found one of the best landing fields of the whole route."

Colonel Rogers and his Administration Secretary George Fleming, an ex-RAF pilot, had done their utmost to accommodate the flight. Tents had been erected, a Chinese cook and a Mess Tent were provided, and he had moved gas and oil to the site. The flyers decided to take a swim in a nearby lake, but the water temperature made it very brief. The ferocious mosquitoes kept them moving and quickly warmed them up again. The group built smudge fires at their encampment and were able to get a modicum of rest.

On August 2 the flight got an early start for their next destination, Prince George, following the Grand Trunk Pacific Railway (now CNR) via Tete Jaune Cache and McBride. Soon after take-off from Jasper, plane #1 caught fire, with Capt. Streett and Sergeant Heriques on board. The oil tank had been over-filled and it vented onto the aircraft's exhaust causing the fire. Sgt. Henriques was flying and he put the machine into a side-slip, which extinguished the fire, and the pair returned to Jasper. However, the other three DH-4B's pressed on to Prince George. Three hours later Capt. Streett continued the flight from Jasper to Prince George.

Alaska Flying Expedition's de Havilland DH-4B's are prepared for takeoff from Henry House Field August 2, 1920. P.A.A.

Jasper National Park Superintendent, Colonel Maynard Rogers, hoped that the flight's stop in Jasper would inspire the Dominion Government to establish a Forestry Patrol Detachment there, with obvious reference to the Air Board Stations initially at Morley and later High River, Alberta. However, this did not come about.

The Air Board had established an Air Station at Morley in mid-1920 to provide forest fire protection to the Dominion Government Forest Reserve

High River based de Havilland DH-4 of the Canadian Air Force G-CYEC (#2714) was likely at the Henry House field at the request of park officials during the summer of 1921. via Larry Milberry

on the eastern slope of the Rocky Mountains. de Havilland DH-4 aircraft were utilized. Some of the northern patrols would undoubtedly have stopped at the Jasper landing field for weather, mechanical related reasons, or for fuel.

Evidence of Air Board usage occurred in the early 1920s with a photograph of a DH-4 at McBride, B.C., 120 miles to the west of Jasper. This flight would have not been possible from the Air Board sub-base at Eckville (Rocky Mountain House), Alberta as they would have had to refuel. (The Air Board was the only operator of the DH-4 in Canada.) This DH-4 at McBride, B.C., has been identified as G-CYEC, which was taken on strength at High River, August 2, 1921. Jasper Park Superintendent, Colonel Maynard Rogers, had earlier contacted the Air Board respecting the use of an aircraft to survey the park's lakes and mountains and potential routes for trail building. An aircraft was then dispatched in late summer 1921 from High River to Jasper, where it remained on detached duty for three days. It is most likely that this aircraft was G-CYEC which is photographed at McBride, B.C.

The following year another American aviator passed through Jasper en route to Alaska. Clarence O. (Ollie) Prest had departed Las Vegas, Nevada, in late July 1921 entering Canada at Lethbridge on August 8, then on to Edmonton flying his Curtiss JN-4D named the "Polar Bear". It was Prest's intention to fly to Siberia. The "Polar Bear" departed Edmonton and flew on to Jasper following the Grand Trunk Pacific railway tracks. After spending a couple of days, Prest left Jasper August 22 or 23 for Prince George.

Major George A. (Tommy) Thompson arrived at Henry House (Jasper) July 13 or 14, 1922. He was flying a German

American flyers, C.O. Prest and C.M. Bach arrive at Henry House August 20 or 21, 1921 enroute to Siberia in their modified Curtiss JN-4. Prest Collection

built Junkers Larsen JL-6 on wheels, G-CADP, from Edmonton to Hazelton. The aircraft had been sold by Imperial Oil to an investment syndicate for prospecting purposes.

By this time, the former Air Board Dominion Air Station at Morley had closed and had moved to a new location at High River. It was now re-organized as a Canadian Air Force Station (No. 2 Squadron), which continued forestry protection patrols through the Government Forest Reserve, eventually establishing substations at Pincher Creek, Coleman, Eckville, Rocky Mountain House, and Grande Prairie.

On Tuesday afternoon, April 16, 1929, pilots "Shorty" Cramer and "Will" Gamble had taken off from Edmonton en route to Prince George. The pair had left the Cessna Aircraft Company plant at Wichita, Kansas in early April and had flown to Chicago before starting an exhibition flight to Siberia and return. There was much concern in Prince George at the Cessna's failure to arrive, until the following day when a telegraph from Jasper reported that the Cessna AW. NC-7107 had landed safely the previous evening at nearby Lucerne on Yellowhead Lake close to the summit of the pass. The flyers were forced to land after experiencing deteriorating weather in a snowstorm. The Cessna successfully took off early on April 17, 1929, but again had to land at

Junkers Larson JL-6 G-CADP seen here at Peace River 1920. via E.L. Myles

On April 17, 1929 Cessna model AW NC-7107 on a flight from Chicago to Siberia landed at Lucerne on Yellowhead Lake, 20 miles West of Jasper. CW

McBride, B.C. because of a heavy rainstorm, arriving the following day at Prince George.

On Sunday, July 21, 1929, Captain Ross G. Hoyt had crashed his U.S. Army Air Corps Curtiss Hawk XP-6B near Valemount, B.C., on a return flight from Whitehorse to Edmonton, Alberta. The Edmonton Journal was quick to pick up on the story and chartered a de Havilland DH-60 Moth from the Edmonton Flying Club, piloted by Leroy Mattern who flew reporter Jack DeLong to the Henry House airfield near Jasper

On Sunday July 21, 1929 Captain Ross G. Hoy of the US Army Air Corps damaged this Curtiss XP-6B pursuit plane near Valemont, BC on the return leg of a New York to Nome flight. USAF 1789A

where the newsman caught a westbound train to Valemont.

The excellent quality natural landing field at Jasper continued to host unrecorded itinerant aircraft traffic through the years, and the site remains little changed to this day.

Leroy Mattern flew a reporter from Edmonton to Jasper Sunday, July 21, 1929 in a deHavilland DH-60 moth.. via Larry Milberry

In early July 1933, an American Bellanca CH-300, Pacemaker NC-403E, touched down on the Henry House, Jasper landing ground. The aircraft had departed New York City and was flown across Canada following the Iron Road (railway). After leaving Jasper, it continued to Terrace, B.C., via Prince George and Hazelton. The pilot, Will Alexander, and three others were a relief expedition for the famous "Round the World" pilot Jimmy Mattern.

On September 9, 1933, Grant McConachie asked pilot Z. Lewis Leigh to fly a 1931 de Havilland DH-80A "Puss Moth", CF-APE, from Edmonton to Jasper with a stop at Edson to pick up a Russian nobleman, Prince Galitzine. On arrival at Jasper, Leigh found a golf tournament in progress on the Henry House airfield and it took several low level passes before the golfers moved off their "fairway" allowing him to land.

While returning by car to the village from Jasper Lodge, Leigh unfortunately gave a man and woman a ride to town. The pair had robbed guests at the lodge and demanded that Leigh fly them to the U.S.A. The pilot convinced the desperados that neither the Puss Moth nor the airfield had lights, so Leigh was then herded to a hotel room in town to await daylight. Leigh and his air engineer, Bill Sutherland, were able to escape and the robbers were later arrested and jailed. The Puss Moth then returned to Edmonton uneventfully.

In August 1934, John A. Wilson, the Controller of Civil Aviation for the Department of Defense, made an inspection of several airfields in a Civil Aviation Branch de Havilland DH-80 "Puss Moth" flown by Inspector Howard Ingram.

Pilot Z. Lewis-Leigh thwarted a hijacking attempt at Jasper September 9, 1933 in deHavilland DH-80A "Puss Moth" CF-APE via Bruce Gowans

An unidentified Travel Air 6000 is parked in front of Bellanca CH-300 NC-403E at Henry House summer 1933. Jasper Archives

Wilson landed at the Henry House airfield near Jasper.

During the spring of 1938, CF-ANM, a 1930 Fleet Model 2, landed at the Henry House Flats field at Jasper. The plane had been purchased on March 12, 1938, in Ontario and was being ferried to Prince Rupert, where it would be operated by the Roman Catholic Episcopal Corporation for missionary work.

The Jasper airfield at Henry House continued to see sporadic use even during Word War II. For example, on April 23, 1944, RCAF Norseman #366 departed Kamloops at 9:15 a.m., later stopping at Jasper en route to Edmonton.

During the immediate postwar period, the RCAF carried out a training exercise to develop procedures for pararescue in remote areas. At least two aircraft participated at the Jasper Airfield - an Expeditor (Beach 18) RCAF No. 1397, and an unidentified Dakota (DC-3). The

Bellanca NC-403E flown from New York on the Jimmy Mattern Relief Expedition landed at Henry House Field early in July 1939. Jasper Archives

Jasper

pararescue course associated with the exercise took place in the summer of 1947.

Few aircraft were based at Jasper, however G.N. Thomson and D.L. Seeley of Jasper purchased CF-THE, a Piper PA-20, in 1954.

The author has only landed at Jasper Airfield once, on July 11, 1972, in my Cessna 170A N-9264A (later C-GHCW), while on a family flight from Dawson Creek to Banff.

The Jasper airfield, in its idyllic setting, has provided a haven from the weather for aircraft traversing the "Yellowhead" route to Kamloops, or via McBride to Prince George. For years, there

Fleet 2 CF-ANM taxis for takeoff. Jasper Archives

A 1930 Fleet Model 2 CF-ANM landed at the Henry House Field March 12, 1938 enroute to Prince Rupert, BC. Jasper Archives

Jasper

were no alternate airfields on either route and many accidents resulted.

Currently Parks Canada has proposed the closure of the Jasper Airfield. This about face of Jasper Park officialdom, is an incredulous affront to pioneer aviators and to that early Park Superintendent of 1920, Colonel Maynard Rogers, who had the foresight to create an aircraft landing field that not only enhanced Jasper National Park but provided aviators with a safe haven while transiting the Rocky Mountains.

Air photo of Jasper looking North. CW

RCAF Expeditor (Beech 18) #1397 at Jasper during the summer 1947 during a para-rescue exercise. DND

RCAF Dakota on short final to Jasper Air Field during the summer of 1947. DND

JASPER ALBERTA

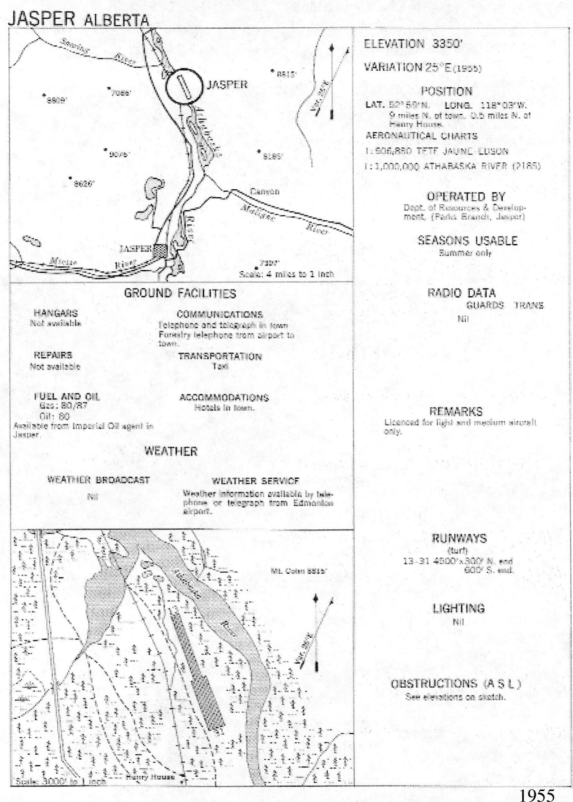

Scale: 4 miles to 1 inch

GROUND FACILITIES

HANGARS
Not available

COMMUNICATIONS
Telephone and telegraph in town
Forestry telephone from airport to town.

REPAIRS
Not available

TRANSPORTATION
Taxi

FUEL AND OIL
Gas: 80/87
Oil: 80
Available from Imperial Oil agent in Jasper.

ACCOMMODATIONS
Hotels in town.

WEATHER

WEATHER BROADCAST
Nil

WEATHER SERVICE
Weather information available by telephone or telegraph from Edmonton airport.

Scale: 3000' to 1 inch   Henry House
Mt. Colin 8515'

ELEVATION 3350'

VARIATION 25°E (1955)

POSITION
LAT. 52°50'N.   LONG. 118°03'W.
9 miles N. of town. 0.5 miles N. of Henry House.

AERONAUTICAL CHARTS
1:506,880 TETE JAUNE CUSON
1:1,000,000 ATHABASKA RIVER (2185)

OPERATED BY
Dept. of Resources & Development. (Parks Branch, Jasper)

SEASONS USABLE
Summer only

RADIO DATA
GUARDS   TRANS
Nil

REMARKS
Licenced for light and medium aircraft only.

RUNWAYS
(turf)
13-31 4500' x 300' N. end
600' S. end.

LIGHTING
Nil

OBSTRUCTIONS (A S L)
See elevations on sketch.

1955

Jasper

140

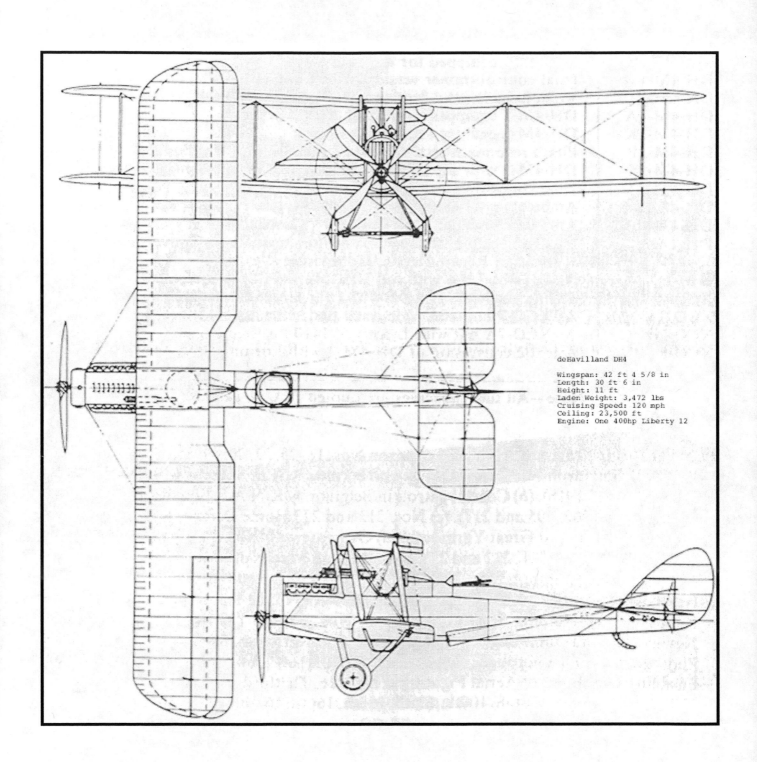

deHavilland DH4

Wingspan: 42 ft 4 5/8 in
Length: 30 ft 6 in
Height: 11 ft
Laden Weight: 3,472 lbs
Cruising Speed: 120 mph
Ceiling: 23,500 ft
Engine: One 400hp Liberty 12

McBride

Located at 53 degrees 19 minutes north, and 120 degrees 10 minutes west, at an elevation of 2,350 feet, McBride is situated in the valley formed by the Fraser River between Jasper and Prince George and provided a natural haven for itinerant aircraft between these points while following the Grand Trunk Pacific Railway.

On August 2, 1920 four aircraft passed over McBride on their way to Prince George from Jasper. The aircraft were de Havilland 4Bs of the United States Army Air Service flight to Nome, Alaska from New York.

The following year, in July 1921, a lone Curtiss JN-4 christened "Polar Bear" also passed over McBride from Jasper en route to Prince George. Pilot Clarence O. Prest of Las Vegas, Nevada was on a flight from Mexico to Siberia.

The Superintendent of Jasper National Park, Colonel Maynard Rogers, had hoped that the use of the Henry House flats by the United States Army Air Service in the summer of 1920, would inspire the use of the same site by the newly-formed Air Board, which by 1922 was established at High River, Alberta with a sub-base at Elkville east of Rocky Mountain House.

Maynard also hoped that the forest fire patrols would include his park and there is evidence this came to pass with possible use of the Henry House field by the Air Board's de Havilland DH-4s. A picture of the DH-4 in a field at McDonald's farm at McBride is evidence that High River based aircraft flew into this area. The pictured aircraft is one of twelve gifted to Canada by Great Britain after the First World War. The registration of the DH-4 has been covered by a sheet held by several McBride residents except for the letter "G", which is in black on a white background as was required by Canadian authorities in the early 1920 period. There were no civil registries of DH-4 aircraft in Canada so it follows that this particular DH-4 was one of the High River based machines. However, there is one giveaway to its identity. Its rudder, by regulation, should have had a large black "G" on it, but this aircraft does not. Obviously the rudder was a replacement not yet painted. Another picture of the same aircraft exists taken in May 1922 at High River, with the only visible identity being a service number F-2714.

The assigned Air Board registration for F-2714 was G-CYEC which was registered for government use (C of R) August 2, 1921, and assigned to the High River Dominion Air Station for photographic and forest protection duties. G-CYEC remained in service until November 2, 1928, four and a half years after it had been on inventory with the RCAF. Local McBride lore tells that the DH-4 was the first aircraft to land at the community and that the aircrew would only agree to a picture being taken if the registration was covered up as "they were not supposed to be here."

High River based deHavilland DH-4 patrolling in the northern Rockies 1924. DND

A de Havilland DH-4 G-CYEC of the High River, Alberta air station lands at McBride summer 1921.
via McBride Public Library

McBride

144

A DH-4, at a maximum range of approximately three hours at 120 miles per hour, would not have enough fuel to travel from the Air Board sub-base at Eckville to McBride and return. It is logical that a fuel cache was used at Henry House for the crew's sightseeing trip to McBride.

Cessna AW NC-7107 powered by a Warner Scarab radial engine landed at McBride April 17, 1929. Janes A.W.A.C.

On Wednesday April 17, 1929, a Cessna AW on an endurance flight from Chicago to Siberia passed overhead at McBride en route to Prince George, but was forced to turn around near the Goat River due to weather and made an emergency landing in a field at McBride. The Cessna NC-7107 became mired in mud and was unable to take off, forcing its pilots Shorty Cramer and Will Gamble to unload most of their gear and remain overnight. Fortunately it froze during the night and Cramer was able to take off the next morning without incident for Prince George where he landed at 10:45 a.m., April 18. Will Gamble and their equipment followed by rail.

Captain Ross G. Hoyt USAAC landed Curtiss Hawk XP-6B near Valemont July 21, 1929. USAF

In the late afternoon of Sunday July 21, 1929, another aircraft passed overhead McBride at 6,000 feet. The aircraft was a Curtiss Hawk XP-6B of the United States Army Air Corps flown by Captain Ross G. Hoyt, who was on the return leg of a record flight from New York to Nome, Alaska. Hoyt had taken off from Whitehorse at 11:00 a.m. and was flying non-stop to Edmonton. Shortly after passing over McBride, the Hawk's

XP-GB Curtiss Conqueror engine started to fail. Hoyt was considering parachuting from his aircraft when he spotted what looked like a possible landing field. By now all power had gone from the engine and he deadsticked the Hawk into the field of soft sand. Unfortunately, just before the aircraft had stopped rolling, the right wheel struck a mound throwing the Hawk on its back. Captain Hoyt was uninjured and crawled from his wrecked plane.

Mr. Cox, the postmaster from the village of Valemount, came to Hoyt's assistance and with

McBride

145

Modern Air Photo of McBride looking North. CW

the help of several residents Hoyt was able to right the Hawk. Hoyt quickly determined that the damaged aircraft would have to be shipped out by rail. He then left the Yellowhead country on Tuesday, July 23, 1929, by rail to Edmonton.

There was no road to McBride until 1968 when the connection was made between Valemount and Tete Jeune Cache through to Prince George. Prior to this time the CNR was the sole means of transport in and out of the community.

The people of McBride were quick to appreciate the value of the airplane. A small airfield came into use during the 1940s on the farm of Phil Jeck, three miles east of town on Jeck Road. Another airfield was established at Crescent Spur in 1960, approximately twenty-five miles west of McBride on the farmland of Vern Adams.

HAPPY LANDINGS!

You Too Can Fly
HERE'S HOW!!

PREPARED AND DISTRIBUTED BY:
ROYAL CANADIAN FLYING CLUBS ASSOCIATION
Journal Bldg., Ottawa 4, Ontario

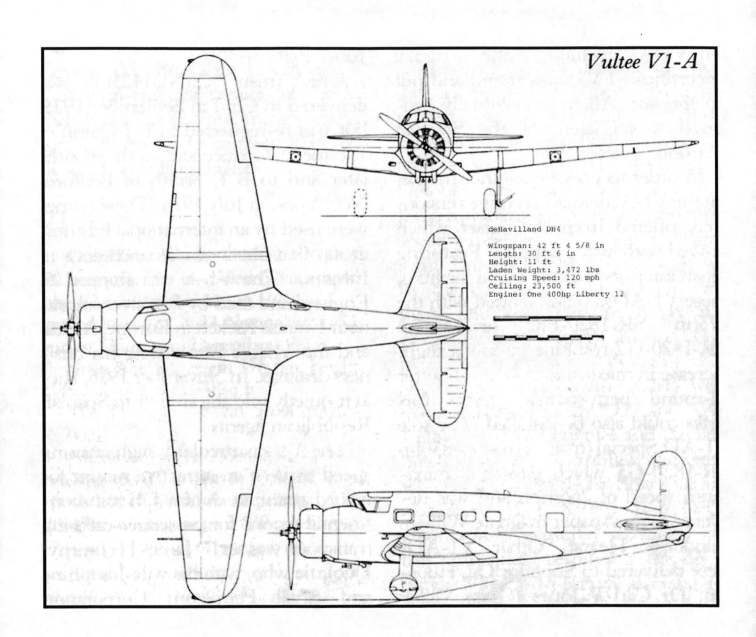

Vultee V1-A

deHavilland DH4

Wingspan: 42 ft 4 5/8 in
Length: 30 ft 6 in
Height: 11 ft
Laden Weight: 3,472 lbs
Cruising Speed: 120 mph
Ceiling: 23,500 ft
Engine: One 400hp Liberty 12

Prince George

In 1906 survey parties arrived at Fort George in preparation for the construction of the Grand Trunk Pacific Railway (CNR), a transcontinental rail line which would have a profound effect on this isolated community. The tracks came through town in 1913 and real estate promoters had a field day promoting the area as the "Hub City", which it indeed was destined to become. The city formed by the land boom was incorporated in 1915 under the name of Prince George.

With the end of World War I, returning aviators and the availability of cheap war surplus aircraft made the federal government start to take aviation seriously and in 1919 established the Air Board to control virtually every aspect of aviation in Canada. Dominion Air Stations were established across the nation, the most westerly being at Jericho Beach in Vancouver. Air Board personnel were to a man veterans who served in either the Royal Flying Corps or the Royal Navel Air Service, both of which were amalgamated as the Royal Air Force in 1918. There was no air force in Canada and Canadian airmen had all served with the services of Great Britain.

On February 23, 1920, the Air Board approached the City Fathers of Prince George as to the city establishing an air harbour, which was the name in use at the time for a licenced airfield. Air Board Inspector S.R. Anderson visited the city by train on return from his inspection and approval of an air harbour at Hazelton for both private and commercial use by both land and float aircraft. The Prince George City Council declined the invitation to have its unlicenced Central Avenue airfield officially listed as an approved air harbour because of the costs involved.

Prince George was destined to play an important part in British Columbia's aviation history, but its first aviation presence would come from the air service of the United States. Brigadier General William "Billy" Mitchell was Assistant Chief of the US Air Service, a division of the Army, and he was the leading advocate of an independent air force. To promote this vision, he dreamed up a series of long distance flights to attract attention to his ideas. In 1919, he advised Colonel "Hap" Arnold, "Better get oriented along the line as to the possibilities from your department (to the) north, having previously demonstrated that we could go across the United States we wanted to demonstrate that we could establish an airway to Alaska and Asia."

A flight was planned to depart New York and fly to Nome, Alaska, 4,000 miles distant from Mitchell Field, New York. Few aircraft had been over much of the route and few established landing fields existed to support the ambitious project. Mitchell arranged contact with his Canadian counterparts at the Air Board to discuss his plans and obtain permission to overfly and land in

Canada, over which a large portion of the flight would pass.

It was agreed that a reconnaissance party, consisting of US Air Service Captain Howard T. Douglas and Canadian Air Board Captain H.A. Le Royer, would travel along the Canadian portion of the route three months before the flight and make arrangements for services and landing sites en route. Captains Douglas and Le Royer arrived at Prince George aboard the Grand Trunk Pacific Railway and immediately set about selecting a suitable landing ground for the upcoming flight. The pair, in liaison with City Council, selected a site on what is known as Central Avenue and across First Avenue, now a part of the city's downtown.

The site was 900 feet long by 300 feet wide. It was quickly cleared and the parameters were marked at the four corners. A large "T" was constructed that could be moved to indicate the landing direction. This was augmented by a smudge pot that would also provide a visual indication of wind direction. The intended route after leaving Edmonton was via Jasper, overhead McBride, and on to Prince George.

The flight, known as the Alaska Flying Expedition, consisted of four de Haviland DH-4B World War I bombers. Each was crewed by a pilot who was an officer and an air mechanic NCO, with the exception of airplane Number 2 which was crewed by two officers, the second being the engineering officer for the flight. The flight departed New York's Mitchell Field on July 17, 1920, and had reached Jasper, Alberta, on

August 1 where the four DH-4Bs and their crews remained overnight.

Early the following day the flight took off from Jasper. Shortly after takeoff the lead plane, Number 1, which was being flown by its mechanic Sergeant Henriques with the flight's leader Captain Street on board, developed an oil fire and returned to land safely at Jasper. The other three aircraft continued via Tete Jaune Cache, McBride to Prince George. As the three aircraft flew over McBride, the Grand Trunk Pacific Agent sent a telegraph message to his counterpart in Prince George advising of their imminent arrival.

The three DH-4Bs arrived at Prince George in the early afternoon just ahead of a rain storm. Aircraft number 2 and 4 landed uneventfully, however number 3 aircraft, flown by Lieutenant Clarence E. Crumrine as pilot with photographic officer and mechanic Sergeant James D. Long, was not so fortunate. Landing too fast Crumrine overshot the marked landing field, struck a small stump at the end of the field which blew a tire, and nosed the aircraft over, which splintered its propeller and damaged a wing tip. The City had

Captain Street's plane #1 in foreground undergoes repairs at the Prince George Central Avenue Airfield (August 1920). Trelle Morrow Collection

Plane #1 after completion of repairs, August 1920. Frank Hewlett Collection

arranged to keep the public and their vehicles and animals away from the three aircraft and officials kept smokers at a safe distance.

Captain Street had sent a telegram from Jasper that he had resolved his difficulties and was on his way to Prince George expecting to arrive about three hours behind the other aircraft. By the time Street arrived there was an intense storm in progress, and the heavy rain and poor visibility initially prevented him from locating the city. But on turning back he was able to identify his position and arrived over the Central Avenue Field where the other crews had lit a series of fires to guide him. Captain Street commented afterwards, "Finally a blaze of light on the ground to my right indicated that a flare had been lighted to guide me. Flying low I observed the three other airplanes of my flight huddled together in blinding rain while around them was grouped a number of motor cars. I made a blind landing. As luck would have it I hit the edge of the field and smashed my left wing and tore away the whole side of the stabilizer. Ten feet more to my right would have given me an open path."

The flight's second in command, Lt. Clifford C. Nutt, witnessed the landing and would later state, "The outline of the field was, of course, indefinable in the rain so when Street came in he had good speed and overshot, rolling out of the field itself into a cut-over stretch beyond where he struck a stump that took about four feet of the left wing and breaking both main spars and tearing all the ribs out, also the left half of his horizontal stablizer and the aileron."

Captain Street and his crews held a conference. If they had to get a new wing from California, the closest location, it could take many days or even weeks. Inquires resulted in locating a local cabinet maker, Charles Sinclair, who was engaged to repair the two damaged spars and ribs as well as the horizontal stabilizer and aileron. As these were repaired, a Prince George tailor covered the surfaces with linen fabric, which was shrunk into place by the application of a concoction of dope made by plane Number 4's pilot Lieutenant Ross C. Kirkpatric. Meanwhile, a propeller for plane

Prince George ladies pose with Lt. Nutts plane #2, August 1920. Trelle Morrow Collection

No. 3 was purchased and delivered, likely by train from Edmonton.

All this activity would take eleven days, and the flight was already behind its anticipated schedule and summer in the north would soon be gone. Street and Nutt decided they were less than happy with the advance parties selection of a landing field and they decided to take the train to the next planned stop in Hazelton to assess its potential and attempt to avoid a repetition of the aircraft damage at Prince George.

Meanwhile, the townspeople made the best of the first flight to the city. Many pictures were taken with the aircraft and crews. The City Board of Trade decided to host the men to a banquet and dance held in their honour on the fifth of August.

Captain Street had been right to suspect that the field selected at Hazelton would be inadequate. He located a much larger site nearby, which unfortunately somewhat spoiled the celebrations planned by that community at the original landing site.

Repairs completed and their hosts properly thanked, the DH-4s lifted off Prince George Central Avenue Airfield at 9:05 a.m. Friday, August 13, 1920, and followed the railway west to make an uneventful flight to Hazelton, and from there on to Nome, Alaska.

The four aircraft would again land at Prince George on their return flight on October 4, where they stayed until October 8 before proceeding via Jasper to Edmonton and back to New York to a tumultuous welcome on October 20, 1920.

The following year on August 23, 1921 yet another American aviator arrived at the Central Avenue Field. Clarence 0. (Ollie) Prest had also been a pilot in the US Air Service in World War I, but was now attempting a record setting flight in conjunction with a movie company. Prest left Las Vegas, Nevada, in his Curtiss JN-4 Jenny, a war surplus trainer that he affectionately named "Polar Bear", declaring that he would fly from Mexico to Siberia, probably attempting to upstage the Alaska Flying Exhibition of 1920.

After giving an exhibition of his flying ability stunting over the town, he likely offered rides for cash to help pay his expenses before departing for Hazelton along the railway line via the Vanderhoof-Smithers route.

The following year a third aircraft came to the Central Avenue Airfield. This time a German Junkers JL-6 with Canadian registration G-CADP and christened the "Vic". This early Junkers and another had previously belonged to Imperial Oil who had used the two aircraft on company busi-

Lt. Kirkpatrick's plane #4 getting loaded for departure to Hazelton, August 12, 1924. Trelle Morrow Collection

Junkers JL-6 G-CADP in flight. Via F. Ellis

ness in the North West Territories. Now purchased by an investment and mining syndicate in Hazelton, ADP was headed west on wheels arriving at Prince George on July 14, 1922.

ADP's pilot was Major George A. "Tommy" Thompson, previously an RFC Veteran of the Great War who had flown the last leg of the first

Prince George

J.A. Wilson RCAF at left exits Curtiss HS-2L that visited Prince George in 1924. P.A.C.

Trans Canada Flight in 1920 from Calgary to Vancouver. ADP would return to Prince George at the end of the decade to make a colourful contribution to aviation in central B.C.

With the formation of the Royal Canadian Air Force on April 1, 1924, John A. Wilson was appointed as Assistant Director and Secretary of the RCAF. During the summer of 1924, Wilson set out on a 10,000 mile inspection trip of aviation facilities across the country. Wilson departed Vancouver's Jericho Beach in a Curtiss HS-2L Flying Boat and visited Prince George before continuing on to Prince Rupert and other coastal centres.

During the summer of 1928, the RCAF commenced a program of aerial photography throughout B.C. that would eventually result in the production of aerial maps of the province. Two Fairchild 71's, G-CYXN and XQ, were dispatched from the Jericho Beach Air Station at Vancouver to Salmon Arm and Prince George. Initially the aircraft assigned at Prince George were flown to Fort George on the Fraser River until another site was located at Summit Lake, 28 miles north of the city where the small detachment established itself for the summer.

Reference has been made by Jack Corless to his family's first flight made at Prince George in 1926 with his father R.F. Corless in an Alexander Eaglerock, which was barnstorming in the area. This must have been an American registered aircraft because the first Eaglerock registered in Canada, G-CAIS, was to B.C. Airways at Victoria, B.C. December 13, 1927. On July 12, 1928, B.C. Airways bought a second Eaglerock, G-CATN. Possibly Corless family records are in error and the date of their flight was 1928.

On October 26, 1928, a new Alexander Eaglerock A-2 arrived from Quesnel at the Central Avenue airfield. The Eaglerock had been flown from the factory in Colorado Springs, Colorado, to Vancouver where it had received its temporary Canadian licence G-CAUZ from the Civil Aviation Branch Department of National Defence. The aircraft then flew through the Okanagan and Cariboo putting on exhibition flights, giving rides, and occasionally doing charters to earn travel expenses along the way.

AUZ had been purchased by the Yukon Airways and Exploration Company Limited of Whitehorse, Yukon, and was being flown by pilot John M. Patterson and company owner Clyde Wann. The pair had christened AUZ the "Northern Light" and the name was emblazoned on its sides. On November 1, AUZ departed Prince George continuing its barnstorming at Vanderhoof.

Earlier, on October 15, 1928, the City of Prince George, at the instigation of Mayor A.M. Patterson, had decided that in view of the growing number of aircraft passing through the community a more suitable and less confining location should be found for the city's airfield. A site was found a mile south of the city's centre just west of Carney Hill and adjacent to the city's Exhibition and Fair Grounds, near the junction of today's Highway No. 16 and 97. The City Council authorized the purchase of 165 acres of land at this location.

Yukon Airways Eaglerock G-CAUZ barnsatormed at Prince George October 26, 1928. Quesnel Archives

A guest speaker at the Board of Trade meeting in April 1929 further inspired airport action. International airman Parker D. Cramer urged that the city quickly develop its airport and outlined the benefits that would ensue. The Board was so impressed that a special committee was formed to help push the airport project to completion. Two veteran Royal Flying Corps members were appointed to the committee, A.B. Young and V.R. Clerihue, as well as the city's Mayor A.M. Patterson.

At the May 1929 Board meeting, A.B. Young advised the group that a Civil Aviation Board, Department of National Defence inspector was expected shortly to review the city's plans and location for the improved airfield. The inspector, Dan McLean had enlisted in the Royal Flying Corps in Canada in 1917, and after returning to Canada after the First World War he continued his university education and later joined the RCAF. At this time civil aviation in Canada fell under the authority of the Department of National Defence, which was administered by the RCAF as the Civil Aviation Branch.

Junkers JL-6 G-CADP at Six Mile (Tabor) Lake, 1928. Attwood Collection

RCAF Fairchild FC-2W G-CYYU at Summit Lake late in 1929. Attwood Collection

RCAF Sub Base at Summit Lake; William Cecil Attwood second from left. Attwood Collection

Prince George

156

On April 1, 1929, Dan McLean was seconded to the Civil Aviation Branch Department of National Defence as Inspector of Western Airways with headquarters in Regina, Saskatchewan. One of his first tasks as Inspector was to respond to the City of Prince George's request to review their chosen site for an airport.

Dan McLean arrived at the end of May 1929 and, in concert with City and Board of Trade representatives, toured the proposed areas and concluded that the Carney Hill location would be potentially suitable for a licenced airfield. The City did not act on McLean's recommendations until the October council meeting when a property acquisition was agreed to and $500 was allocated to commence clearing of the Carney Hill site. Work began in the first week of November 1929. Clearing, grading, and leveling of the site continued for the next two years and by April 1932 the city airfield had two gravel runways 2,200 x 300 feet wide.

The RCAF photographic detachment from the Jericho Beach Air Station was again present for the summer months of 1929 and Fairchild 71, G-CYXQ, was assigned to the Summit Lake subbase north of Prince George. XQ arrived at Summit Lake on June 9 and remained until October 17, 1929. The pilot was F/O Windsor with photographer air mechanic William Cecil Attwood. RCAF Fairchild G-CYXN was also present in October 1929, flown by F/O A.L. Laurie Morfee.

A mining promoter and businessman resident of Prince George had noted the possibilities of aircraft for transport to remote locations and the ability of this mode of transport to maintain the secrecy of destinations and mining claims. R.F. Corless had a number of interests in Prince George, including the Hudson and Essex car deal-ership on George Street. Corless was aware of a derelict Junkers JL-6 that had been sitting on the bank of the Skeena River next to the Mission Point airfield at Hazelton, and in 1928 he negotiated a purchase of the machine which he brought to Prince George on a railway flatcar.

Corless's son Tom had also become interested in aviation and travelled to Calgary where he received flying instruction from the Great Western Flying School and earned his licence. Meanwhile, Corless senior had taken the Junkers, G-CADP, to his car dealership where he had his employees assist air engineer Emil Kading restore the machine to airworthiness. Henry Gross, a local tinsmith, was employed to make repairs to ADP's damaged metal surfaces. Corless also hired a very experienced pilot, Wilhelm "Bill" A. Joerss, who had served with the German Air Service during the First World War. Joerss had been refused a licence because of his German citizenship and the regulation that a Canadian pilot had to be a British subject.

ADP's repairs completed, the aircraft was moved to the Fraser River for flight testing and then to Six Mile (Tabor) Lake. Corless senior made application to the Civil Aviation Branch at Vancouver for recertification of G-CADP, and the newly appointed District Inspector of B.C. and the Yukon, R. Carter Guest, dispatched a member of his department to assess the airworthiness of ADP. This was most likely F/L A.L. Johnson, an engineering officer.

Even over a decade after the conclusion of the First World War prejudices were still evident and, though unstated, this probability clouded the attitude of the attending inspector at Tabor Lake. After a survey of ADP the official took a screw driver and stabbed several holes in the Junkers' corrugated aluminium skin. This action enraged

Emil Kading works on Junkers G-CADP at Six Mile Lake, 1928. Attwood Collection

the owner's son Tom who, after a brief vocal outburst, landed a blow on the inspector's nose which sent him backwards into the lake. Needless to say the licence application was rejected on grounds of deterioration and age of the aircraft.

As soon as the inspector had left town, ADP left on a series of very serviceable flights at the needs of her owner's, flown by Bill Joerss who knew his trade well. The aircraft was frequently seen throughout northern B.C.

The Prince George Citizen edition of February 7, 1929, proclaimed the news that Western Canada Airways had asked City Council of business possibilities should the airline establish itself in the city. The Council's response must have been positive as WCA dispatched two float aircraft to the area. A Fokker Univeral was based at Six Mile (Tabor) Lake and a Junkers W-34 was based at Summit Lake, where an RCAF Fairchild 71 from Jericho Beach had set up a sub-base the previous year and continued in summer months

until October 1929. The Junkers operation worked in concert with the RCAF aerial photographic detachment under charter to the federal and provincial agencies responsible. When this work was completed Western Canada Airways withdrew both aircraft from Prince George for the winter.

WCA had located a base at Six Mile (Tabor) Lake and the company manager Leigh Brintnell took exception to ADPs clandestine operations. In June 1929, he wrote a letter of protest to the Controller of Civil Aviation:

"We are operating at the present time at Six Mile Lake, twelve miles from Prince George, and it is noted that the old Junkers F-13 which Imperial Oil used to have has been reconditioned and is now flying again. I do not wish to make this an official complaint but would like to submit these suggestions to you so that you can take care of them as you deem advisable. The machine has no official licence and I believe its licence was G-

CADP. The pilot flying it is an old time German war pilot and has no licence either. We have kept our engineers from examining this machine officially as we did not wish to be inflicted in any way in the event of a crash. Unofficially, we feel this machine is very unsafe to fly as half an aileron pulled away in the air the day before I arrived", signed Leigh Brintnell, Western Canada Airways, Prince George, BC.

Prince George Citizen ad, July 1930

and purchased two Junkers F-13 aircraft - one rebuilt, CF-AMX, and one new, CF-ALX. The company decided to base CF-ALX at Tabor Lake and hired Corless's former pilot, Wilhelm "Bill" A. Joerss, to fly it as he was well known in the central B.C. area. ALX arrived at Prince George early in May 1930, and in a ceremony at Tabor Lake in June was christened "City of Prince George" by Mayor Patterson's daughter Norine.

ADP continued the renegade operations until September 20, 1929, when the aircraft made a landing on Stuart Lake in heavy waves during a storm, resulting in damage to the floats and the breaking of engine mounts. While the Junkers sat on the shore of Stuart Lake it was badly vandalized and three days later was seized by the RCMP. The Junkers firm in Germany got wind of the plight of ADP and offered that if the aircraft was shipped back to Germany they would, without charge, rebuild and install a new engine and ship it back to North America. The owners reluctantly declined the offer and old "Vic" never flew again. But the aircraft had more than proven its worth to the prospecting and mine development interests of the Corless family.

The Air-Land Manufacturing Company was established at Vancouver November 29, 1929,

Joerss did well in Prince George that summer and, being an election year, the "City of Prince George" was chartered by both Liberal and Conservative candidates to conduct their campaign tours. The Air-Land Manufacturing Company would have competition this year, however, as Western Canada Airways again based a Fokker Universal flown by P.B. Calder at Six Mile (Tabor) Lake. Bill Joerss ended his season at

Air Land Manufacturing Co. Junkers F-13 CF-AMX and Western Canada Airways Fokker Super Universal G-CASQ at Summit Lake 1930. J. Cruikshank Collection

Prince George

159

Cessna AW NC-7107 lands at Prince George April 18, 1929, flown by Parker D. "Shorty" Cramer, who is enroute to Siberia. CW

Prince George on August 20, 1930, when he flew ALX to Vancouver and soon thereafter left for Atlin, B.C.

Parker D. "Shorty" Cramer landed a very mud covered new Cessna AW NC-7107 at Prince George at 10:45 a.m. on April 18, 1929. Cramer had left Edmonton on the afternoon of April 16 for Prince George, but was forced to land at Lucerne on Yellowhead Lake west of Jasper due to deteriorating weather. The following day NC-7107 was again forced down due to weather at McBride in a confining field that necessitated Cramer to off-load all of his equipment as well as his co-pilot Will Gamble.

The pair was outbound on an endurance flight from the Cessna Aircraft Factory in Wichita, Kansas via Chicago for Siberia and return. The Cessna returned through Prince George on Tuesday, April 30, 1929, departing the same day for Edmonton where they landed at 10:00 p.m.

Alaskan pilot Clayton Scott and his girlfriend Myrtle Smith arrived at Prince George on August 10, 1930, from Hazelton in Travel Air 6000B,

NC-377M. Scott was ferrying the aircraft from Whitehorse, Yukon, to Seattle, Washington. The aircraft had been seized at the Yukon city by Canadian Customs. Scott departed on August 11 for Vancouver B.C.

American aviator Frank G. Dorbandt and mechanic Lon Cope landed at Prince George on Tuesday, October 21, 1930, in Bellanca CH-300, NC-259M, on a flight from Seattle to Anchorage. Dorbandt telegraphed the office at Pacific International Airways at his destination advising that he had been commissioned by the Air-Land Manufacturing Company at Vancouver, B.C. to search for Junkers F-13, CF-AMX, lost in the Liard River area in the Yukon. NC-259M departed on October 22 for Hazelton and Atlin where it arrived on October 26, 1930.

On November 10, 1930 two more American aircraft of Pacific International Airways arrived in Prince George at 2:00 p.m. en route to Atlin, B.C. to relieve their pilot Frank G. Dorbandt in the search for Junkers F-13's pilot Paddy Burke missing since October 11, 1930.

One aircraft, a Consolidated Fleetster, NC-75OV, a model 17-2C, was flown by Joe Barrows with company president Edwin Ted Lowe, Junior also on board. The other machine, a Fairchild 71, was flown by Harry Blunt. Both aircraft left for Smithers on November 12.

On Friday, November 12, 1930, Alaskan pilots Noel and Sig Wien arrived at Prince George en route from Detroit, Michigan, to Nome, Alaska, in their new orange and black Stinson Junior SM-

Pacific International Airways Consolidated Fleetster NC-750V enroute to Alaska via Prince George October 10, 1930.
(Pictured at Lulu Island, Vancouver)

2AB, NC-490H. The pair later departed for Telegraph Creek.

Corless purchased a Stinson SM-8A Junior Detroiter, CF-ANE, in Vancouver from Commercial Airways on February 12, 1931, and son Tom S. Corless flew it home on March 9. Tom later experienced an engine failure on June 12 when landing twenty miles west of Takla Lake, and the Stinson Junior was damaged beyond repair.

Jimmy Mattern left New York City on June 3, 1933, in his Lockheed Vega sponsored by the Stanavo Oil Company. This was his second around-the-world record attempt. Mattern flew eastward across the Atlantic with landings at Norway and Moscow, and had planned to cross Siberia and land at Nome, Alaska. However, poor weather forced him to turn back from his Alaska landing and, after his engine's oil pressure began to fail, he made a forced landing on the tundra near Anadyr, Siberia, where he waited for two weeks before a group of Eskimos found him. Soviet aviator Sigismund Levanevsky then flew him to Nome. Meanwhile, a concerned group of supporters in New York organized a rescue mission which was sponsored by a New York brewery and in early June 1933 they set out for Alaska in a Bellanca CH-300 monoplane, NC-403E. They left Edmonton travelling via Jasper and landed at Prince George for fuel on June 5. The

Bellanca NC-403E at Carney Hill Airfield July 26, 1933. L. to R.: unknown, mechanic; Bill Alexander, pilot; Thomas Abbey, New York policeman and Kings Brewery representative; Jimmy Mattern; Fred Ferrerman, mechanic. via Frank Hewlett

group, consisting of pilot Will Alexander and three passengers, quickly left for Smithers and followed the Yukon telegraph line north of Hazelton. The Belenca ran into bad weather forcing them to turn around, eventually landing at Terrace.

Mattern was later picked up at Nome by a chartered Lockheed Vega from Juneau and the group assembled at Hazelton where they took off for Prince George on the late afternoon of July 26. Mattern was to receive a tumultuous welcome from the crowd that gathered at the new Municipal airfield at Carney Hill. The event received a prominent position on the front page of the Prince George Citizen on the same date.

American pioneer aviator Frank Dorbandt was chief pilot for Ptarmigan Airlines, a new airline that was planning to start scheduled service between Fairbanks and Anchorage, Alaska, using what would be that territory's first Ford Tri-Motor. On May 21, 1934, Dorbandt left Seattle's Boeing Field intending to make a nonstop flight to Prince George en route to Alaska. Dorbandt underestimated his fuel requirements and was forced to land near Nazco, where the pilot and eight passengers spent the night. The next morning, Dorbandt left the passengers in order to get out of the very confined field and flew to Quesnel for fuel. He then flew to Prince George, where he unloaded all of the freight and baggage before returning to a larger field at Nazco to pick up his passengers and return to Prince George. There the disheveled group spent a comfortable night before leaving for Hazelton on May 23.

Prince George Municipal Air Field was becoming well known and was fast becoming a preferred stopping point for fuel for wheel aircraft en route to Alaska. The Alaska Highway had yet to be built and the usual route continued from Prince George via Hazelton and the Yukon Telegraph line to Atlin and Whitehorse, Y.T.

1934 was an exciting year for the city's aeroplane buffs with the appearance of the huge Ford Tri-Motor in May and then, two months later on July 26, a flight of ten US Army Air Corps Marten B-10 Bombers, commanded by Lieutenant Colonel Henry "Hap" Arnold, which arrived on their way to Fairbanks, Anchorage, and Juneau. They had left Washington, DC, on July 19. The flight was intended to demonstrate the aerial might of the United States and its ability to defend Alaska against any potential enemy.

The US bombers arrived in three flights, followed by two Douglas biplanes that were accompanying the bombers to take aerial photographs

1948 air photo of Carney Hill Field. National Air Photo Library via Trelle Morrow

National Air Photo Library. via Trelle Morrow

ELEVATION - 1910'

POSITION (approx.)
LAT. 53°53'N. LONG. 122°46'W.
One mile S. of city centre, adjacent to Exhibition and Fair Grounds.

OPERATED BY
City of Prince George

REMARKS
Airfield on 165 acres of land
Airfield unlicenced until December 1, 1938

RUNWAYS
TURF & GRAVEL
15-33 3000' x 300'
18-36 2600' x 300'

OBSTRUCTIONS (ASL)

April 1932

Prince George

en route. The officers of the squadron were hosted to a luncheon by the Board of Trade at the Prince George Hotel, while the remainder of the aircraft crews were provided with a meal at the field after which they arranged for fueling and servicing of the aircraft. The ten bombers and their two camera planes departed later in the afternoon for Whitehorse cheered by hundreds of the area's citizens.

P.A.A. Consolidated Fleetster NC-750Y refuelling at Carney Hill Field, 1934.
Trelle Morrow

Another Pacific Alaska Airways aircraft arrived at Prince George during 1934 - a Consolidated Model 17-A Fleetster, NC-705Y. PAA purchased all three of the models built in 1933 and in turn sold two of them, NC-703Y and NC-704Y, to the Soviet Trading company Armtorg for use in the rescue of a stranded Russian aviation expedition.

On August 15, 1935, American long distance pilot Wiley Post and entertainer Will Rogers were killed in the crash of Post's float-equipped Lockheed Orion Explorer, NR-12283, near Point Barrow, Alaska. Pictures and movie film of the tragedy were rushed by air to Seattle by two rival news companies. The Associated Press (AP) film was flown by Alex Holden in a float aircraft via Juneau and down the inside passage by Pacific Alaska Airlines. The International News Service (INS) film was flown by Noel Wien and Victor Ross in Wien's Bellanca CH-300 "Pacemaker" on wheels, and carried INS newsman Alfred Loman.

The INS trio left Fairbanks at 2:30 p.m. August 17, landing at Whitehorse for fuel and a brief rest before making a night takeoff on the unlighted field with only the lights of the Pacific Alaska station manager's car at the far end of the runway to guide him.

Martin B-10 Bombers enroute to Alaska landed at Carney Hill Field July 26, 1934. USAF Archives

Wien's Bellanca seen here at Seattle August 18, 1935, after flight from Fairbanks via Prince George. Wien Collection

Noel Wien's biographer, Ira Harkley, wrote the following description of the flight:

"Wien disliked the night flying except with a full moon. But here he was flying in blackness over mountain country that matched any in the world for inhospitability to aircraft. He had let an insistent customer push him into a flight that all his knowledge told him should not be attempted. He regretted it.

The distance was 740 miles from Whitehorse to Prince George. He flew at eight thousand feet, holding about 100 degrees, trying to maintain a constant distance from the peaks of the Coast Mountains that were faint silhouettes in the dark sky. He could see nothing below. On regular order, Lomen dipped the hose into a can and Noel wobbled fuel into the plane's tanks.

Noel kept the Wasp turning at 1650, resisting the impulse to throttle to full power. He had fuel enough to fly all-out, but his long habit of babying his equipment could not be broken. At 1650 (R.P.M.) he would burn fourteen gallons an hour.

A surge of pleasure came with the recognition that his navigation, clairvoyant as it was, was on the nose: a little more than two hours out of Whitehorse he picked up in the starlight the faint outline of Edziza Peak in British Columbia. It was to his left, where it should be, its 9,100-foot thrust standing alone above a 5,000-foot plateau about twenty-five miles southeast of Telegraph Creek on the Stikine. He had flown 270 miles, and this was his first checkpoint. On the nose.

Edziza's snowfield shone dully in the feeble light.

Noel turned a few degrees left beyond Edziza. He would cross the Skeena a few miles beyond Edziza but he was not certain he could see it. The rough land below lay in darkness. He did not see the Skeena. A checkpoint he could not miss, though, was the group of thin lakes, much like Atlin, Teslin, and their companions. He should reach the first one, Takla, about 2:15 after passing Edziza. The others would be ahead and to the right, lying haphazard like strands of spaghetti thrown onto the ground. They should reflect the starlight, weak as it was.

He sighted them! Steel-colored slivers that told him he was still on course. Now he felt safe. A hundred or so miles east of the lakes was the broad valley cut by the Finlay and Parsnip rivers. He would turn left a little, pick up the valley, and fly south to Prince George. A yellow glow to the left told him dawn was coming. After a flight of 7 hours 15 minutes, he landed at Prince George at 6:00 A.M., fifteen and a half hours and 1,340 miles out of Fairbanks, and nearly forty-eight hours since he had slept.

There was no way of knowing, of course, but Alex Holden in the opposition PAA Fairchild was still about an hour and a half the other side of Juneau. Noel and the INS film were well ahead in the race, but the edge might not last. Holden landed at Juneau at 7:30 a.m. and his AP film was hastily handed to pilot Bob Ellis who took off immediately in the speedy Vega. Even on floats it cruised about five miles an hour faster than the Wien Bellanca on wheels. But Ellis had 900 miles to cover to reach Seattle. Even flat out, it would take him 6 hours 30 minutes, yet PAA swaggered with confidence. None of its people had reported sighting Wien at any station in Alaska. Obviously the cautious Wien had decided to wait even longer, wherever he had sat down, for the Chilkat weather to subside. His fuddy-duddy style of flying could cost him this time.

At that moment Wien had only half as far to go to reach Seattle as did his PAA opposition. But he had been at Prince George an hour and a half and now it looked as if he could be there much longer. He had spent a half hour poking about the airfield trying to find a customs officer. He would be checking out of Canada here. At seven he found someone who knew the name and home telephone number of the local customs official. Noel called. The official informed Wien that (1) he had regular hours; (2) the present time was not among them; (3) he would not consider arriving at the field before his appointed time; and (4) he did not at all appreciate being disturbed at home at that hour. At this news Al Lomen nearly dropped dead from acute outrage. Noel shrugged.

At 8:00 A.M. the customs man arrived at the airfield. When Noel told him what the aircraft was carrying, from where to where, the man said, "Why, my good fellow, you have no need for customs. There is nothing at all to clear with me." He seemed pleased to be delivering the tidings that the Bellanca and its film had lost two hours for nothing.

Tanks and cabin cans had been topped. Wien, Lomen, and Ross piled back into the airplane and Noel took off to follow the Fraser River south and then west to its mouth in the Strait of Georgia at Vancouver, ninety miles north of Seattle. None of the three men now had much confidence that they could win the race. Bad enough to lose out on flying strategy and ability; unbearable to lose by needlessly wasting time.

As they approached Williams Lake, Noel saw ahead a layer of clouds that appeared to be quite low. When he reached Williams Lake he found that the five-thousand to six-thousand-foot mountain tops bordering the river were in clouds. Worse, a thin layer seemed to be forming below. If that layer became solid, Noel thought, and the overhead one lowered, he could be forced to turn back. He would not fly through a socked-in canyon that twisted in its course. He wondered also about conditions at Seattle. Its notorious morning fog often lasted long enough to become afternoon fog. The layer below remained broken, and Noel caught occasional glimpses of the river below. The

overcast remained at a kindly altitude. They flew on, hoping and wobbling.

About three hours out of Prince George, Noel reached Hope and made the sharp right turn with the Fraser River. When they reached the flat land that stretches from east of Chilliwack to the great sound, Wien saw with a flood of relief that there was no coastal fog. He left the river, turned south over the flat land, skirting the Skagit Range and Mount Baker, past Abbotsford and into the United States over Bellingham and Everett, searching ahead for signs of Seattle fog.

There was no fog. Seattle sparkled in a noon sun.

Noel Wien landed the Bellanca at Boeing Field at 12:30 p.m. August 18, fourteen hours and ten minutes after departing Fairbanks, Alaska. The P.A.A. Lockheed Vega did not arrive with the Associated Press film until mid-afternoon. Noel Wien and the International News Service had won the race. "

On August 18, 1935, Pacific Alaska Airways Lockheed 10A Electra, NC-14259, flown by Joe Crosson, departed Fairbanks with the bodies of Post and Rogers. Crossen landed the Electra at the Prince George Carney Hill Field later in the day where a large crowd had gathered. Pioneer B.C. aviator Sheldon Luck was also at the airfield flying "Puss Moth", CF-AGW, and recalled talking with Crossen and his co-pilot before the Electra departed for Vancouver, B.C.

Sheldon Luck and his air engineer Ron Campbell had flown to Prince George from Calgary seeking work for the DH-80A "Puss Moth" on behalf of Advance Air Services, who had received encouragement from the Prince George Mayor after Canadian Airways had closed their base there.

R.F. Corless was back in the air at Prince George after April 23, 1936, on which date he had

Bellenca refuelling at Carney Hill Field, Prince George, likely flown by Noel Wien on his flight to Seattle, August 18, 1935.
Trelle Morrow Collection

Pacific Alaska Airways Lockheed 10A "Electra" NC-14259 at Prince George August 19, 1935, flown by Joe Crosson.

Canadian Airmen pose with P.A.A. Electra August 19, 1935. Left to right: Ron Campbell, SheldonLuck, Ian Hunter, Jack Hunter (D.O.T.)
Ron Campbell Collection

purchased CF-AUL, a 1933 Swallow four seat biplane manufactured in Wichita, Kansas and powered by a 90 hp Curtiss OX-5 engine.

AUL had crashed in the USA and the wreck imported and rebuilt at Vancouver in 1933 by J.R. Clancey. Tom Corless flew the aircraft for over two years and a natty logo "Corless Fort George" was emblazoned on one side of the float aircraft. The Swallow was damaged beyond repair in June 1936 at Seaton Lake near Lillooet when the air-

Y.S.A.T. Waco Custom, possibly CF-AZM, at McLean's Auto Court Landing, Fort George, with pilot Alex Dame, Summer 1938. Sheldon Luck

craft's float support structure collapsed on takeoff.

Jaun Trippe's Pan American Airways (PAN AM) subsidiary Pacific Alaska Airways (PAA)'s use of Prince George as a base for their itinerant fleet would increase dramatically during the next decade. Tabor Lake and Summit Lake continued to be used by float aircraft with business at Prince George as well as the occasional use of the Fraser River at Fort George for docking.

The city had been operating its Municipal Airport at Carney Hill since April 1932, but it did not receive a licence from the Department of Transport until December 1, 1938, when it was issued to the city. A year later in 1939 the city received a federal grant to upgrade the field as part of the air route to Alaska.

Grant McConachie had been operating sporadically in the central interior for years, starting with his Independent Airways operations with the Two Brothers Mine from Burns Lake. By 1937 he was operating United Air Transport. A post office contract was in the offing to fly mail from Vancouver to Fort St. John to hook up with the air mail route from that city to Whitehorse and Edmonton.

McConachie knew that he would be at a disadvantage should he apply because he was operating an Alberta based airline. He then approached Ginger Coote, who owned the Bridge River and Cariboo

Airways, and the pair made an application for the contract in Ginger Coote's name.

The application was successful and the first flight departed Ashcroft at 9:30 a.m. on Sunday, January 15, 1938, in a WACO Custom, CF-AZM, flown by Sheldon Luck. The first airmail flight made stops at Williams Lake and Quesnel and arrived at Prince George at 12:19pm - 31 minutes after leaving Quesnel.

Sheldon Luck flies inaugural airmail flight to Prince George January 16, 1938, with Cariboo dignitaries. L to R: Jack Wilson, Lawyer; G.B. Wilson., YSAT Business Manager, Prince George; Louis Le Bourdais, MLA Cariboo; Ginger Coote; W. Gray Turgeon, MP, Cariboo; Sheldon Luck. Sheldon Luck

Aboard the flight were local MP Mr. J.G.Turgeon and M.L.A. Louis LeBourdais who were greeted by a large crowd including Prince George Mayor A.M. Patterson and J.O. Wilson of the Board of Trade who took the group to lunch while the plane was being serviced. Shelden Luck resumed the inaugural flight at 2:00 p.m. for Fort St. John, returning to Prince George the following day, Monday, at noon.

Ginger Coote became manager of B.C. operations for United Air Transport. Initially the mail was picked up in Ashcroft from the overnight train from Vancouver, but within a few months the flight started from Vancouver.

The name United Air Transport was found to be in conflict with United Air Lines in the United States and McConachie soon changed the company's name to Yukon Southern Air Transport.

An interesting aircraft passed through the Carney Hill Municipal Field during the summer of 1939, flown by Alaskan pilot Joe Crossan. The Vultee VIA, NC-22077, had been purchased by Alaska Star Airlines on February 22, 1939, from Canadian Colonial Airlines and was previously registered CF-AWQ. United Air Transport pilot Sheldon Luck was at the field at the time of its landing. The Vultee was southbound to Seattle at the time.

In 1939 Pan American Airways needed to install a series of navigational aids and communications stations to support its flights from Seattle to Alaska transiting through the B.C. central interior. As federal regulations restricted the operation of radio stations to Canadian citizens, PanAm President, Jaun Trippe, contacted Grant McConachie with regards to possible cooperation between the two companies to allow Yukon Southern to apply for licences to operate the communications stations on PanAm's behalf. McConachie agreed and this deal was responsible for a large amount of sub-contract work eventually coming McConachie's way.

Sheldon Luck taxis to Prince George dock in Fleet 50 Freighter CF-BDX followed by Norseman CF-AZE on August 4, 1938. Sheldon Luck

Fairchild FC-2W G-CARM on Fraser River at Fort George, 1938.
Sheldon Luck

Y.S.A.T. Fokker Universal G-CAHJ at Fraser River dock. Sheldon Luck

Fairchild FC-2 G-CARM at front and Waco Custom CF-BDR at Y.S.A.T., Prince George dock. Sheldon Luck

Vultee V1-A at Prince George. Trelle Morrow Collection

Yet another flight of eight US Army Air Corps bombers touched down at Prince George as reported in the May 29, 1941, edition of the Prince George Citizen. Page one of the newspaper gave it a full review. The eight B-18 Douglas "Bolo's" were en route to Alaska almost six months before the Pearl Harbour attack.

With the attack on Pearl Harbour on December 7, 1941, and the invasion of the western Aleutian Islands by Japan on June 7, 1942, military aircraft in transit to Alaska increased dramatically. RCAF Station Prince George was operational in July 1942. The US Army Air Force constructed many buildings and stationed men and equipment on site. Besides the North West Stage Route from Edmonton to Fairbanks and the coastal route from Seattle to Anchorage, US authorities planned a third alternate Staging

Yukon Southern's B.C. interior route grew. Twin engine Barcley-Grows came into use followed by larger Lockheed aircraft, which were used on both regular passenger and mail flights. The Carney Hill Municipal Airport was fast becoming too confining for the larger aircraft using the facility. A new airport site consisting of 2,034 acres was located six and a half miles southeast of the city on high bench land above the Fraser River. A runway was completed in 1940 and the land purchased for the Department of National Defence. Construction commenced immediately and the main runway 14-32 was completed in 1941.

Starting in 1940, Pan American Airways was making frequent, often daily, flights through Prince George. They built a radio station and located administration staff on site to handle company traffic.

Yukon Southern Air Transport's Prince George staff, July 1940. L. to R: Alberta,
Vinson Office - Olive Vinson; Coglin Taxi Office - Alex Dame, Pilot; Mechanic;
Bert Coglin, owner of taxi company.   Sheldon Luck

Prince George

USAAC Douglas B-18 "Bolos" pass through Prince George (Carney Hill Field) enroute Alaska, May 1941. Trelle Morrow

Air photo of Prince George looking East, October 1, 1944. RCAF PB-9717

accompanied by WO2 E.B. Hackett, an RCAF photographer. The pair were on a photographic survey of airport facilities in B.C. and in that regard would operate from Fort George until October 6 photographing Vanderhoof, Fort St James, Prince George's new airport, as well as other Army installations and the Quesnel and Williams Lake airports.

On their arrival at Prince George the pair had found that there were no rooms available for rent due to wartime expansion. Williamson luckily ran into Russ Baker, the future president of PWA, who lent Williamson and Hackett his hotel room for a week. The rest of Williamson's crew, Al Campbell and Jim Millar, slept in a tent at Fort George near Norseman #2480.

The US Army Air Force established an Airways Communication System (AACS) Service Station here in 1943 to provide scheduling, weather, and radio service to their aircraft.

Route from Seattle to Prince George and on to Whitehorse. With the commencement of Lend Lease to Russia there were thousands of aircraft moving to Alaska.

An RCAF Norseman on floats, #2480, arrived at the seaplane dock at Fort George on September 29, 1942, flown by F/S George Williamson and

RCAF aircraft were frequent visitors - Hurricane and Kitty Hawk fighters, Bollingbroke, and later Hudson and Ventura bombers, as well as Anson, Beachcraft 18 Expeditors, and DC-3s (Dakotas) en route to coastal or inland destinations. Prince George was part of the Inland Staging Route conceived as a

RCAF Station Prince George looking Northwest, November 11, 1943. RCAF 51-1509

CPA Lockheed 18-56A CF-CPB loading mail at Prince George 1942. North Peace Museum Archives

Prince George

173

RCAF Tower and Administration buildings, March 1944.
USAAF

D.O.T. Radio Range Transmitter site at Prince George,
March 1944. P.A.C.

second line of attack in the event the Japanese established a foothold at the RCAF flying boat stations on the coast. Fighters could quickly relocate and operate against an enemy from any one, or all, of the RCAF stations at Williams Lake, Dog Creek, Quesnel, Prince George, Vanderhoof, Smithers, or Woodcock.

On March 31, 1944, the old city airport at Carney Hill was closed and all traffic began to use the new facility, where construction was completed on August 9, 1945. With the war over, control of RCAF Station Prince George was passed by the Department of National Defence to the Department of Transport on August 1, 1946, and an airport licence issued.

On May 2, 1951, Central B.C. Airways commenced a regular scheduled service from Prince George to Terrace using an Avro Anson MKV, CF-GDW, flown by Harry Taylor. On the inaugural flight, company president Russ Baker and his wife Madge went along to greet civic officials en route.

Prince George airport runways had not been constructed with longevity in mind, and during 1951 Canadian Pacific Airways, who had absorbed YSAT earlier, had to take their

Central BC Airways Junkers W-34 CF-ASN crashed at Summit Lake, March 1948.
PAC PA-102416

DC-4 aircraft out of use and replace them with DC-3s as the former were sinking into the asphalt. This was further emphasized on November 23, 1953, when a USAF B-29 made an emergency landing on runway 19-01 and its main wheels sank several inches into the runway. The runway was not rebuilt until 1959.

On November 8, 1954, an Aeronca 7AC, CF-HSR, landed at Prince George on a delivery flight from Vancouver to Prince Rupert for Pacific Wings. This was the first landing made by the author at Prince George. My second landing was much more memorable and occurred March 30, 1956. By this time I was employed by Russ Baker's Pacific Western Airlines.

Prince George Terminal 1951. CW

CF-BVK was a Fairchild 71C originally built in the USA in 1929 as a model FC-2. It was sold to the RCAF as G-CYXB, who operated it until 1942 when it was sold to a commercial operation who installed a Pratt and Whitney R-985 engine in 1946. By October 1949 BVK belonged to Russ Baker's Central B.C. Airways, who later changed their name to Pacific Western Airlines.

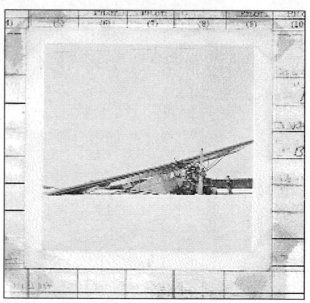

Pacific Western Airlines 1929 Fairchild 71 CF-BVK's dramatic arrival on March 30, 1956, flown by Jimmy Dunbar with the author. CW

BVK was reportedly wrecked October 11, 1955, when it hit a log on takeoff at Ocean Falls and overturned while the wreckage was under tow. The Canadian Civil Aircraft Register showed it as damaged beyond repair. However BVK was hauled to PWA's Sea Island hangar in Vancouver and repaired. PWA had acquired a contract on the western sector of the DEW line construction and in February 1956 BVK was prepared to be dispatched to Hay River, North West Territories and points due north.

Chief engineer Ted Dobbin and Superintendent of Maintenance Frank Coulter had been unable to find a tail wheel. BVK had been originally equipped with a tail skid but had spent almost its entire life on floats. So BVK was mounted on two main wheels, and a tail ski was fixed under the tail. The author was also being transported to Hay River and in company with pilot Jimmy

Prince George

C.P.A. Bristol Britannia 314 at Prince George's third airfield in early 1960"s.
Trelle Morrow

Dunbar and a cabinload of supplies and barrels of oil set off at first light from the grass area parallel to Vancouver's runway 08. We turned up Howe Sound past Squamish to Lilloet and then followed the Fraser River to Prince George and landed on runway 23, which was covered with snow but had been compacted to provide a firm landing surface.

Unknown to Dunbar and myself, the bungees, which controlled the for and aft position of the tail ski, had let go allowing it to turn off center and when the tail ski touched the surface it immediately sent BVK into a wild ground loop tearing off the right main wheel and damaging the right wing and horizontal stabilizer. I would be here for a week before the company dispatched another machine in which I left the city on April 5, 1956, via Monkman Pass for Fort St John, Grimshaw, and Hay River. This aeroplane was Junkers W-34, CF-ATF, which was the last surviving W-34 in the world.

The Prince George Flying Club was established in 1959 and put on its first air show on May 17.

Canadian Pacific Air Lines had been operating Douglas DC-6B aircraft on the Vancouver/Prince George scheduled service since 1957, and briefly in the early 1960s they operated Bristol Britannias. By 1961 traffic had increased requiring the reactivation of the World War II control tower. By 1968 CPA was using Boeing 737s to service the community's needs.

The author again flew at Prince George during the summer of 1975 as a relief pilot for Northwood Mills flying their bright orange Mitsubishi MU-2 registration CF-CEL.

Northwood Mills Mitsubishi MU-2DP CF-CEL flown by author at Prince George 1975. CW

Prince George

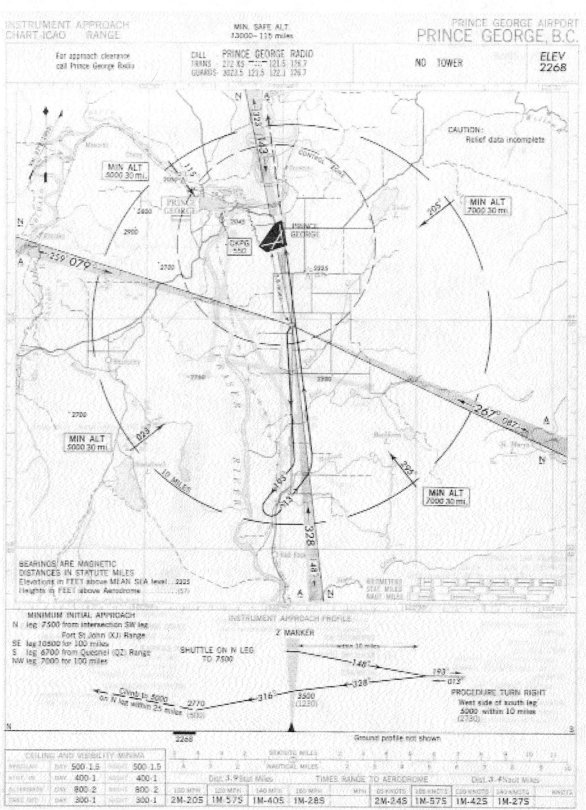

January 10, 1956

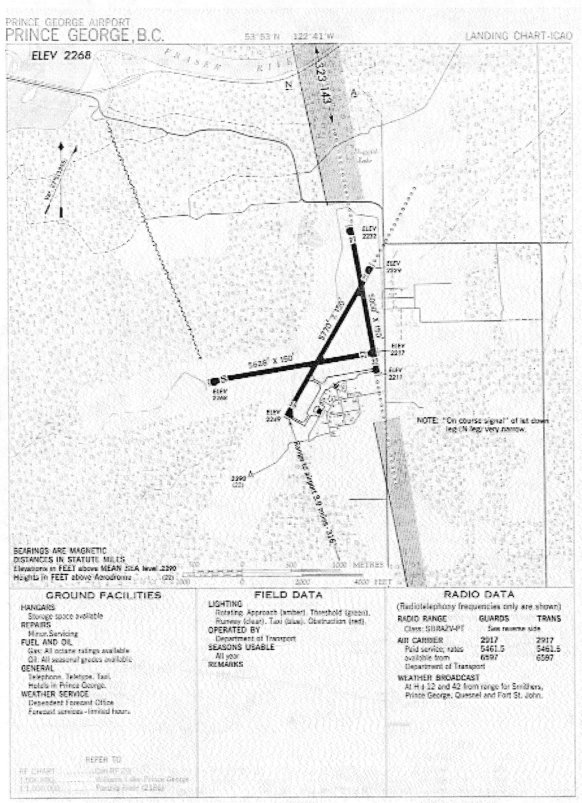

January 10, 1956

Prince George

178

Prince George

179

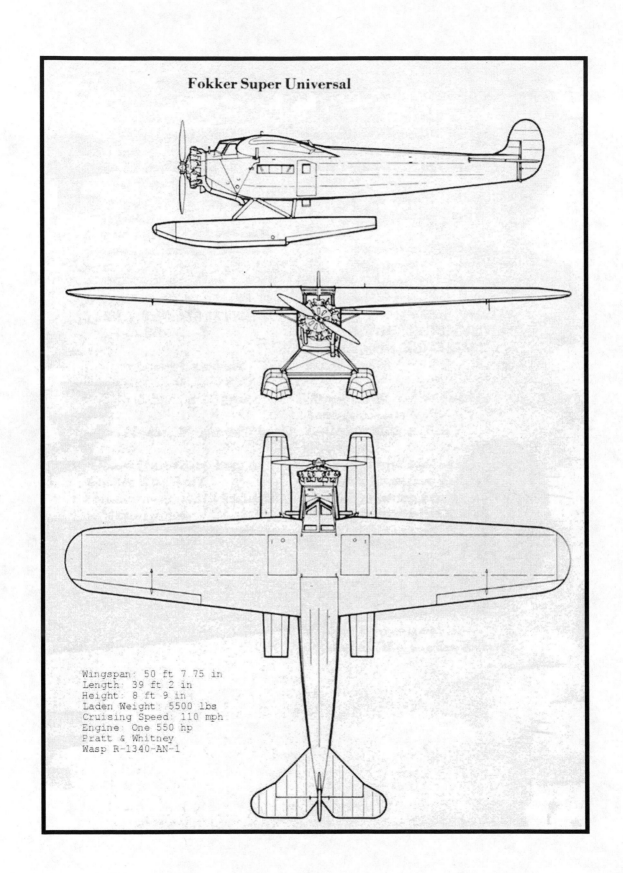

Fokker Super Universal

Wingspan: 50 ft 7.75 in
Length: 39 ft 2 in
Height: 8 ft 9 in
Laden Weight: 5500 lbs
Cruising Speed: 110 mph
Engine: One 550 hp
Pratt & Whitney
Wasp R-1340-AN-1

Prince George

Vanderhoof

On November 1, 1928, an aircraft landed in Mr. Snell's sheep pasture near the village of Vanderhoof. The new Alexander Eaglerock A-2, G-CAUZ, was on a delivery flight to Whitehorse, Yukon, for Yukon Airways and Exploration Company. The two men on board were Clyde Wann, the ramrod of the company's operations, and John M. Patterson his pilot. They had left Colorado Springs on September 7, 1928, and had stopped at every town along the way giving exhibitions and rides to earn travel expenses.

The citizens of Vanderhoof had witnessed other airplanes flying overhead for several years. The four American Army de Havilland DH-4Bs of the 1920 Alaska Flying Expedition flew overhead shortly after 10:00 a.m. on Friday, August 13. Their pilots had taken off from Prince George and were heading to Hazelton. The flight had originally left New York and was en route to Nome, Alaska, which they later reached on October 4, 1920.

The following year on August 26, 1921, another American pilot flew overhead in his Curtiss JN-4 Jenny which he had named "Polar Bear".

Yukon Airways Eaglerock G-CAUZ landed at Vanderhoof November 1, 1928; Pilot John Patterson at centre.
Vanderhoof Archives

Vanderhoof Airfield looking South, October 1, 1943. RCAF PB-8720

RCAF Fairchild FC-2W's G-CYXQ left, and 'XN" right, on photographic duty, 1929. Attwood Collection

U.S. Army Air Corps. Pilot Captain Ross Hoyt landed this Curtiss XP-6B Hawk at Vanderhoof July 19, 1929. USAF #1789 AC

On July 14, 1922, the German Junkers JL-6, G-CADP, passed overhead on its way from Edmonton to Hazelton flown by a former RFC pilot, Major George "Tommy" Thompson, who had been the second pilot to cross the Rocky Mountains in 1920. Thompson was delivering the aircraft to an investment and prospecting syndicate in Hazelton.

On September 22, 1928, the Nechako Chronicle reported that aerial maps were being made of the area. In fact the RCAF were producing a photographic mosaic of the entire area for use by map makers.

The following year the RCAF were back again on June 9, 1929, in a Fairchild 71 seaplane, G-CYXQ, which was based at Summit Lake north of Prince George and flown by F/O Windsor with photographer William Cecil Attwood. The pair remained in the area until October 17, when they flew back to the Jericho Beach Air Station at Vancouver.

The Jenny's owner and pilot was Clarence "Ollie" Prest who was attempting to go one better than the US Army Air Service flight of the previous year. Prest declared that he was flying from Mexico to Siberia.

It is highly likely that XQ landed on the Nechako while on their photo flights of the area as it had landed at many other communities when photographing them.

1929 would be a bumper year for aviation enthusiasts at Vanderhoof with the arrival of two aircraft on wheels. Around noon on Friday, July 19, 1929, an American military aircraft on a long distance flight from New York to Nome, Alaska passed overhead for Whitehorse. US Army Air Corps Captain Russ G. Hoyt had departed Edmonton in his Curiss Hawk XP-6B pursuit ship at 5:30 a.m. on a 1,090 mile leg to Whitehorse, but when overhead Hazelton at 10:30 a.m. he realized that he was bucking very strong winds that would prevent his reaching Whitehorse without refueling. Captain Hoyt reversed his course and landed at Vanderhoof at 2:00 p.m. He refueled and waited overnight for better weather, departing the following morning, Saturday, July 19 at 4:00 a.m. Hoyt flew on to Whitehorse where he landed after a five and one half hour flight.

Junkers F-13 CF-AMX landed at a farm field at Vanderhoof in late June 1931. CMFT Collection

In late June 1931, a salvage crew had towed Junkers F-13, CF-AMX, by water to Fort St. James, where the aircraft was put on wheels and flown from a tennis court on the lakeshore. Its pilot, Bill McClusky, had stripped the aircraft of all but bare essentials, with only enough fuel to allow a flight to a farm field at Vanderhoof (possibly belonging to pioneer farmer Fred Borhaven), where he landed a short time later.

After the arrival of his engineer Ted Cressy and helper Len Fraser, by truck the party reloaded and refueled AMX and the aircraft and truck departed for Vancouver.

In July 1934, a seaplane operating on behalf of the Two Brothers Mining Company landed at nearby Nulki Lake while on a flight to Edmonton from Stuart Lake. This was likely one of two Fokker Universal aircraft operated under the name of Independent Airways by Grant McConachie, but actually registered in the name of B. Phillips of Edmonton. The two aircraft were G-CAHE and G-CAHJ. A third Fokker Universal, G-CAFU, was also used in mining operations in the area and all three of these machines were registered to McConachie's United Air Transport the following year, 1935. In October 1934, the

Grant McConachie operated Fokker Universal's G-CAHJ as well as "AHE" and "AFU" into Nulki Lake at Vanderhoof in July 1934. Sheldon Luck

Vanderhoof

Air photo of Vanderhoof looking North, December 15, 1943. RCAF TE-7

WWII buildings at Vanderhoof, August 2000. CW

Nechako Chronicle reported yet another seaplane landing on the Nechako River east of town.

The Cocker and Emslie farm (formerly the Borhaven farm) was the site of construction of

the first airfield in October 1937. Intended as an emergency field, it was officially opened in March 1938. It received little use. However, in November 1941 a Pan American Airways Lockheed en route from Seattle to Alaska landed for an unknown reason.

The attack by Japan against Pearl Harbour brought a flurry of military activity on Canada's West Coast and Vanderhoof was chosen as the site of an intermediate airfield on the route between Prince George and Smithers, which would later be referred to as the Inland Staging Route.

Early in 1942 a half section of land, including the Cocker and Emslie farm, was expropriated. The Department of National Defence then carried out an airport survey and let a contract to Bennett and White Construction Company for the clearing and preparation of three gravel runways.

Vanderhoof was one of a series of airfields that were constructed or upgraded to handle military aircraft. These airfields were constructed as a second line of defence in the case of the Japanese gaining a foothold on the coastal airports and flying boat stations. In this event, fighter squadrons would have moved inland for the defence of these areas. In the meantime each station was manned and equipped to provide services to military and airline traffic as needed.

Between October 1 and October 6, 1942, RCAF Norseman #2480, a float aircraft operating from the Fraser River at Fort George, flew daily photographic surveys of Vanderhoof and Prince George. The aircraft was flown by F/Sgt George Williamson with photographer W02 E.B. Hackett.

Western Air Command of the RCAF ordered the construction of RCAF Vanderhoof barracks, mess hall, and other buildings built to house a radio range station to allow aircraft to carry out an instrument approach to the airfield, as well as being a navigational aid to overflying aircraft. On May 20, 1943, Western Air Command issued Secret Organization Order Number 126 stating that henceforth RCAF Vanderhoof would become part of the Interior Staging Route and designating it as Number 14 Staging Unit.

On August 26, 1943, RCAF Bollingbroke #9066 arrived on a photographic mission at Vanderhoof. This aircraft was flown by George Williamson who was now commissioned as a Flying Officer.

After Japan capitulated, the Department of National Defence turned over the Vanderhoof air-

Vanderhoof Flying Club occupies WWII RCAF Operations Building at Vanderhoof, August 2000. CW

WWII D.O.T. and RCAF married quarters at Vanderhoof Airfield, August 2000. CW

field to the Department of Transport. In 1946, RCAF airfield custodian Scotty Almond turned over operations to the D.O.T., who maintained the field until April 1959 when control was passed to the Village.

During 1946 a group of local men, Mr. Johnson and the two Lee brothers, purchased three surplus aircraft from the War Assets Disposal Corporation with the intent of starting a flying school and charter service. However, tragically the two Lee brothers were killed on a flight to Calgary to pick up one of the aircraft and the project was soon abandoned.

A public wharf and dock was established by the Village on the Nechako River for use by local and transient float planes. In 1949 Russ Baker founded Central Airways at nearby Fort St. James and on May 5, 1951, the airline started a scheduled service from Prince George to Terrace via Smithers and with a flag stop at Vanderhoof. The first flight was in Avro Anson Mk-V, CF-GDW, flown by Harry Taylor, with Russ and Madge Baker along to take care of the dignitaries at each stop. Central B.C. Airways soon became Pacific Western Airlines, which hired the author during the winter of 1955.

At noon on November 9, 1954, an Aeronca 7AC Champion, CF-HSR, stopped at Vanderhoof on the way from Prince George to Smithers, having barely enough fuel and being wary of the inclement weather. HSR's 18 year old pilot was taking no chances and stopped to top up the "Aerknocker's" single tank. No other aircraft was in sight and after the fuel attendant came from town the author pressed on toward Smithers, a destination that was not to be reached on this wintery November day.

In February 1953, Vanderhoof pilot Gerald Johnson purchased an Aeronca 7AC Champion.

In 1959, R.R. Devauld purchased CF-LRB, a Champion 7GC.

In 1960 Clifford Andros purchased CF-MHH, a Champion 7GC.

In 1961 McDougall Excavating Limited purchased CF-NSH, a Piper PA-18 Super Cub.

In 1965 Darrel F. Cursons purchased CF-SPH, a Champion 7ECA.

In September of 1964, local enthusiasts organized the Vanderhoof Flying Club and started a series of successful air shows at the airport. This tradition was further enhanced by another club, the Blue Mountain Flyers.

Gerry Haldemen's Harrison Airways of Vancouver commenced a tri-weekly scheduled service to Vanderhoof and Burns Lake commencing on November 2, 1972 using DC-3 aircraft. The service lasted for less than three years, when Harrison sold its A and B licences to Fred May's Tradewinds Aviation, and its C and D licences to Mark Brady's Futura Aviation, both of Vancouver. The latter organization employed the author from September 1975 until 1978.

Mitsubishi MU-2 CF-AMP and pilot Chris Weicht. CW

On July 23, 1988, Mitsubishi C-FAMP, on charter to the Canadian Government, departed Prince George on a short flight to Vanderhoof. The author was the Captain with First Officer son Andrew Weicht. The purpose of this flight was to take the Secretary of State for Transport, Gerry St. Germain, a former RCAF pilot, to officially open the Vanderhoof Air Show. After landing we taxied to the VIP parking area passing row upon row of visiting aircraft, many with pup-tents parked under their wings. Startled occupants quickly emerged, hands cupped over their ears to help reduce the deafening scream of the MU-2's Garrett TPE-331 jet prop engines.

We parked next to a group of aircraft on static display and my eyes were drawn to an immaculate Messerschmitt BF-108, "Taifun", resplendent with black crosses and in the camouflage in use by the Luftwaffe during World War II. I knew an old friend was also present at Vanderhoof that day - Franz Stigler former Hauptman in Jagdverband 44 in the European theater of World War II.

VANDERHOOF B.C.

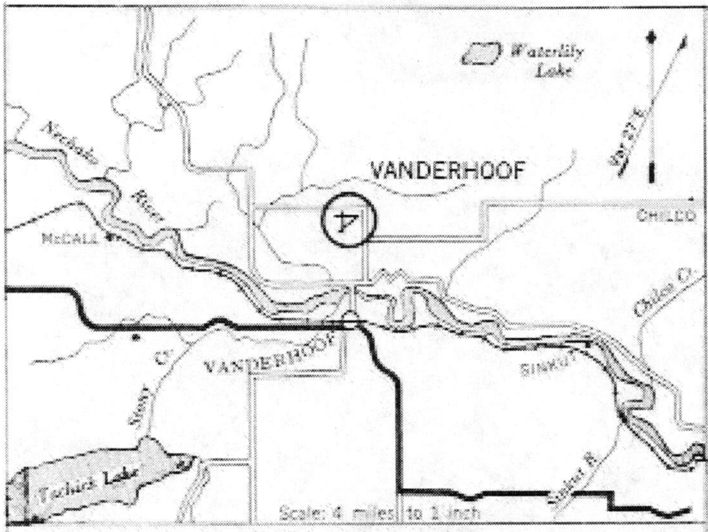

ELEVATION 2225'

VARIATION 27°E. (1955)

POSITION
LAT. 54°03'N. LONG. 124°00'W.
2.5 miles N. of Vanderhoof.

AERONAUTICAL CHARTS
1:506,880 SMITHERS-FORT ST JAMES
1:1,000,000 PARSNIP RIVER (2186)

OPERATED BY
DOT

SEASONS USABLE
All year

RADIO DATA
GUARDS TRANS
Nil

REMARKS
To be used in daylight only.
Runways are unserviceable in wet
weather

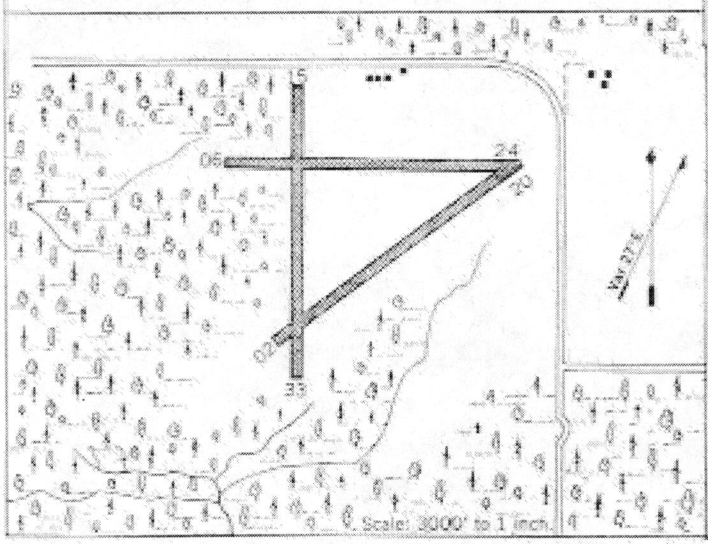

RUNWAYS
Gravel
02 - 20   5600' x 200'
06 - 24   5600' x 200'
15 - 33   5400' x 200'

LIGHTING
Nil

OBSTRUCTIONS (ASL)
N. Ridge (2800') 3 miles

GROUND FACILITIES

HANGARS
Nil

COMMUNICATIONS
Telephone, Telegraph.

REPAIRS
Servicing only

TRANSPORTATION
Bus.

FUEL AND OIL
Gas: 80/87 & 91/98 octane.
Oil: 80 and 100

ACCOMMODATIONS
Hotel in town

WEATHER

WEATHER BROADCAST
Nil

WEATHER SERVICE
Nil

August 10, 1955

RESTRICTED

VANDERHOOF
B.C.

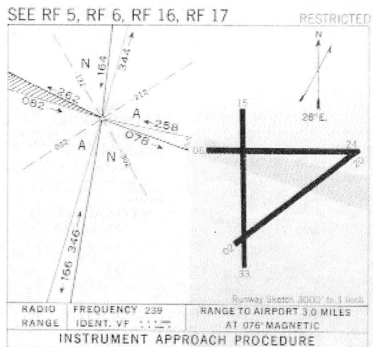

RADIO	FREQUENCY 239	RANGE TO AIRPORT 3.0 MILES
RANGE	IDENT. VF ...	AT 076° MAGNETIC

INSTRUMENT APPROACH PROCEDURE

("Z" Marker)

1. Twenty minutes before E.T.A. at range station call range requesting altimeter setting.

2. Initial approach E. leg 6000' a.s.l.   (N. leg 10,000')
   (W. leg 9000')   (S. leg 10,000')

3. Shuttle— If necessary use E. leg down to 6000' a.s.l. making procedure turn left, to north of E. leg.

4. Upon arrival at cone proceed out W. leg (final approach leg) for 3 minutes (6 miles) descending to 4500' a.s.l.

5. Make procedure turn left (to south of W. leg) for return to station (final approach). Altitude over range station 3200' a.s.l.

6. Passing cone, change heading 6° left to 076° Mag. and let down to minimum 2730' a.s.l. following E. leg.

7. Ground contact not made at authorized minimum (see below) seconds after passing cone. Pull Up, full power to 6000' a.s.l. straight ahead.

MINIMUM SAFE ALTITUDES
For 1000 feet clearance

Orientation within 25 miles 6500' a.s.l.
Orientation LOST (within 100 miles) 10,000' a.s.l.

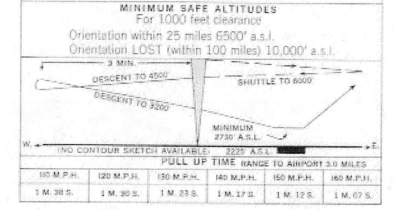

(NO CONTOUR SKETCH AVAILABLE)   2225' A.S.L.

PULL UP TIME RANGE TO AIRPORT 3.0 MILES

110 M.P.H.	120 M.P.H.	130 M.P.H.	140 M.P.H.	150 M.P.H.	160 M.P.H.
1 M. 38 S.	1 M. 30 S.	1 M. 23 S.	1 M. 17 S.	1 M. 12 S.	1 M. 07 S.

POSITION

Air Navigation Chart:
SMITHERS - FORT ST. JAMES
54°03'N. 124°00'W.
2.5 miles N. of Vanderhoof.

ALTITUDE 2225'
VARIATION 28°E.

LANDING THRU OVERCAST			
DAY		NIGHT	
CEILING	VIS	CEILING	VIS
500'	1	500'	2

TAKE OFF THRU OVERCAST			
DAY		NIGHT	
CEILING	VIS	CEILING	VIS
300'	1	300'	1

RUNWAYS
Gravel
06 - 24 5600' x 200'
15 - 33 5600' x 200'
02 - 20 5600' x 200'

LIGHTING
Portable electric flare path on request on runway 06 - 24 only.

OBSTRUCTIONS (A.S.L.)

N. Ridge (2800') 3 miles

RADIO DATA

	RECS	TRANS
RADIO RANGE:	3017.5	239
CLASS: BRAZVP - DT	3105	
(Call "VFF" W/T)	3117.5	
	4495	
	6210	

CONTROL TOWER:

(No frequencies guarded)

RUNWAY ELEVATIONS
06 - 2224'   24 - 2225'
15 - 2224'   33 - 2218'
02 - 2223'   20 - 2225'

October 5, 1945

Vanderhoof

189

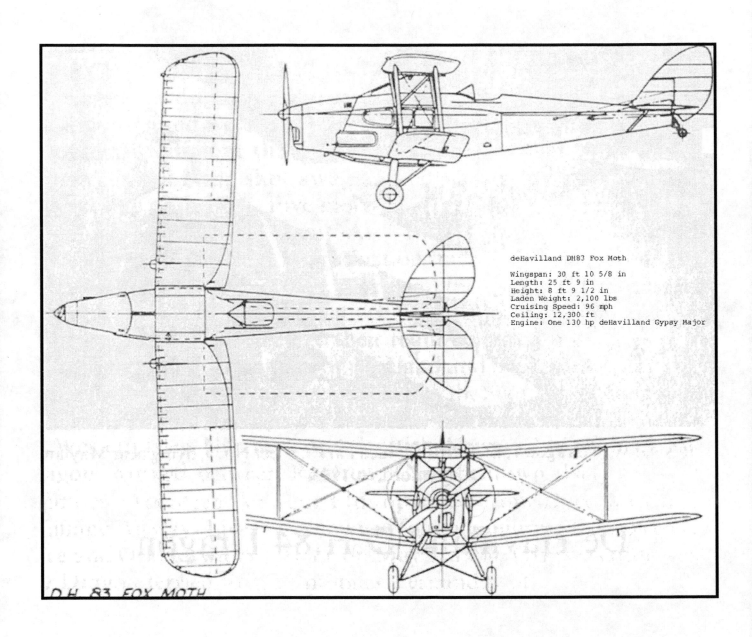

deHavilland DH83 Fox Moth

Wingspan: 30 ft 10 5/8 in
Length: 25 ft 9 in
Height: 8 ft 9 1/2 in
Laden Weight: 2,100 lbs
Cruising Speed: 96 mph
Ceiling: 12,300 ft
Engine: One 130 hp deHavilland Gypsy Major

D.H. 83 FOX MOTH

Fort St. James

The first European presence at Fort St. James occurred during 1806 when Simon Fraser established a fur trading post here for the Northwest Company.

The town site is located at the south east end of fifty nine mile long Stuart Lake, in the Omineca District. This lake and a chain of others provide a ready access to a huge area of natural resources not easily accessible except by these water routes or by air.

The first use of an aircraft for prospecting the vast Omineca came from the Railway Employees Investment and Industrial Association of Hazelton, B.C., who in the summer of 1922 purchased a Junkers JL-6, G-CADP, from Imperial Oil at Edmonton, Alberta. This low wing monoplane had previously been christened the "Vic" and had been used the previous year by I.O.L.'s pioneering flight to Norman Wells, NWT.

"ADP" was flown to Hazelton, and then throughout the area, by Major G.A. "Tommy" Thompson, until the summer of 1923 when an airworthiness inspection by Earl McLeod of the Jericho Beach Air Station rendered it unser-viceable. The Junkers sat idle until 1929, when it was purchased by interests in Prince George who made repairs; again it was inspected and found unservicable by Jericho Beach personnel. A confrontation resulted in Junkers ADP being flown away unlicenced in the summer of 1929, and again flown throughout the Omineca on prospecting forays by former German Air Service pilot Wilhelm A. "Bill" Joerss.

On September 20, 1929, Junkers ADP was landing on Stuart Lake at Fort St. James when the heavy waves caused by a storm severely damaged her floats and broke the wooden engine mounts. The Junkers was pulled up onto the beach and left for the winter. Unfortunately, when her owners returned the following spring, they found the air-

The last flight of Junkers JL-6 G-CADP occurred in a storm on Stewart Lake September 20, 1929. It is pictured here with sister ship G-CADQ in 1921.
via F. Ellis

Fort St. James

craft severely vandalized and the aircraft was abandoned and never flew again.

The Air Land Manufacturing Company at Vancouver acquired two Junkers F-13's at the end of May 1930, CF-ALX and CF-AMX. "ALX" was based at Prince George's Six Mile (Tabor) Lake and flown by Bill Joerss, who flew the Junkers on several occasions to Fort St. James. The second Junkers, CF-AMX, was sent to Atlin with pilot Paddy Burke, who in October became the subject of a lengthy search after his aircraft went missing in the upper reaches of the Liard River in the Yukon.

The Air Land Manufacturing sent its other Junkers, CF-ALX, that was in Vancouver, to join the search for Paddy Burke and "AMX", departing Vancouver on floats on November 11, 1930, flown by pilot Bill Joerss and Robert I. Van der Byle, with engineer Ted Cressy.

"ALX" was flown up the Fraser River to Prince George, then on November 13 via Fort St. James to Takla Landing, where they refueled and took off for Dease Lake. An hour into the flight they ran into a heavy snowstorm, forcing Joerss to deviate north east of their route and land at Thutade Lake, where they stayed at a cabin until the weather improved.

Junkers F-13 CF-AMX arrived at Fort St. James June 8, 1931. National Museum Science Tech. #5037

Fort St. James

The following morning they found that freeze-up had begun in earnest and an inch of ice covered the lake. Attempts to break the ice to allow a take off failed. Joerss eventually decided to strip the aircraft of all but bare essentials and fly out by himself by taking off the float plane on top of the ice. His plan worked and he took off for Takla Landing where he arranged for two Indians to mush to Thutade Lake and bring Van der Byl and Cressy out. Joerss then flew to Burns Lake and Vancouver, as the Junkers was useless without skis at that time of the year.

The rescue party missed the stranded pair who had secured other guides and hiked to Takla Lake. They were able to obtain a canoe there and they made their way to Fort St. James, where they arrived December 19, 1930.

"AMX" and its passengers were eventually found, but pilot Burke had died. The owners of the Junkers salvaged the aircraft, which was undamaged. It was flown south with pilots Joerss, Van der Byl, and engineer Kading, leaving Atlin on February 23, 1931, later landing at Dease Lake and Telegraph Creek, remaining there until February 28 when they departed for Fort St. James, but did not arrive.

Two and a half hours after take off, "AMX"s engine swallowed a valve and they were forced down on the Driftwood River just north of Bulkley House (north west end of Takla Lake). The aircraft was undamaged and was pulled up high on the river bank until repairs could be made.

The March 12, 1931, issue of the Prince George Citizen reported to its readers that they had "arrived at Fort St. James at noon March 6, having mushed out from Bulkley House". Apparently Indians at Trembleur Lake had sup-

plied them with horses to enable them to complete their journey.

On June 5, 1931, the Air Land Manufacturing Company again despatched a salvage crew, this time comprising of pilot Bill McClusky, engineer Ted Cressy, and helper Len Fraser. The trio drove from Vancouver to Fort St. James with a set of floats and the engine repair parts needed for "AMX", arriving at Fort St. James on June 8.

The crew built a raft using "AMX"s floats and hired a small boat to tow it to the beached Junkers, which they reached four days later. To their chagrin, the float fittings were not compatible and a decision was made to raft "AMX" back to Fort St. James, which they reached several days later.

McClusky, Cressy and Fraser decided that they would install wheels on the Junkers and, after a search for a suitable take off area at Fort St. James, decided to use two tennis courts near the Hudson's Bay store, which would allow a departure out over Stuart Lake.

With an extremely short runway, McClusky decided he would strip the aircraft to bare essentials and would fly it to Vanderhoof, where the others could join him on his flight back to Vancouver. His take off was uneventful and half an hour later he phoned from Vanderhoof for the others to join him with their truck.

G.W. "Grant" McConachie's Independent Airways at Edmonton was on the verge of bankruptcy, but a chance meeting with mining promoter Barney Phillips in 1932 was to change this. Phillips had come into possession of a map indicating a lost gold mine near Two Brothers Lake (later known as Toodoggone Lake). Phillips hired McConachie to fly his last airplane, a de

Grant McConachie's Fokker Universales G-CAHE, AHJ and AFU, at Takla Lake.
CAI Archives

Junkers "ABK" switching floats for skis at Fort St. James. Sheldon Luck

Havilland DH-80A "Puss Moth", CF-APE, with Phillips and three prospectors, into the lake in the spring of 1933.

The arrangement between Phillips and McConachie proved successful and a new company, United Air Transport, was formed to provide transportation to the mine. Two Fokker Universals, G-CAHE and G-CAHJ, operated out of a forward base at Takla Landing. Supplies were brought by barge to Takla Landing during ice-free months from Fort St. James.

In 1936, United Air Transport began flying the mail from Prince George to Fort St. James and on to Takla Landing, which was flown by McConachie, Sheldon Luck and Ginger Coote, whose airline (Ginger Coote Airways) was in the process of amalgamating with U.A.T. Pilot Russ Baker, an employee of Ginger Coote, soon arrived in a de Havilland DH-83 "Fox Moth", CF-APL. However Baker left the company, accepting an offer from Canadian Airways to operate a base for that company at Fort St. James, at first with Fairchild FC-2W2 CF-AUT, and later with Junkers W-34 CF-ABK.

Competition between airlines for business became fierce with much rate cutting and the inevitable overloading to satisfy the customers. On May 23, 1937, CF-BDT, a Waco ZQC-6 operated by Pacific Airways of Vancouver, crashed at Tchentlo Lake seven miles north west of Fort St. James, while attempting to land in severe turbulence. One passenger died, another was severely injured, as was the pilot Charlie Elliott. The engineer, Bill Martin, was able to get help and Russ Baker flew in and picked up the survivors, but Elliott died seven days later in hospital at Prince George.

Soon after World War II, Russ Baker formed Central B.C. Air Services at Fort St. James, and was able to secure a B.C. Government Forest Service Contract. In May 1951, CBCA started a

Canadian Airways Junkers W-34 CF-ABK in flight North of Fort St. James at Nation Lakes. PAC PA-88951

scheduled service from Prince George to Terrace using an Avro Anson. Still later in 1955, the airline became Pacific Western Airlines, initially based at Vancouver.

The seaplane base at Fort St. James remained active over the years with service provided by a number of local air services. Still later, the Village of Fort St. James began the operation of a 2,800 foot long airfield 2.4 miles south of the settlement.

On July 12, 1991, the village of Fort St. James unveiled a one third scale Junkers W-34 mounted on a pedestal at the waterfront and declared that henceforth July 12 would be known as "Junkers Day".

The author visited the site in August 2001 to reflect on the community's association with bush flying.

Fort St. James

195

Canadian Airways base at Fort St. James, Winter of 1939. Junkers W-34 CF-ABK, Bellanca CH-300 "Pacemaker" CF-BFB, and Fairchild 71 CF-AQP. Sheldon Luck

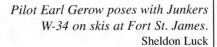

Pilot Earl Gerow poses with Junkers W-34 on skis at Fort St. James. Sheldon Luck

Central B.C. Airways President Russ Baker with Junkers W34 at Fort St. James, 1947. PAC PA-102385

Fort St. James

We DON'T WANT TO FLY TO China!

—We DON'T have ambitions to operate a "Trans World" airline.

—We DON'T have Stewardesses.

—We DON'T even believe uniforms trimmed with gold braid are much help in handling freight.

But . . . WE ARE DETERMINED TO GIVE

A Practical Air Charter Service

to

Central and Northern B.C.

★★★ Our flight and ground crews are already veterans in the District.

★★★ Our aircraft, all fresh from the factory and fully radio-equipped, will operate at rates you can afford to pay, when and where you want them, all the year round.

★★★ Our constant aim will be to give you increasingly good service, at minimum cost, to bring the speed and comfort of air-travel within everyone's grasp.

★

BRING US YOUR PROBLEMS—WRITE OR WIRE

Central British Columbia Airways

Head Office: KELLER HOUSE, PRINCE GEORGE

Operating Bases: Fort St. James and Prince George

Central B.C. Airways advertisement in Prince George Citizen,
May 2, 1946. P.G. Citizen

July 12 was declared "Junkers Day" by Fort St. John in 1991, and a 1/3 scale W-34 was mounted in a waterfront park. Veteran pilots Ernie Harrison, Pat Carey and Sheldon Luck, pose for the occasion. Sheldon Luck

1/3 scale model of Junkers 34 at Fort St. James, August 2000. CW

Fort St. James

FORT ST. JAMES, BC
STEWART LAKE (SEAPLANE)

Modern air photo of Fort St. James looking North. CW

GROUND FACILITIES

Gas and oil available

Minor repairs at workshop

ELEVATION - 2230'

POSITION
LAT. 54°27'N.   LONG. 124°17'W.
SE end of Stuart Lake at mouth of Stuart River.

OPERATED BY
Pacific Western Airlines

REMARKS
Strong W. wind creates swells - unsafe for some aircraft.
Sheltered moorings behind breakwater.
Breakup May 1
Freezeup November 1
Ski-planes in winter

LANDING AREA
STUART LAKE
N-S 5 miles x 1.5 miles
NW-SE 5 miles x 1.5 miles
E-W 5 miles x 1 mile

OBSTRUCTIONS (ASL)

Fort St. James

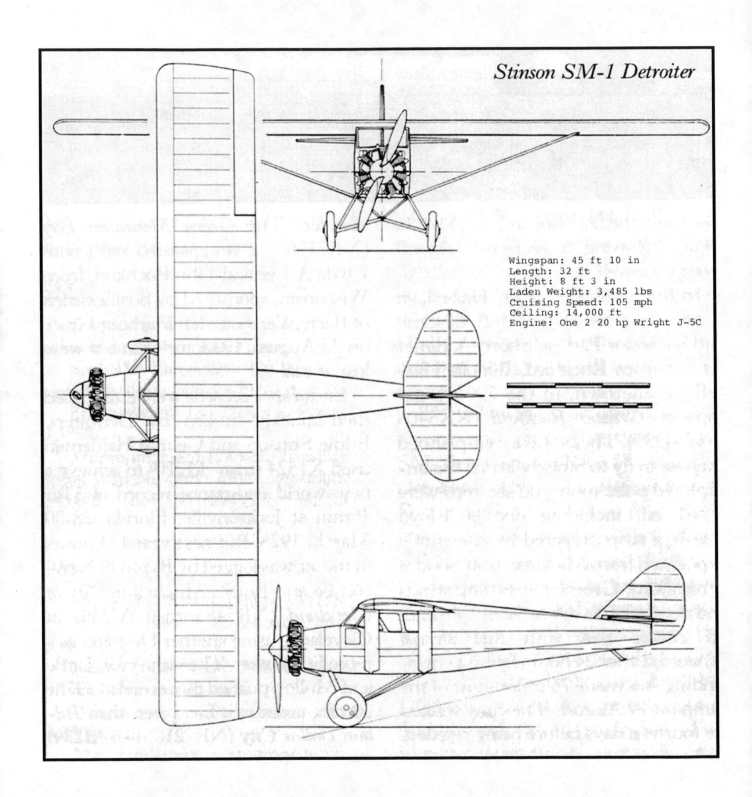

Stinson SM-1 Detroiter

Wingspan: 45 ft 10 in
Length: 32 ft
Height: 8 ft 3 in
Laden Weight: 3,485 lbs
Cruising Speed: 105 mph
Ceiling: 14,000 ft
Engine: One 2 20 hp Wright J-5C

Smithers

The January 23, 1920, edition of the Omineca Herald announced that a flight of aircraft proceeding from New York to. Nome, Alaska, would be landing in the area during the following summer. The Interior News announced that on June 16, 1920, they had interviewed members of the advance planning party for the flight. Captain Howard T. Douglas of the United States Air Service and Captain Le Royer of the Canadian Air Force advised that the flight would stop at Hazelton, forty-five minutes northwest of Smithers. The pair had selected a site behind that community's hospital and the planned arrival date was set for July 20 the following month.

Because of a landing mishap the aircraft were delayed at Prince George and did not arrive at Hazelton until August 13. Smithers' residents had to be content with watching the flight of four de Haviland DH-4Bs fly over their community.

In August 1921 yet another American aircraft overflew the Village of Smithers en route to Hazelton. It was "Ollie" Prest who had served in the United States Air Service in the First War and later became a stunt flyer for the movie industry. Prest left Las Vagas, Nevada, in July 1921 announcing his intention to fly his Curtiss JN-4 from Mexico to Siberia.

The Interior News edition of April 10, 1929, announced the report of the Smithers Chamber of Commerce under the banner "Put Smithers on the Air Map." The speaker had announced, "The aeroplane will open up the north and Smithers must awaken to the new era in transportation. We must have an airport." The lightly attended audience agreed and a motion was passed that the group would start searching for a suitable site for aircraft alighting.

Pacific Airways' Junkers F-13 CF-AMX at Lake Kathlyn in 1934, flown by Don MacLarin on mine exploration. B.V. Museum

Likely the first aircraft to land near Smithers was Junkers JL-6, G-CADP, which had sat derelict at Hazelton since 1922 and was later purchased in 1928 by Richard F. Corless of Prince George and overhauled at his auto dealership garage in that city. The aircraft was refused a Canadian licence, but Corless operated it anyway, landing at Smithers' Kathlyn Lake. A 1929 newspaper reported "Three Prospectors Fly into Tatla Lake". (This should probably read Takla Lake.)

Later in 1929, World War I Ace Donald McLaren landed Junkers F-13 CF-AMX at Kathlyn Lake on a prospecting charter. Also G-CAEB, the Vickers Viking operated by a mining syndicate, made several visits to the lake.

On July 17, 1929, the Smithers Chamber of Commerce bought a 247 acre ranch from E. Hill. The funding came from aviation minded individuals and from funds raised by the Chamber. The turf field was located two miles south of the village.

In early November 1928, G-CAUZ, the "Northern Light", arrived at Smithers to barnstorm the community, giving a stunting exhibition followed by short flights to eager Smithers residents. The Alexander Eaglerock, owned by the Yukon Airways and Exploration Company of Whitehorse, later departed for Hazelton.

The April 4, 1930, edition of the Interior News declared the new aviation field well underway

G-CAUZ, an Alexander Eaglerock owned by Yukon Airways, barnstormed at Smithers in late November 1928. B.V. Museum

stating that it occupied an area of 25 to 30 acres and that with eleven men working on it they would have everything completed save the burning of the stumps. The newspaper further stated that the landing area would be 1,200 feet long and was considered adequate for any modern airplane.

On May 3, an American Travelaire, NC-377, arrived over Smithers intending to land at the new aviation field for fuel. The aircraft had landed previously at Hazelton, but that town was out of aviation fuel so NC-377 flew back to Smithers.

Pacific International Airways Consolidated Fleetster NC-750V, and Fairchild 71 at Smithers, November 1930. Worthy Lake Collection

The aircraft's pilot, J.C. McFayden of Lakeport, California, circled the town for over an hour. He had seen the aviation field but decided that it was not suitable for the big eight-seat monoplane. Finally he dropped a note asking that three smudge pots be lighted at a suitable landing area. City officials sped in their automobiles to the Sproule Ranch and lit the requested signal fires. McFayden landed safely and was able to secure fuel and accommodation for the night. Taking off the following morning at 5:20 a.m. the crimson coloured Travelaire was observed over the 9th linemans cabin of the Yukon Telegraph between Hazelton and Telegraph Creek. The aircraft apparently ran into bad weather, which forced a landing on the ice at Dease Lake.

On November 12, 1930, two American aircraft arrived at Smithers en route to Atlin to assist in the search for Paddy Burke missing in Junkers CF-AMX. The Pacific International Airways aircraft, a Consolodated Fleetster, NC-750V, was flown by J.W. Joe Barrows, and a Fairchild 71

was flown by H.L. Harry Blunt. The airline president A.E. Ted Lowe and his wife were also in the Fleetster. Because of the weather both aircraft remained at Smithers until Saturday, November 22, when the two aircraft changed from wheels to skis for their flight north by way of Telegraph Creek for Atlin. On Saturday, November 14, 1930, one of the aircraft attempted to depart in deep snow but aborted the takeoff after dragging his wing over a tree.

In March of 1933, the Smithers Chamber of Commerce made a request to the Federal Government Department of National Defence and Department of Labour for assistance in upgrading the airfield. They specifically asked to be included in the Unemployment Relief Program, which used single unemployed men for manual labour at airport sites.

Another aircraft to use this field was an American Bellanca CH-300 Pacemaker, NC-403E, powered by a Wright J-6 Whirlwind engine. The aircraft was being flown from New York to Alaska in an attempt to rescue Jimmy Mattern who had crashed in Siberia while attempting to set a round-the-world record flight.

Bellanca CH-300 Pacemaker NC-403E of the Mattern Relief Expedition, Summer 1933. B.V. Museum

The Mattern Relief Expedition, organized by supporters in New York and funded by the King's Brewery, departed New York proceeding west. On June 5, pilot Will Alexander took off from Prince George and may have stopped in Smithers and/or Hazelton before heading up the old telegraph line for Telegraph Creek and the Yukon.

Poor weather forced the aircraft back and it eventually landed in Terrace. Mattern had meanwhile been rescued and flown to Nome, Alaska, by Russian pilot Sigismund Levenevsky. After, the Relief Expedition realized that they then needed a floatplane to get Mattern, they chartered one from Juneau. They flew to Nome and returned with Mattern via Juneau to Lake Lakelse at Terrace on July 26, 1933, where, because of the shortness of the strip, Mattern alone flew the Bellanca while Bob Ellis of Alaska Southern Airways flew the relief expedition in his float-equipped Lockheed Vega, NC-366H. The two aircraft flew to Hazelton where Ellis discharged his passengers and returned to Juneau.

At this point the author finds a bit of a conundrum. The Bellanca was known to be at Hazelton on this day, so why would the group stop in Smithers (only forty-five miles away en route to Prince George? Local lore and a photograph of the Bellanca at Smithers definitely position the aircraft at this community's airfield - a pitstop after a ten minute flight is not within reason, saving the possibility that Hazelton was out of fuel. This author's conjecture about what really happened is that pilot Will Alexander landed at Smithers when westbound from Prince George on June 5 to his ultimate landing at

RCAF Norseman at Smithers. B.V. Museum

Terrace. After refueling, he headed for Telegraph Creek, bypassing Hazelton and eventually turned around because of weather. He may or may not have landed at Hazelton before proceeding to Terrace.

By 1936, ownership of the Smithers airfield had passed to the Village of Smithers, who in turn applied to the Civil Controller of Aviation Department of National Defence, Ottawa, for an airport licence, dated March 1936. The Department of Transport carried out a survey and determined the original airfield site inadequate and instead selected an alternate location that would

Smithers Airfield looking West, December 15, 1943. RCAF TE-4

be acceptable to development for the Department of National Defence. The new site was two miles northwest of the town adjacent to Lake Kathlyn and this land was expropriated in November 1941.

Flight Sgt. George Williamson, RCAF, was pilot on a photographic survey of RCAF airport sites in the interior. Williamson recalls that early in the war Pan American Airways used the old Smithers airfield on a scheduled flight from Seattle to Fairbanks on the inland route through B.C., using Boeing 247D and Lockheed 10A aircraft. PanAm maintained staff at Prince George and operated weather and communications stations at Takla and Dease Lake to support their flights on the interior route to Alaska. Williamson further states that initially the new airfield was 3,500 feet long and had a 16 foot hump in the centre of it.

RCAF Station Smithers, August 26, 1943, looking South.
RCAF PB-32

Williamson and photographer W/O Hackett were at Smithers from September 26 through the 27, 1942, on an RCAF photographic assignment, flying Norseman #2480 on floats which they operated from Lake Kathlyn. By this time the

RCAF Lockheed 10B #7648 of No. 13 (O.T.) Squadron, visits Smithers 1942.
B.V. Museum

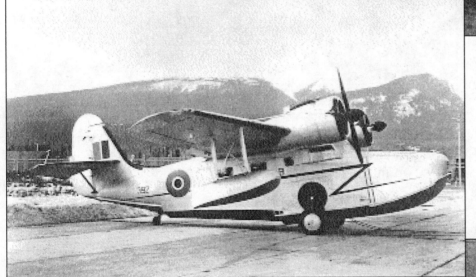

RCAF Grumman Goose #392 of No. 166 SAquadron on ramp at Smithers.
B.V. Museum

RCAF Station Smithers, 1943, looking West to Hudson Bay Mountain.
B.V. Museum

Department of National Defence contractor had removed the hump from the single runway.

On August 12, 1942, the first aircraft officially landed at the new airport. The Department of Transport aircraft was calibrating the radio navigation facility for the approach to the single runway.

On May 6, 1943, the field's 4,400 foot runway was officially opened as RCAF Smithers.

RCAF Lockheed Vega Ventura G.R. Mk5 #2250 of No. 149 Squadron at Smithers January-March 1944. B.V. Museum

The building contractor, Tomlinson Construction Company, had finished most of the support facilities with final completion in November. The station was conceived as part of the Home War Establishment's second line of defence to back up operational stations on the coast in the emergency of an enemy gaining a foothold between Alaska and Washington in the United States.

The station's first Commanding Officer F/0 (later promoted to F/L) A.W. Scott arrived August 6, 1943. The station was used as a base for itinerant aircraft and some training aircraft from other areas. The station's complement averaged 100 men, with its highest strength January 31, 1944, of 167 men.

From January 20 to March 1, 1944, Number 149 Squadron RCAF assigned a detachment of three Lockheed Vega Ventura GR MKV bomber aircraft to be temporarily stationed at Smithers. Also on January 20, Number 135 Squadron RCAF detached three Hawker Hurricane MKXII fighters from Terrace to Smithers on a training mission until March 9, 1944.

Owing to the decreased Japanese threat on the Pacific coast, many RCAF units and stations were disbanded during 1944. RCAF station Smithers was officially closed on March 31, 1944. However, the RCAF re-classified its unit to become Number 17 Staging Unit on April 1, 1944, with a compliment of 60 men under F/L A.W. Scott. As a detachment of Prince Rupert, the station provided services to itinerant American and Canadian military aircraft.

On November 28, 1944, Western Air Command RCAF received a request from the Canadian Army to assist in quelling a mutiny of the 15th Infantry Brigade who had seized the Army camp at Terrace in reprisal against orders for posting to the European theatre. The 1,600 men were conscripts from an eastern province who had been drafted for home-front duty only.

Number 8 (BR) Bomber Reconnaissance Squadron immediately dispatched eight Vega Venturas from Patricia Bay at Victoria to Smithers. The aircraft were unarmed, but an accompanying Dakota (DC-3) which transported the squadron's support staff, carried the munitions potentially required. Army officers at Terrace

Dakota #976 of No. 164 Squadron at Smithers December 1944. B.V. Museum

USAF B-36 Bomber similar to one that crashed Northwest of Smithers on February 14, 1950. Convair

Department of Transport staff on site. However, late on February 13, 1950, a drama was played out in the skies above the Bulkley and Skeena Rivers.

The Cold War between the Western Allies and the Soviet Union was at its height and each day Strategic Air Command of the US Air Force sent armed flights toward the USSR in anticipation of attacking that nation should it begin belligerent activity.

A Strategic Air Command B-36B, armed with a nuclear weapon, was returning from Eielson Air Force Base Fairbanks, Alaska, to Carswell Air Force Base at Fort Worth, Texas. The B-36 bomber was the largest production-built bomber ever constructed. The six piston, four jet-engined aircraft had a wingspan greater than the Boeing 747.

were able to subdue the mutineers before the use of the Venturas was required.

Number 17 Staging Unit at RCAF Smithers was disbanded on August 11, 1945, with its last Commanding Officer F/0 G.N. Whalley.

At the end of the war the Smithers airport was passed from Department of National Defence to the Department of Transport, and an airport licence was issued on April 1, 1946. Limited activity was reported from 1945 to 1951. Snow on the runways was compacted during the winter and the radio range communications and weather facilities were kept operational by the

The code number of this B-36B was #2075 and it was under command of Captain H.L. Barry with fifteen crew members and one special passenger, Lt. Col. Daniel V. MacDonald from the US Air Force office of Plans and Operations. Six hours into the flight Captain Barry declared an emergency in the vicinity of Hecate Strait near the Queen Charlotte Islands.

The aircraft commander advised his intention to ditch 90 nautical miles south of Prince Rupert. The 11,000 pound nuclear bomb was jettisoned into the sea and the crew bailed out after the aircraft was put on auto pilot with a southwesterly course set.

Eventually, after an extensive search, code named "Operation BRIX", twelve survivors were picked up and five, including the co-pilot, were listed as missing.

In the early hours of February 14, 1950, many residents of the Bulkley, Skeena, and Kispiox Valley likely heard a distinctive aircraft engine noise quite unlike other aircraft that had flown overhead in the past. A few years later an explanation unfolded.

U.S.A.F. Grumman SA-16A "Albatross" at Smithers September 1953 on search and rescue duty. B.V. Museum

On September 4, 1953, a US Air Force aircraft from Ketchikan, Alaska, was searching for a missing de Havilland Dove executive aircraft en route to Bellingham, Washington. The search aircraft discovered wreckage at an altitude of 6,900 feet on Kiloget Mountain, thirty miles northwest of Hazelton. It turned out that this was B-36B #2075. The crash site was almost 200 miles from the point where it was abandoned by its crew. Several unsuccessful attempts were made to reach the crash site, until early August 1954 when a US Air Force investigative team arrived in Smithers. A former RCAF hangar was commandeered with the blessing of the Department

USAF Sikorsky H-19 #13865 used in retrieval of classified material and destruction of wreck of Convair B-36B Bomber Northwest of Smithers, Augusut 1954. B.V. Museum

of National Defence, Ottawa. The tenants, B.C. Forest Service and Central B.C. Airways, were temporarily evicted. The team spent nine days in their mission to retrieve sensitive material and destroy the wreckage on Kologet Mountain. A shroud of secrecy was maintained, but uncon-

Smithers

firmed rumors exist that skeletal remains were brought back to Smithers and returned to the United States. Almost 50 years later parts of the USAF report on this incident still remain classified.

On May 2, 1951, Central B.C. Airways started a regular service from Terrace to Prince George via Smithers using an Avro Anson MKV, CF-GDW, flown by Harry Taylor. The Smithers Chamber of Commerce and civic officials welcomed the arrival of the first scheduled flight with Central B.C. Airways President Russ Baker on board.

On March 16, 1953, Canadian Pacific Airlines commenced service three times a week using DC-3 and later DC-4 aircraft between Edmonton and Terrace, with stops at Prince George and Smithers.

In the early afternoon of November 9, 1954, a teenage wanabe pilot was flying westbound from Prince George to Smithers in a 1946 Aeronca 7AC, CF-HSR - an aircraft that had been sold in Vancouver to a Prince Rupert man, and I had been given the opportunity to deliver it for expenses and much needed flying time.

HSRs range was about 250 miles and, in an attempt to increase this, the aircraft's seller, Pacific Wings, had strapped two five gallon gas cans into the back seat. The "Airknocker" had no radio, and in fact no electrical system, so as I roared across the sky I was unaware of an extensive bank of fog and low stratus that obscured the town of Smithers to my arrival.

I was faced with a quandary. My single fuel tank was nearing empty. My destination was unobtainable. I had no alternative but to turn

C.P.A. Douglas DC-4 at Smithers 1952. B.V. Museum

Modern air photo of Smithers Airfield looking North. CW

In 1955 the single runway 14-32 was extended to 5,000 feet of length. At this time Canadian Pacific airlines started using Convair aircraft on the route. After the Prince Rupert airport opened in 1961, the Smithers airport was no longer required as an alternate and CPA reduced its service to weekend flights only. By 1970 Smithers had a new terminal and was serviced by Pacific Western Airlines using a Nord aircraft, later replaced by a Convair 640, and by 1973 a Boeing 737 jet service.

back, but to where? I realized that I did not have enough fuel to make Vanderhoof, so I had to land. After assessing several potential areas, I selected one about 25 miles west of Burns Lake between Telkwa and Houston in a field next to Highway 16. The landing was a little bumpy but uneventful. I taxied to a gate at the highway and a passing travelling salesman stopped and helped me lift one wing then the other over the gate posts allowing me to park on the gravel of the road-edge. I filled my single tank from the five gallon cans and was almost finished when a logging truck stopped. Its owner owned the farm I had landed on and, after insisting that I stay the night, he got out the Aquivit and beer. I spent a cold night in my sleeping bag in a small farm shed. Early next morning the logger and his wife gave me breakfast and suggested that I stay and marry their large blond daughter and they would keep the plane. I managed to decline without hurting the fifteen year old's feelings and compensated the logger with a ride around his homestead, taking off and landing on the highway. After making good my escape I made the short flight to a landing at Smithers.

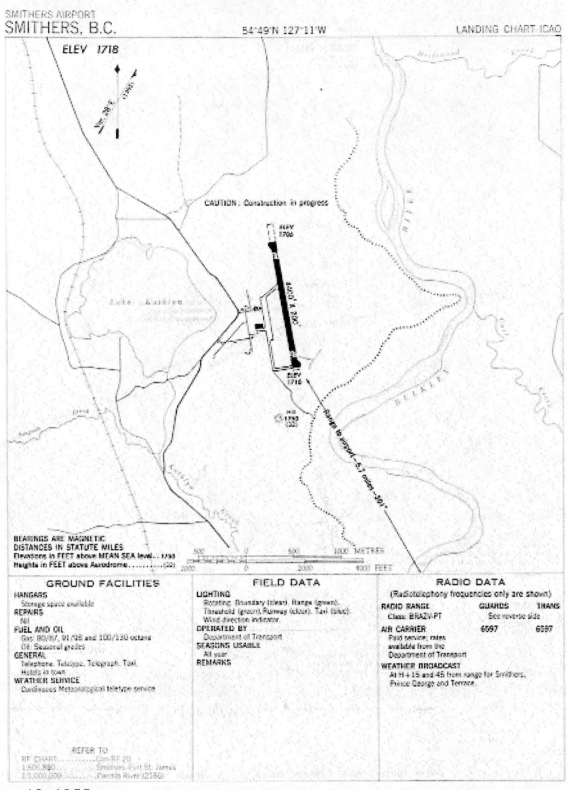

August 12, 1955

Smithers

212

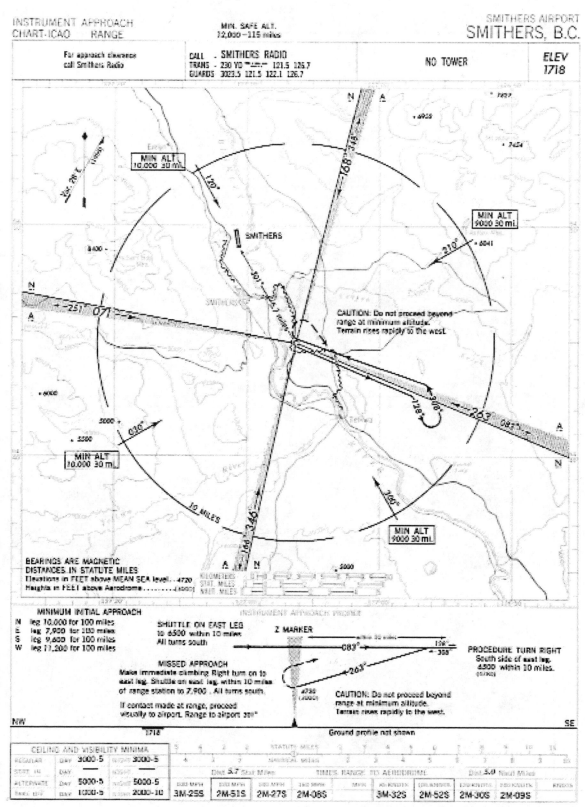

INSTRUMENT APPROACH
CHART-ICAO   RANGE

MIN. SAFE ALT.
12,000—115 miles

SMITHERS AIRPORT
SMITHERS, B.C.

For approach clearance
call Smithers Radio

CALL . SMITHERS RADIO
TRANS - 230 YO ▀▄▀▄ 121.5 126.7
GUARDS 3023.5 121.5 122.1 126.7

NO TOWER

ELEV
1718

MIN ALT
10,000 30 ml.

MIN ALT
9000 30 mi.

SMITHERS

CAUTION: Do not proceed beyond
range at minimum altitude.
Terrain rises rapidly to the west.

MIN ALT
10,000 30 ml.

MIN ALT
9000 30 ml.

BEARINGS ARE MAGNETIC
DISTANCES IN STATUTE MILES
Elevations in FEET above MEAN SEA level . . 4720
Heights in FEET above Aerodrome . . . . . . (3000)

KILOMETERS
STAT. MILES
NAUT. MILES

INSTRUMENT APPROACH PROFILE

MINIMUM INITIAL APPROACH

N leg 10,000 for 100 miles
E leg 7,900 for 100 miles
S leg 9,600 for 100 miles
W leg 11,200 for 100 miles

SHUTTLE ON EAST LEG
to 6500 within 10 miles
All turns south

Z MARKER

PROCEDURE TURN RIGHT
South side of east leg.
6500 within 10 miles.

MISSED APPROACH
Make immediate climbing Right turn on to
east leg. Shuttle on east leg within 10 miles
of range station to 7,900 . All turns south.

If contact made at range, proceed
visually to airport. Range to airport 301°

CAUTION: Do not proceed beyond
range at minimum altitude.
Terrain rises rapidly to the west.

NW   SE
1718   Ground profile not shown

CEILING AND VISIBILITY MINIMA			
REGULAR	DAY	3000-5	NIGHT	3000-5
STAT. IN	DAY		NIGHT	
ALTERNATE	DAY	5000-5	NIGHT	5000-5
TAKE OFF	DAY	1000-5	NIGHT	2000-10

STATUTE MILES
NAUTICAL MILES

Dist. 5.7 Stat. Miles   TIMES RANGE TO AERODROME   Dist. 5.0 Naut. Miles

100 MPH	120 MPH	150 MPH	240 MPH	MPH	90 KNOTS	120 KNOTS	150 KNOTS	250 KNOTS	KNOTS
3M-25S	2M-51S	2M-27S	2M-08S		3M-32S	2M-52S	2M-30S	2M-09S	

August 12, 1955

Smithers

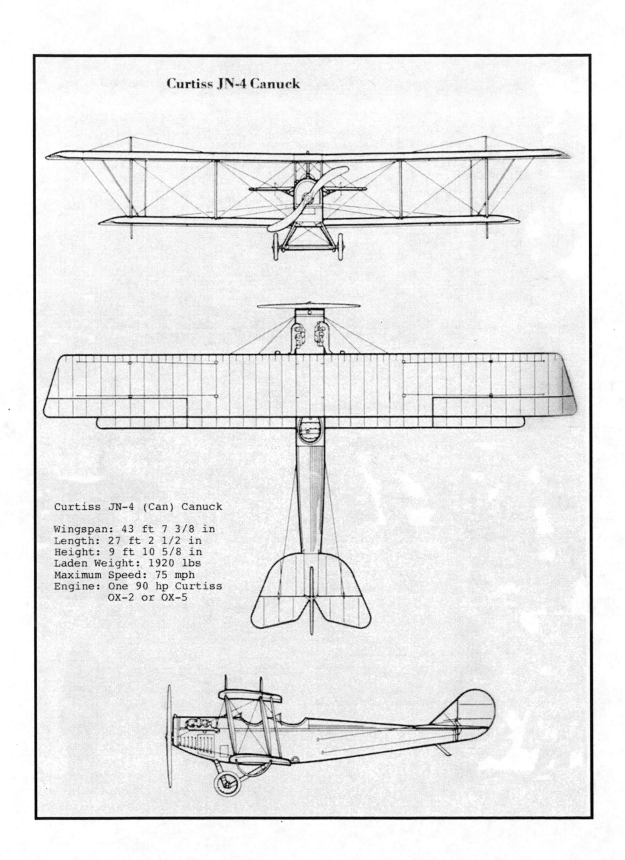

Curtiss JN-4 Canuck

Curtiss JN-4 (Can) Canuck

Wingspan: 43 ft 7 3/8 in
Length: 27 ft 2 1/2 in
Height: 9 ft 10 5/8 in
Laden Weight: 1920 lbs
Maximum Speed: 75 mph
Engine: One 90 hp Curtiss
        OX-2 or OX-5

Hazelton

Preparations for the landing of the first aircraft at Hazelton began in the spring of 1920 with the arrival of Captain Howard T. Douglas of the United States Army Air Service and Captain H.A. LeRoyer of the Canadian Air Force who also represented the Canadian Air Board. The pair arrived on the Grand Trunk Pacific Railway, which is now the CNR, and were selecting potential sites for the Alaska Air Expedition from New York to Nome, Alaska, which would depart New York on July 15, 1920.

U.S. Air Service de Havilland DH-4B on short final to Northeast at Mission Point Field, Friday, August 13, 1920. Hazelton Museum

Douglas and LeRoyer initially selected a landing site close to the community hospital, but the advance party had underestimated the length of take off required by the expedition's four de Havilland DH-4Bs. This prompted the expedition leader, Captain Street, and Lieutenant Nutt to also take the train west from Prince George to examine the landing field before the expedition continued its flight beyond Prince George.

Landing DH-4B taxis past SMOKE Pot Wind Indicator at Mission Point Field. Hazelton Museum

Aircraft at Mission Point. The three boys are from the Parent family. The author interviewed Delcort Parent in 1998 when he was 83. Trelle Morrow Coll.

Street found the site chosen inadequate and selected another one across the Bulkley River at its junction with the Skeena River known as Mission Point and now called Anderson Flats.

This was the site of George Biernes's oat field. Mission Point and Mission Flats had previously been the site of a Methodist Church Mission. Captain Street arranged with Biernes to cut a section of his oat field to allow the landing of the DH-4Bs. He then returned to Prince George.

On Friday 13, 1920, the four aircraft took off from Prince George at 9:05 a.m. and after a flight of three hours landed at the Mission Point Aviation Park, as the field at Hazelton had become known. The landing field chosen by Street at Mission Point had worked out well, however before the four aircraft could take off the field would have to be compacted. The large number of townspeople who had come to witness the event were pressed into service tramping up and down the length of the field to pack the loose hay and dirt into a useable runway.

DH-4B plane #2 taking off at Hazelton toward Southwest, August 14, 1920. B.V. Museum

The crews of the four DH-4Bs stayed overnight at Hazelton and were hosted to a dinner and dance by the community's veterans of the First World War. On Saturday, August 14, the weather was reported good at their next destination and all four aircraft took off at 2:30 p.m. Expedition pilot Lieutenant Clifford Nutt wrote a synopsis of the flight and his report of the flight from Hazelton to Wrangell Alaska follows:

US Air Service DH-4B parked at Mission Point Field, August 13, 1920.
P.R. Archives

"Our next jump was to land us in United States territory again, but to reach Wrangell we had to jump over the Coast Range mountains, at least that is what we thought we had to do from our maps, which showed the trend of a river or of a mountain system, and depicted everything else as perfectly smooth, level country. In point of fact, the region has never been explored or surveyed. Fortunately, we had a clear day for our take-off. When we began to ascend for our hop over the mountains, we found that the mountains rose too, and higher than we had. Instead of being 5,000 and 7,000 feet as shown on our map, when we reached a height of 7,000 we found we needed 3,000 more to get over the top, and when we tried to skirt the range, we found it wasn't really a range at all with a valley on the other side, but just close packed mountain peaks filled with snow and ice between. These glaciers looked like level seas of dark green water."

Hazelton family pose with DH-4B while Sergeant Mechanic works on aircraft.
P.R. Archives

The flight continued successfully, landing at Wrangell, Alaska; Whitehorse and Dawson City, Yukon; Fairbanks, Ruby, and Nome, Alaska; arriving at the latter city on August 23, 1920. Eight days later the group reversed course and on September 29 three of the four aircraft again landed at the Mission Point airfield. The three machines remained at Hazelton until October 4, as they waited for Captain Douglas who had

Hazelton

217

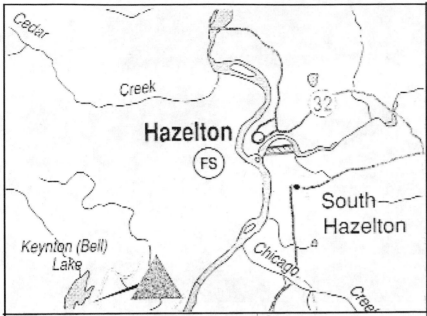

ELEVATION - 850'

POSITION
LAT. 55°15'N.   LONG. 127°39'W.
1/4 mile E. of Village at Mission Point

OPERATED BY

SEASONS USABLE
Limited maintenance.
No snow removal or compaction

GROUND FACILITIES

HANGARS
Nil

COMMUNICATIONS
Telephone Telegraph
in Hazelton

REPAIRS
Nil

TRANSPORTATION
Highway and Railway

FUEL & OIL
Gas - 80 octane
Oil - seasonal grades

ACCOMMODATION
Limited in town

REMARKS
To be used in emergency only.
Licenced by Canadian Air Board 1922 for use by land and sea aircraft

LANDING AREA
TURF
1800' x 600'

OBSTRUCTIONS (ASL)
Mountainous terrain

DH-4B circling overhead Mission Point Field prior to landing, August 13, 1920. Hazelton Museum

1922

returned from Alaska by the Canadian Pacific Steamship Princess Alice to Prince Rupert. He then had taken the train to Hazelton, from which point he had arranged with Captain Street to fly back to New York, replacing crewman Sgt. Henriques who took the train.

The following year, at the end of August 1921, another American aviator landed at the Mission Point field. Clarence "Ollie" Prest, a World War I aviator with the United States Air Service, had departed Las Vegas, Nevada, in late July 1921 and crossed into Canada at Lethbridge on August 8. Prest worked his way to Edmonton, barnstorming as he went giving rides and doing aerobatics at small towns to earn his expenses.

Prest, accompanied by air mechanic L.M. Bach, was flying a Curtiss JN-4D Jenny which he had christened the "Polar Bear" and had stated his intent of flying from Mexico to Siberia. Leaving Edmonton August 18 or 19, he flew via Jasper and Prince George before arriving at Hazelton. Prest entertained the townspeople with stunts and offered rides for cash. However, on one of his takeoffs his engine quit leaving him no other option than to land in a small field down the Skeena River. The aircraft was not badly damaged and no one was hurt. With the help of willing locals, he was able to bring his "Polar Bear" to town in a canoe. It was then

transported to a workshop next to the Hudson Bay Company store and repaired. Prest had originally intended to fly along the Yukon telegraph route to Telegraph Creek, on the route of the 1920 return flight of the Alaska Flying Expedition However, he was suspicious of the quality of fuel obtained locally and decided to ship the aircraft to Prince Rupert on the Grand Trunk Pacific Railway departing Hazelton on September 1, 1921.

"Ollie" Prest removing parts from the "Polar Bear" at Hazelton August 1921.
Hazelton Archives

Hazelton

"Ollie" Prest's "Polar Bear" after his landing mishap at Hazelton August 1921.
Hazelton Archives

"Polar Bear" crosses Skeena River by canoe after its crash downstream from Hazelton. Hazelton Archives

TheCanadian Air Board had come into existence after the First World War and one of its mandates was to regulate aviation in Canada by licencing pilots, aircraft, landing grounds, and seaplane landing areas which it categorized as Air Harbours. In the first list of licenced Air Harbours October 17, 1920, no landing fields were licenced in B.C.

During February 1922, Hazelton was visited by Canadian Air Board Inspector S.R. Anderson who was inspecting the Mission Point Airfield as an approved Air Harbour for both land and sea aircraft. Sea aircraft were to use the adjoining waters of either the Skeena or Bulkley Rivers.

In the Air Board's report of 1922 it gives its first published list of approved Air Harbours across the country. In B.C. only one approved landing field is named - Hazelton. The report states that "alighting areas are available for land and sea-planes and the field available is 600 x 1,800 feet"; it also states that Customs are available.

Up to now all the aircraft using the Mission Point airfield had been passing through to other destinations, but the aircraft had a profound affect on the community and many started to see the benefits and possibilities available from air travel. One such group was the Railway Employees Investment and Industrial Association of Hazelton. They purchased a German Junkers JL-6 aircraft from Imperial Oil in Edmonton and in mid-July 1922 G-CADP, previously christened the "Vic", was flown westward on wheels by Major George A. "Tommy" Thompson with stops at Henry House in Jasper and Prince George. On its arrival in Hazelton the Junkers was mounted on floats. It was used on prospecting and hunting expeditions flown by Tommy Thompson. During the summer of 1922, ADP became the first aircraft flown to the Queen Charlotte Islands.

As mentioned earlier, the establishment of the Air Board had brought aircraft registration and licencing. During the early summer of 1923, F/0 Earl L. McLeod was dispatched from the Dominion Air Station at Jericho Beach Vancouver to inspect certain aircraft for certification. McLeod travelled by train to Prince George and on through Smithers to Hazelton where he had been instructed to inspect Junkers JL-6, G-CADP, for serviceability. He reported the aircraft as unserviceable. McLeod then received a telegram to report to Prince Rupert for Fisheries patrol duty.

Air Board InspectorLt. Earl MacLeod flew a Curtiss HS-2L from Prince Rupert to inspect worthiness of Junkers ADP, seen here on Skeena River at Hazelton, August 6, 1923. Earl MacLeod Estate

The owners of ADP were hoping for continued use of the aircraft. Mr. Len S. Bell, the President of the Railway Association, and George Beirnes, a big game hunter and guide, continued to attempt to get the aircraft back to work. It seems that Tommy Thompson got cold feet at this time. When Earl McLeod again inspected the aircraft on August 6, 1923, he found another pilot present, a W.H. McCardle who was unsuccessfully attempting to carry out engine repairs.

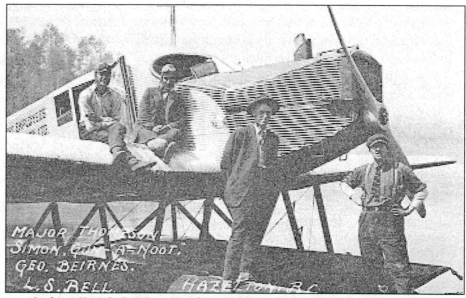

Junkers JL-6 G-CADP at Hazelton 1923. L. to R.: Major "Tommy" Thompson; pilot Simon Gun-A-Noot; native guide George Birnes; owner of Mission Point Field; and Len S. Bell, President of Owner Association. Earl MacLeod Estate

During September 1998 the author visited Hazelton and interviewed Eric Jantze, a longtime resident who remembered as a small boy watching George Biernes charging up and down the river trying, without success, to get the Junkers to fly. Eric Jantze's stepfather had been a fitter, or engine mechanic, in the RAF and he was asked to assess the cost of overhauling the B.M.W. IIIA engine. However, the Railway Association's President considered the RAF mechanic's estimate too high. Jantze further recalls that they were able to get the aircraft to fly once more, but the engine quit 300 feet above the town. In its attempt to get back on the water, its floats hit the roof of a barn on the corner of the Mission Point airfield, and for years after you could still see the skid marks.

Hazelton

In the year of its operation at Hazelton, the Junkers covered a considerable amount of the province's northland. Flying into this unmapped territory in 1922 was a very risky enterprise. The possibility of survival in the event of a crash would be very slim. However, the aircraft often carried a very bush-smart guide, Simon Gun-A-Noot. Simon was a native and an outlaw who had eluded the Provincial Police for thirteen years when they were trying to arrest him for two murders, for which he later was acquitted.

ADP was ignominiously hauled up on the bank of the Skeena River where the machine sat for six years, until 1929 when it was sold to R.F. Corless of Prince George. Eric Jantze remembers it leaving Hazelton on a railway flatcar.

In February 1924, Earl McLeod was back in Hazelton. He had been detailed by the Commander of the Jericho Beach Air Station at Vancouver to lay out a series of fuel caches in anticipation of a need by an around-the-world flight. Colonel E.L. Broome, an English engineer, had organized the flight in a Vickers Viking, G-EBGO, flown by RAF S/L MacLaren.

Mission Point Airfield continued to be an important stop for fuel, weather, and accommodation for aircraft en route to the Yukon and Alaska, as there was no airfield at either Terrace or Prince Rupert until years later. The accepted drill seemed to be to fly west from Prince George to Hazelton, refuel, then follow the Yukon telegraph line northward to Telegraph Creek, Atlin, and into the Yukon. Pilots frequently sent out requests to telegraph linemen along the route to light fires to indicate the way.

The telegraph line operated to provide communications between southern B.C. and the Yukon until it was abandoned in 1936 when replaced by wireless radio. Linemen were stationed in cabins along the route, connected by a well-maintained trail. The first cabin was twenty-eight miles from Hazelton, the next was twenty-four miles north of the first cabin, and then the cabins were seventeen miles apart.

Cessna AW NC-7107 shown here at Fairbanks, landed at Mission Point April 20, 1929. Harbottle Collection

One such flight was made in early November 1928 by an Alexander Eaglerock, G-CAUZ, a new aircraft that was being flown from the factory in Colorado Springs, Colorado. It was headed for Whitehorse, Yukon Territory, flown by John M. Patterson and accompanied by the aircraft's owner, Clyde Wann of the Yukon Airways and Exploration Company.

Yukon Airways Eaglerock G-CAUZ barnstormed at Hazelton November 1928. Hazelton Archives

NC-7107, a new Cessna AW, landed at Mission Flats on April 20, 1929, flown by pilot Parker D. Cramer and Willard Gamble, who had departed Chicago in early April intending to fly to Siberia and return. The following day NC-7107 took off for Whitehorse.

Cramer eventually landed at Nome, and on April 26 overflew Little Diomede Island, Siberia. On April 27, at 4:55 a.m., they started their return flight via Fairbanks, Whitehorse, and Atlin. They then followed the Yukon telegraph line to Hazelton where they landed on Tuesday, April 30. After refueling at Mission Flats they departed for Prince George and Edmonton where they landed in darkness at 10:00 p.m.

On April 29, 1930, an American Travelaire, NC-377M, from San Francisco landed at Hazelton's Mission Point field at 1:00 p.m. The eight seat, bright scarlet-coloured monoplane was flown by J.C. McFayden of Lakeport, California, with two passengers on board and was en route to Whitehorse. On May 3, 1930, McFayden discovered that there was no fuel available at Hazelton and took off for the new Smithers Aviation Park.

Pilot McFayden had evidently failed to clear Customs inbound through Canada, and NC-377M

Travel Air 6000 NC-377M flown by Clayton Scott, landed at Mission Point Field August 9, 1930. Hazelton Archives

Pacific International Airways NC-259M, a Bellanca CH-300 "Pacemaker" flown by Frank Dorbant and Lon Cope, landed at Hazelton October 22, 1930. Worthy Lake Collection

was impounded on its arrival in Whitehorse by Canadian Customs. The aircraft remained there until August 6, 1930, when an American pilot ferried it via Atlin and Telegraph Creek to Hazelton, where it arrived on August 9. Pilot Clayton Scott and his girlfriend, teacher Myrtle Smith, picnicked at the Mission Flats Field, departing the following day for Prince George and eventually Vancouver and Seattle.

Hazelton

Bellanca CH-300 "Pacemaker" NC-403E of the Mattern Relief Expedition, landed at Mission Point Field on June 5, 1933. Hazelton Archives

Five Eastman E-2 "Sea Rover's" arrived at Hazelton in June 1932, en route to Dease Lake. Shown here at Juneau, Alaska. L. Jarmin Collection

On Wednesday, October 22, American pilot Frank Dorbandt of Pacific International Airways landed his Belanca CH-300 Pacemaker, NC-259M, at Hazelton to refuel. He was en route to Telegraph Creek to participate in the search for Captain E.J.A. "Paddy" Burke who was missing in the Liard River area since October 10.

Dorbandt had been en route from Wenatchee, Washington, to Anchorage, Alaska, when he received an appeal from the Government Gold Commissioner, Mr. Wright, for assistance in the search, while Dorbandt was stopped in Hazelton. He was accompanied by air engineer Alonzo "Lon" Cope.

A Pacific International Airways American Consolidated Fleetster flown by Joe Barrows, accompanied by a Fairchild 71 flown by Harry Blunt, passed overhead Hazelton en route to Atlin on November 22, 1930. The two American aircraft had stopped at Smithers and were now en route to assist in the search for Burke.

When in June 1933 a round-the-world record attempt by Jimmy Mattern ended in his crash in Siberia, a group of supporters in New York organized a relief expedition. Financed by the King's Beer Brewery of New York, the group left New York heading for Alaska. On the morning of June 5, the Bellanca CH-300 with registration NC-403E took off from Prince George and, after landing at Hazelton for fuel, turned northwest. With no knowledge of what lay ahead, the Bellanca followed the old government telegraph line toward Telegraph Creek. However, low cloud, fog, and poor visibility forced pilot Will Alexander to turn around toward Hazelton, where he may have stopped again for fuel before continuing his flight along the Skeena River toward the coast.

Alexander landed in a hay field at Terrace. After a several days wait, the group chartered a float plane from Juneau, Alaska, then flew to Nome where they picked up Mattern and flew back to Terrace on July 26, 1933. The chartered aircraft, flown by Bob Ellis, dropped Mattern at Lake Lakelse and flew on to Hazelton. Mattern then retrieved the Bellanca from the hay field and in turn flew to Hazelton, landing at the Mission

Point Airfield. He picked up the relief party waiting there for him. The reasoning for this exercise related to the limited dimensions of the hayfield at Terrace being inadequate for a takeoff in a fully loaded Bellanca. Mattern and Alexander and the other two group members may have stayed overnight before proceeding east for Ontario and eventually New York. Bob Ellis flew the Alaska-Southern Airways Lockheed Vega floatplane NC-366H back to his base at Juneau, Alaska.

Hazelton pioneer Eric Jantze recalls five flying boats arriving and landing on the river, one of which clipped a cottonwood tree on landing. These were in all likelihood the five Eastman E-2 Sea Rovers, CF-AST, ASU, ASV, ASW, and ASY, all built in 1930 in Detroit, Michigan, and powered by Curtiss R-600 Challenger engines. The five Sea Rovers were being flown across Canada along the Grand Trunk Pacific Railway line and had departed Walkerville, Ontario, on May 25, 1932, as part of a mining expedition mounted by the Mitchell Exploration Company of Canada. The organization was later dubbed the Mitchell Drinking Expedition by one of its pilots, Frank Barr. The group arrived in Hazelton in early June 1932 later departing for Juneau, Alaska, where they arrived at 2:00 p.m. on June 11, 1932.

White Pass Airways' Ford Tri-Motor NC-5092 landed at Mission Point Field flown by Vern Bookwalter, Fall 1934. (Pictured at Skagway, Alaska) Via Jim Ruotsala

Canadian Airways Fairchild 71 CF-ATZ (seen here the previsous winter) arrived at Hazelton flown by "Punch" Dickens, July 29, 1935. Walter Gilbert Collection

Eric Jantze also reported a Ford Tri-Motor at Hazelton during the 1930s.

White Pass Airways of Whitehorse purchased a Ford Tri-Motor in Seattle during the fall of 1934 and hired an experienced pilot to fly it. Vern Bookwalter landed NC-5092 at Hazelton's Mission Point Field en route to Whitehorse, where the Ford went to work on scheduled flights from Skagway, Alaska, to Whitehorse, Mayo, and Dawson City.

Hazelton

225

Mission Point Field in 1998, looking Southwest. CW

well within the range of the Hurricane and Kitty Hawk fighters to initially utilize these fields. Smithers is approximately 45 miles east of Hazelton. Another emergency field was developed at Woodcock, between Cedarvale and Kitwanga in the narrow Skeena Valley, twenty miles west of Hazelton.

Hazelton had been bypassed by so-called progress. The community had been at the head of navigation for stern-wheelers on the Skeena River from Prince Rupert until the Grand Trunk Pacific Railway came west before World War I toward the coast and Prince Rupert. Grand real estate and industrial plans were made and eventually abandoned. After the war, a new and more exciting transportation vehicle made its grand entrance when in 1920 the first aeroplanes arrived. Hazelton was foreseen as the hub of air traffic to Alaska. Twenty years later, however, technology and politics would again determine Hazelton's fate. Aircraft no longer needed to stop every few miles and instead flew non-stop to their destinations.

Previously in 1934, another Ford may have landed at Hazelton flown by American Pilot Frank Dorbandt en route to Alaska during May.

On July 29, 1935, a Canadian Airways Fairchild 71C seaplane, CF-ATZ, arrived at Hazelton from Juneau, Alaska, via Telegraph Creek. The aircraft had been chartered by the Department of National Defence to fly the Civil Aviation Branch Western Airways Inspector on a survey flight of 8,400 miles to assess potential airports and airways in the northwest. Inspector Dan McLean was flown by Canadian aviation pioneer C.H. "Punch" Dickens with William Sutherland as engineer. After assessing the Mission Point Field, the group left for Prince Rupert.

War clouds were on the horizon by 1936 and the Department of National Defence began looking for airport sites throughout the province. By 1940 construction plans for new airports at Smithers and Prince George were underway as part of the North West Staging route. Airport sites were planned at intervals of 300 miles, which was

1957 - William A. Jenkins of New Hazelton purchased CF-KBT, a Piper PA-14 Family Cruiser.

1960 - Wilderness Game Guides Ltd., purchased CF-MOK, a Champion 7GCB.

1962 - W.H. Davidson purchased CF-NZP, a Piper PA-12 Super Cruiser

1971 - Ronald Burleigh purchased CF-YHK , a Champion 7GCB

Mission Point Airfield no longer hosted the arrival and departure of aviation and reverted back to a rough field on a point of land at the junction of the Skeena and Bulkley Rivers across from old Hazelton, a delightful community in an Alpine setting that rivals many similar areas in the Rockies or the Alps.

The last aviation reference the author could find to the Mission Point Airfield at Hazelton was in the 1967 edition of the Fostair Pilots Guide, which lists a 1,400 foot long grass strip one quarter mile east of Hazelton, and further states 80 octane fuel was available.

The author visited Hazelton in the summer of 1999 and drove to the site of the Mission Point field, which is now grown over with weeds and grass.

While enjoying a picnic in my VW Camper, it was not difficult to imagine the aviation activity at this long forgotten airfield that was in 1922 the very first to be licenced in B.C.

DEPARTMENT OF TRANSPORT INFORMATION CIRCULARS TO CIVIL AIR PILOTS AND AIRCRAFT OWNERS 1927-1940

0/23/36   31/8/36

Landing - Hazelton BC

A small landing field at Hazelton, B.C. has been used occasionally for a number of years by aircraft, particularly of American registration, flying through to Alaska.

The field is unlicensed and is strictly limited in dimensions with a rolling surface and poor approaches, as a result of which a number of minor accidents have occurred from time to time.

While it is realized that the field in question is the only one in the vicinity of Hazelton, its use is discouraged for all types of aircraft and pilots should bear in mind that they bear the onus of responsibility in landing at this field.

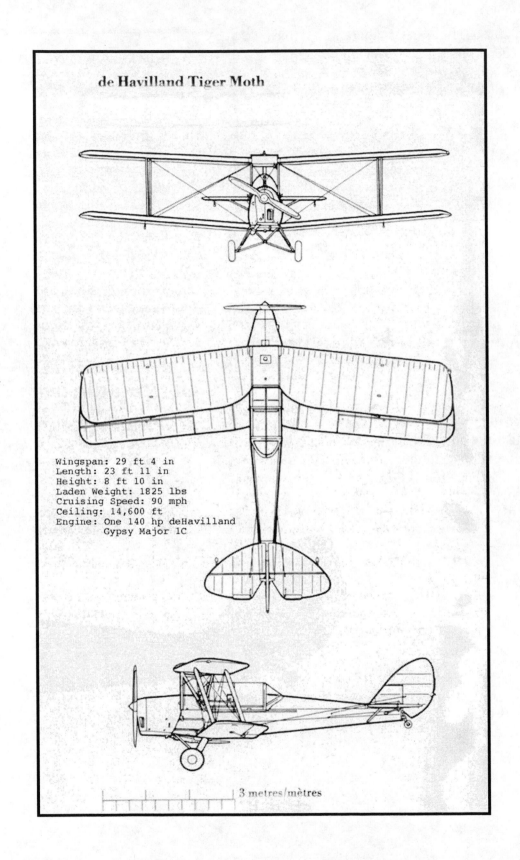

de Havilland Tiger Moth

Wingspan: 29 ft 4 in
Length: 23 ft 11 in
Height: 8 ft 10 in
Laden Weight: 1825 lbs
Cruising Speed: 90 mph
Ceiling: 14,600 ft
Engine: One 140 hp deHavilland
        Gypsy Major 1C

3 metres/mètres

Woodcock

Woodcock was constructed in 1943 as an emergency airfield between Smithers and Terrace for aircraft operating visually en route from Prince George west to coastal stations. It was built by the Department of National Defence as part of the Home War Establishment. Preliminary clearing at the site, forty-four miles north-north-east of the Terrace airport, started in the spring of 1942.

On September 24, 1942, RCAF Norseman #2480, a float equipped aircraft operating from Lake Lakelse at Terrace, made a series of photographic over-flights of the future Woodcock airfield site, as well as at Kitwanga. The pilot was F/Sgt George Williamson with photographer W02 E.B. Hackett.

Before the onset of winter 1942, airfield preparation by a DND contractor had been completed and preliminary runway preparation was well underway, but work on the Woodcock site came to a halt during the winter of 1942-43 due to heavy snowfall. An aerodrome maintenance crew and a Defence unit were stationed here throughout the winter, but for duty purposes only.

Woodcock Airfield looking North, August 26, 1943. RCAF PB-16

On May 1, 1943, the RCAF Station diarist reports that as of this date the runway had not been completed. Again on June 1, the diary records that all buildings structures with the exception of the wireless building are 50% completed and work has commenced on the sewage disposal plant.

On August 16, 1943, two aircraft thought to be Harvards flew overhead at 12:15 p.m. flying east at 5,000 feet.

WOODCOCK B. C.

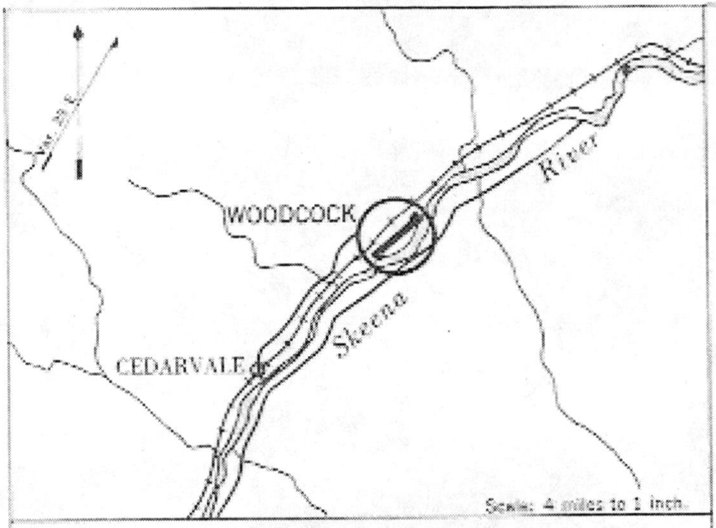

ELEVATION 537'

VARIATION 28°E. (1948)

POSITION
LAT. 55°04' N.   LONG. 128°15' W.
44 miles N.N.E. of Terrace airport.

AERONAUTICAL CHARTS
1 : 506,880 PRINCE RUPERT - STEWART
1 : 1,000,000 SKEENA RIVER (2187)

OPERATED BY
DOT

SEASONS USABLE
All year
No snow removal or compaction.

RADIO DATA
GUARDS TRANS
Nil

REMARKS
TO BE USED IN EMERGENCY ONLY

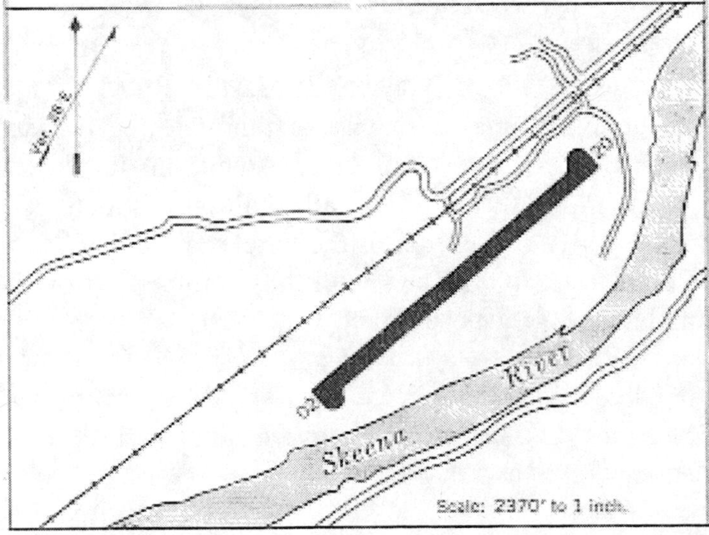

RUNWAYS
(asphalt)
02 - 20   5200' x 200'

LIGHTING
Nil

OBSTRUCTIONS (ASL)
N. & N.W. - Ground rising (4000') 2.4 m
S.E. - Ground rising (6000') 4 miles.
S.S.E. - Mtn. Seven Sisters (9140') 8 m

Scale: 4 miles to 1 inch.

GROUND FACILITIES

HANGARS
Nil

COMMUNICATIONS
Telephone. Telegraph in town

REPAIRS
Nil

TRANSPORTATION
Highway   Railway

FUEL AND OIL
Nil

ACCOMMODATIONS
Very limited accommodations available
at field.   Not available in town.

WEATHER

WEATHER BROADCAST
Nil

WEATHER SERVICE
Weather information available by telephone from Prince Rupert weather reporting station.

Scale: 2370' to 1 inch.

December 28, 1955

Woodcock

230

Woodcock Runway 20, Summer 1999. Tony Vincenzi Collection

View of Woodcock looking South. Tony Vincenzi Collection

The station received a telegram on August 18 advising them to expect Bolingbroke #9066, which would be arriving to conduct a photo survey of the station. On the following day a Bolingbroke was observed flying eastbound at 5,000 feet.

On August 22, a Beechcraft 18 Expeditor, CF-DTN, arrived at the airfield. The Department of Transport aircraft landed at 3:15 p.m. and DOT inspectors Lawson and Tait assessed the condition of RCAF Woodcock and its facilities. The aircraft departed at 4:10 p.m.

The following day an RCAF Cessna Crane, #8672, landed with S/L A.S. McNeil as a passenger.

On August 24, a telegram was received from RCAF Patricia Bay, Victoria, advising them to expect Bolingbroke #9066 to carry out photographic work over the station.

At 12:20pm on August 25, a Ventura or Lodestar was observed flying west at a considerable height and at 2:00 p.m. on August 26 Bolingbroke #9066 flown by F/O George Williamson was observed above the station.

That morning the Bolingbroke had departed Smithers at 10:00 a.m. and had flown to Terrace to photograph the RCAF station there. #9066 took off from Terrace at 1:15 p.m. proceeding to Woodcock where photographs were taken by WO2 Hackett. The aircraft landed and a short time later took off for the return trip to Smithers.

Another RCAF photographic aircraft, Ventura #2204, passed overhead at 5:40 p.m., September 7 en route to RCAF Annette Island, Alaska. The aircraft returned to land at Woodcock on September 9, and the crew overnighted at the station.

At 4:40 p.m. on September 18, 1943, RCAF Goose #941 made what might be termed a "pit stop" at the Woodcock station. On board were S/L Nass from Western Air Command, Mr. C. Gerow from Air Force Headquarters Ottawa, and Lieutenant Spear of the Canadian Army. The aircraft was flown by F/0 Heaslip and W/O Miller. The Goose departed for Terrace at 5:45 p.m.

1980 view of Woodcock Airfield looking North. CW

On September 22, a DOT aircraft landed at RCAF Woodcock. The Lockheed 12, CF-CCT, arrived at 2:05 p.m. with Mr. A.D. Dan McLean, the Controller of Civil Aviation with the Department of Transport, and J.R. Robertson. Both gentlemen were from Ottawa and were accompanied by two other DOT officials, J.L. Tape and N.G. Clarke of Edmonton. CF-CCT was flown by Jack Hunter and took off at 3:20 p.m.

Scottish Aviation Twin Pioneer C-GNIS at Woodcock in late 1980's.
Dirk Septer Collection

On September 23, an RCAF Cessna Crane landed and departed, and on the following day RCAF Goose #941 arrived.

This was the last Station Diary record except for a notation on September 30, 1943, which reads "Cloudy and cool. Heavy snow noticeable on surrounding mountain peaks."

RCAF Station Woodcock would become No. 15 Staging Unit whose operations were unrecorded in the period October 1, 1943, to March 31, 1944, except for the brief mention of the crash of RCAF Hurricane #5404 on December 21, 1943, at Kitwanga.

At the end of World War II, title of Woodcock airfield passed from the Department of National Defence to the Department of Transport. The 5,200 x 200 foot paved runway continued to be used for emergency purposes only by aircraft experiencing weather-related difficulties en route to Smithers through the narrow Skeena River valley between Terrace and Hazelton.

The airport is located on the north side of the Skeena River approximately four miles from the small community of Cedarvale. Road access to

C-GNIS after being vandalized Spring 1991. Tony Vincenzi Collection

the airport requires crossing the highway bridge at Kitwanga and driving southwest on the north side of the Skeena River for thirteen miles.

In later years Woodcock has been used for sky diving and other parachute sport activities, and aircraft left at the site for extended periods have been vandalized. The westerly end of the airfield runway has been displaced, reducing the length available to 3,350 feet.

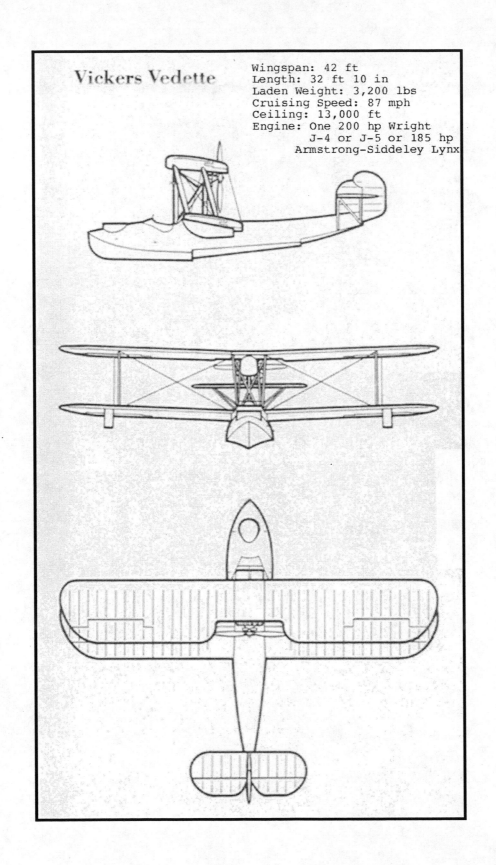

Vickers Vedette

Wingspan: 42 ft
Length: 32 ft 10 in
Laden Weight: 3,200 lbs
Cruising Speed: 87 mph
Ceiling: 13,000 ft
Engine: One 200 hp Wright
        J-4 or J-5 or 185 hp
        Armstrong-Siddeley Lynx

Terrace

The first aircraft to land at Terrace did so on July 5, 1933. This aircraft, a Bellanca CH-300 Pacemaker NC-403-E powered by a Wright J-5 engine, had flown from New York and was on a rescue mission for Jimmy Mattern.

Mattern was making a second attempt to set a record on an around-the-world flight in an easterly direction. His Lockheed Vega, sponsored by the Standard Aviation Oil Company (STANAVO), left New York June 3, 1933, crossing the Atlantic reaching landfall in Norway then on to Moscow and across Siberia planning to land in Nome, Alaska. However, poor weather forced him to turn around. His Pratt and Whitney Wasp engine began losing oil pressure and he was forced to land on the Siberian tundra near the village of Anadyr.

Mattern waited for over two weeks with his damaged Vega until rescued by a group of Eskimos. Mattern was then picked up by the Soviet aviator Sigismund Levanevsky who flew him to Nome, Alaska, in a Russian Dornier-Wahl flying boat.

Bellanca NC-403E at the Frank Brothers hayfield at Terrace, mid July 1933.
Donald S. Cooper Collection

Meanwhile, in New York the Mattern relief expedition was organized, sponsored largely by the King's Brewery of New York, with pilot William Alexander and two air mechanics, Fred Fetterman and a brewery representative, and Thomas Abbey who was a policeman.

On July 5, 1933, with no knowledge of the route ahead, the Bellanca flew from Edmonton westbound making stops for fuel at Jasper, Prince George, and Smithers, and then turned northward at Hazelton intending to follow the old telegraph line toward Telegraph Creek. The flight ran into low cloud and fog in the mountainous passage

Ivan Frank drives team and mower alongside BellancaNC-403E, the first aircraft at Terrace, July 1933. Donald S. Cooper Collection

and returned via Juneau where they arrived at 7:00 p.m. July 25, 1933.

Later Ellis flew the group to Terrace, where he landed the Vega on Lake Lakelse. Mattern was then taken by car back to the Frank Brothers' hay field, as there was concern about the takeoff at the field. Ellis then flew to Hazelton in the Vega with the expedition, and Mattern alone flew the Bellanca to the field at Hazelton as it was believed that this location would better accommodate the takeoff of the loaded Bellanca.

and Alexander decided to turn back and follow the Skeena River to the coast.

Arriving over Prince Rupert they hunted for a place to land the Bellanca, circling over the city. Believing the plane to be in trouble, City authorities cleared the main street for a possible emergency landing. However, Alexander instead decided to fly east again and arrived at Terrace. He selected a large hay field and made a good landing on the bench land belonging to the Frank Brothers Dairy. At this point the group did not know that Mattern was down in Siberia, but after several days of waiting for improved weather the message came that Mattern was now in Alaska.

The expedition arranged to get a ride on the Grand Trunk Pacific Railway gas speeder to Prince Rupert, where two members of the group managed to get a ride in a Junkers on floats bound for Juneau. In Juneau, they chartered Alaska Southern Airways' Lockheed Vega, NC-366H "Chicago", flown by Bob Ellis and Murrell Sasseen, who flew them via White Pass and Burwash, Y.T., to Nome. They picked up Mattern

Terrace pioneer Don Cooper recalls that prior to the Bellanca's takeoff it had been arranged that Frank Brothers Dairy would cut the hay in the field, take out two fences, and cut down several trees that were in the departure path. Mattern was then able to depart the Terrace field without incident.

The Bellanca flew to Prince George and eventually to Toronto, where the group was met by another Vega which STANAVO had painted to match the aircraft crashed in Siberia. Flying this new aircraft, Mattern returned to New York where he received a tumultuous welcome.

When Jimmy Mattern got his pilot licence it was endorsed by Orville Wright. When Neil Armstrong, a personal friend of Mattern, went to the moon, he took Mattern's licence with him and it was inscribed "Carried to Tranquility Base, Moon. Apollo 11, July 16-24, 1969" and was signed by Neil Armstrong and Buzz Aldrin.

There is a side story to pilot Will Alexander's 1933 visit to Terrace. During the war of 1914-18 he had been a pilot in the United States Air Service and had crashed. Fortunately assistance was close by. A medical attendant at the scene pulled Alexander from the wreck. When the relief party climbed out of the Bellanca at Terrace they were greeted by a group of local men. One of these men was Fred Hall and it was he who had pulled Alexander from his crashed aircraft twenty-six years earlier. Alexander had not been able to thank Hall at the time, but he now presented the Terrace man with his gold watch.

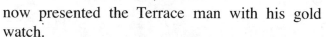
RCAF Station Terrace looking West Southwest, August 26, 1943. RCAF PB-20

The airport at Terrace was completed in mid-1943 by contractors to the Department of National Defence as part of the Home War Establishment.

Previous to the construction, a photographic survey of the Terrace area was completed during the period September 22-26, 1942. The RCAF Norseman #2480 was used, flown by F/Sgt George Williamson with W02 Hackett as photographer. Williamson and Hackett arrived at Lake Lakelse on September 23 and erected a tent near an old Fisheries wharf. The RCAF had created a second line of defence at the lake and had stationed a corporal and two airmen to guard the fuel cache and ammunition dump hidden in the bush near the shore. The small detachment lived in a Forestry cabin and had a telephone line to the Forestry office in Terrace, but Terrace was only manned on Wednesday afternoons. The routine

RCAF Norseman #2480 (seen here on wheels at Pat Bay), landed at Lake Lakelse September 23, 1942. RCAF Photo

was the detachment would give its food order to the Forestry official, who would relay it to an Army camp, who delivered the next day. Needlesss to say, Williamson had no rations and had missed the once a week telephone connection, which meant a sixteen mile walk to town.

The reason for the existence of the Lake Lakelse detachment coincided with orders given to No. 7 (BR) Squadron at Seal Cove in Prince Rupert who were ordered, in the event of an attack, to fly their float equipped Blackburn Shark aircraft to the lake and disperse them along its shoreline.

Blackburn Shark of No. 7(BR) Squadron, Prince Rupert. CW Collection

Terrace Airfield looking North, January 24, 1944. RCAF TE-18

No. 7 (BR) Air Gunner John Moyles tells of a Shark flight he was on with F/Sgt Jerry McKenna. On returning to the coast from patrol, they encountered dense fog but were able to find the mouth of the Skeena River. The patrol continued up the river in the fog and managed to make a safe landing at Lake Lakelse. At their landing site they discovered lots of fuel and a dilapidated cabin with a food cache that consisted of cans of pork and beans and stale coffee. McKenna and Moyles sat out the weather for three days and, except for the effect of the bean diet, Moyles recalls that it was a nice holiday.

After the completion of RCAF Station Terrace, two squadrons were stationed there. No. 135 (F) Fighter Squadron Hurricanes were based there from November 17, 1943, to March 11, 1944. No. 149 (BR) Squadron's Lockheed Vega Ventura aircraft were on site from November 18, 1943, until March 15, 1944. The Squadron's last patrol from Terrace occurred February 19, 1944, in Ventura 2204 flown by F/L Watts and his crew.

From June 22-27, 1944, an 8 (BR) Squadron detachment was stationed at Terrace on exercises with the unit's Ventura G.R. MK4 aircraft.

In November 1944, due to heavy losses in Canadian infantry units in Europe, the Canadian government reluctantly approved an overseas posting of army conscripts who had signed on for home front duties only. Known as the "Zombies", this group was supported by extreme right-wing political and church leaders. Isolated incidents occurred across the country, but the worst was at Terrace where 1,600 men of the 15th Infantry Brigade seized arms and mutinied, taking control of the Army camp on November 25 and 26, 1944.

On November 28, the Brigade Commander requested assistance from the RCAF to demonstrate to the mutineers that force was at hand. Western Air Command dispatched eight Lockheed Vega Venturas from 8 (BR) Squadron and based them at Smithers in case the situation got out of hand. The aircraft were unarmed, but an accompanying Dakota (DC-3) transported the ground crews and an appropriate selection of munitions. However, the following day the 15th Brigade's Senior Officers were able to regain control and diffused a potentially ugly situation.

There were 1,284 officers and men at the station in 1945. With the end of World War II, the RCAF turned over operation of the Terrace Airport to the

Hawker Hurricanes of No. 135(f) Squandron RCAF were stationed at Terrace November 17, 1943 - March 11,1944.
RCAF photo

Twelve Lockheed-Vega Ventura G.R.MKV's of No. 149(B) Squadron RCAF were at Terrace from November 18, 1943 - March 15, 1944. RCAF Photo

Department of Transport in 1946, and a temporary licence for day operations only was issued April 15, 1946, followed on July 8, 1947, with a permanent licence.

May 2, 1946, the Terrace Flying Club purchased de Haviland DH-82C Tiger Moth serial #655 from the War Assets Disposal Corporation. It was assigned registration CF-CHY. The club sold the Moth on March 2, 1948.

Terrace

Inaugural flight of Central B.C. Airways flight from Terrace to Prince George May 2, 1951, with Avro Anson Mk5 CF-GDW flown by Harry Taylor, Madge and Russ Baker are at centre. C.A.I. Archives

Madge Baker went along to take care of dignitaries and the press en route.

Canadian Pacific Airlines also began scheduled service in 1951 and, at the same time, winter maintenance resumed and the airport was again licenced for night operation.

A late 1970's air photo of Terrace looking North. CW

The electric-flame path, a night-landing system, used by the RCAF was discontinued and winter maintenance was also discontinued in 1949.

On May 2, 1951, Russ Baker's Central B.C. Airways commenced its first scheduled service from Terrace to Prince George. CBCA acquired an eleven passenger World War II Avro Anson MkV for the service, flown initially by Harry Taylor. On the inaugural flight, Russ and wife

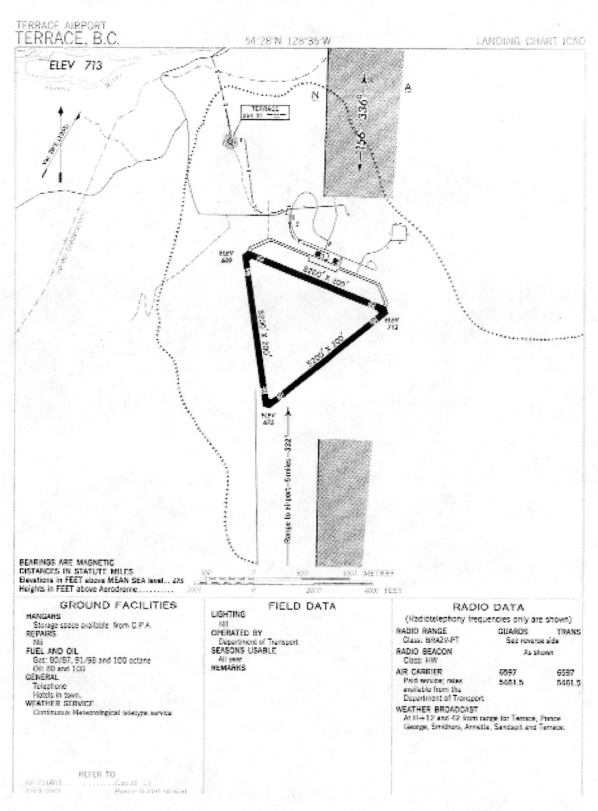

ELEV 713

BEARINGS ARE MAGNETIC
DISTANCES IN STATUTE MILES
Elevations in FEET above MEAN SEA level... 475
Heights in FEET above Aerodrome..........

GROUND FACILITIES

HANGARS
Storage space available from C.P.A.
REPAIRS
Nil
FUEL AND OIL
Gas: 80/87, 91/98 and 100 octane
Oil 80 and 100
GENERAL
Telephone
Hotels in town.
WEATHER SERVICE
Continuous Meteorological teletype service

REFER TO

FIELD DATA

LIGHTING
Nil
OPERATED BY
Department of Transport
SEASONS USABLE
All year
REMARKS

RADIO DATA
(Radiotelephony frequencies only are shown)

	GUARDS	TRANS
RADIO RANGE Class: SRA2V-FT	See reverse side	
RADIO BEACON Class: HW	As shown	
AIR CARRIER Paid service; rates available from the Department of Transport	6597 5461.5	6597 5461.5

WEATHER BROADCAST
At H+12 and 42 from range for Terrace, Prince George, Smithers, Annette, Sandspit and Terrace.

March 16, 1956

Terrace

241

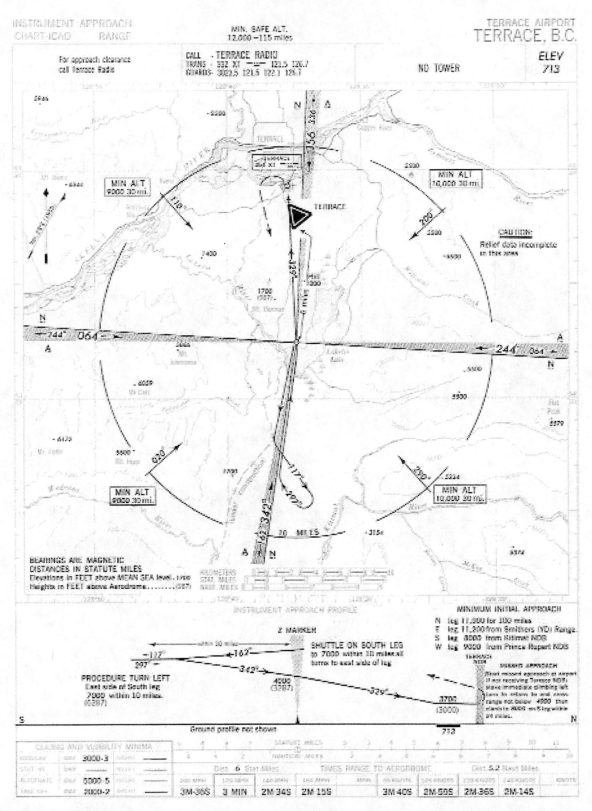

March 16, 1956

Terrace

242

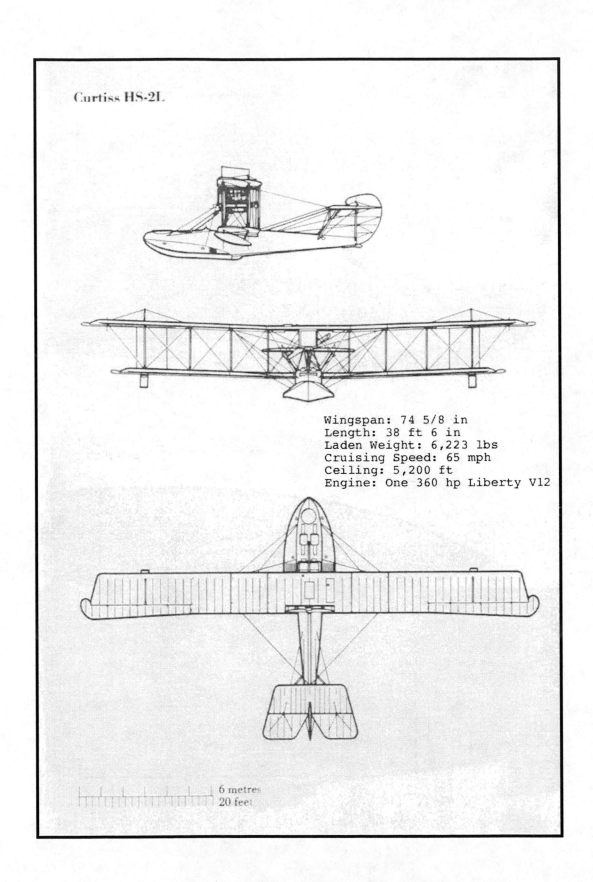

Curtiss HS-2L

Wingspan: 74 5/8 in
Length: 38 ft 6 in
Laden Weight: 6,223 lbs
Cruising Speed: 65 mph
Ceiling: 5,200 ft
Engine: One 360 hp Liberty V12

6 metres
20 feet

Terrace

242

Prince Rupert

It was August 1961 before Prince Rupert had its first airport. It was built by the Federal Government on Digby Island on the west side of Prince Rupert Harbour, across from the city itself.

But the presence of aviation in this city goes back forty years previous, to 1921, and has been continuous from that date.

The Prince Rupert Daily News edition of September 5, 1921, announced the arrival of the first aircraft "*not glorying over the air with her man-made wings, but riding on an ugly old flat car and reduced to the earthly methods of locomotion did the first airplane ever to come to this city reach here at 5:30 last evening.*"

Clarence O. Prest, formerly of Buffalo, New York, but now living in Las Vegas, set out from Nevada in his war-surplus trainer, a Curtiss JN-4 "Jenny", in an attempt to fly from Mexico to Siberia. His aircraft,

"Ollie" Prest's reassembled JN-4 "Polar Bear" at Acropolis Hill, Prince Rupert, September 13, 1921. P.R. Archives

"Polar Bear" over-flies Prince Rupert. P.R. Archives

"Polar Bear" on take-off across bridge joining two tennis courts, September 13, 1921. P.R. Archives

Prest's JN-4 on short final at Acropolis Hill landing ground, September 1921. P.R. Archives

on a local flight, forcing him to land in a field next to the Skeena River. After local repairs were made he shipped the Polar Bear to Prince Rupert on the Grand Trunk Pacific Railway on September 1, 1921.

Prest planned to use the railway docks at the coastal city to take off on his next leg to Wrangell, Alaska. However, the City Fathers asked Prest to delay his departure so that he could partake in the city's Agricultural and Industrial Exhibition, which would take place the following week commencing September 13 on Acropolis Hill, now known as Roosevelt Park.

A tennis court and playing field were linked together for the event with a planked bridge across a small gully. This proved to be sufficient for Prest to take off, but he was concerned about his ability to stop on landing as the Polar Bear had no brakes. A local pioneer, George Frizzel, came up with a solution - by stringing a seine net across the field to stop the Jenny, if need be.

christened the "Polar Bear", entered Canada on August 8, 1921, and he leisurely proceeded to barnstorm his way northward toward his goal.

By the latter part of August 1921 he was in Hazelton, but he had an engine failure on takeoff

The promoters of the celebrations and the spectators were thrilled by the event in which a series of flights were successfully completed for two days. However, on the last flight of the second day Prest ran into the seine net and into the rocks at the end of the field, breaking his propeller and damaging a wing.

To add insult to injury, before Prest could complete his series of exhibition flights he was arrested and jailed for participating in "gainful activities", referring to his barnstorming and giving joy rides in a multitude of B.C. and Alberta towns.

Fortunately, Prince Rupert's City Fathers were able to intervene on Prest's behalf and he was released from jail.

Prest ordered a new propeller from Seattle, Washington, which arrived by steamship. On September 22, 1921, Prest departed for Wrangell but returned due to poor weather. Then, on September 26, a storm hit the city and during the night the Polar Bear broke loose from its tie-downs and was badly damaged. Prest was forced to cancel his plans, but on leaving by steamship for the south he is quoted as remarking that he "will be back next year."

"Ollie" Prest poses with "Polar Bear" in front of seine net on Acropolis Hill, September 1921. P.R. Archives

The "Polar Bear" over runs on landing and hits seine net, September 13, 1921. P.R. Archives

The second aircraft to arrive in Prince Rupert was a flying boat. Lieutenant Roy Jones had served as a pilot with the United States Air Service during World War I. After being discharged, Jones purchased the hull of a Curtiss MF Seagull Serial #5822 from the United States Navy and also bought a 180 HP Hispano-Suiza (Hisso) engine from the US Army. These were shipped to Seattle, Washington's Lake Union, where with the help of Bill Boeing and Eddie Hubbard, Jones' flying boat was assembled. It was subsequently registered in Canada as N-ABCS.

The "Polar Bear" after windstorm damaged it, September 26, 1921. P.R. Archives

The first aircraft to fly up the BC Coast, a Curtiss MF Flying Boat christened "Northbird" and given Canadian registration N-ABCS (via Underwriters Laboratories) although of U.S. ownership. P.R. Archives

Monday, July 17, where after clearing customs they left for Alaska.

Another aircraft visited during the early summer of 1922 - the German-built Junkers-Larsen JL-6, G-CADP "Vic". The aircraft was owned by the Railway Employees Investment and Industrial Association Ltd. and was operated from Hazelton for prospecting and exploration purposes. ADP was flown by Major George "Tommy" Thompson who two years earlier had flown the last segment of the 1920 Trans Canada Flight from Calgary to Vancouver. The "Vic" had an interesting, and latterly, checkered history. (see Hazelton and Prince George)

Prince Rupert had been selected as a sub-base of the Jericho Beach Air Station to enable that Station's aircraft to provide air transport to the Department of Fisheries and make aerial inspections of the area.

Jones had worked for the Standard Oil Company in Alaska before the war and his intention now was to start an airline in southeast Alaska. Jones christened his aircraft the "Northbird" and he, in company of his air mechanic Jerry Smith, left Seattle in early July 1922 for Ketchikan. They made stops for fuel along the way arriving in Prince Rupert on

The first Canadian aircraft to fly up the coast was a Curtiss HS-2L, G-CYDX, which departed Jericho Beach early on July 23, 1923, making stops at Alert Bay, Bella Bella, and possibly Swanson Bay, arriving at Prince Rupert at 5:00 p.m. The flying boat was flown by Squadron Leader Earl Godfrey, with Harold Davenport as crewman.

Junkers JL-6 G-CADP flown by "Tommy" Thompson Taxi's in Prince Rupert Harbour, Summer 1922.
P.R. Archives

Junkers "ADP" docks at Prince Rupert, 1922

The first Canadian aircraft to fly the coast to Prince Rupert was G-CYDX, a Curtiss HS-2L flown by S/L Earl Godfrey, from the Jericho Beach Air Station, July 23, 1923.
P.R. Archives

Prince Rupert

RCAF Station Prince Rupert at Seal Cove looking West.
RCAF PR-819

proved to be a farsighted decision as the cove was used continuously by first the Airforce and later commercial operations and is still in use today. Lt. McLeod made his first flight around the Queen Charlotte Islands from Seal Cove on August 29, 1923.

After the success of the New York to Nome flight of 1920, General William Billy Mitchell, Assistant Chief of the United States Air Service, conceived of the idea of a world flight as a way of getting public respect and recognition, as well as congressional funding for his struggling air service.

The aircraft chosen for this flight were five Douglas DWC "World Cruisers". Four of the aircraft would take part and one would be held in reserve. The DWCs were two-place aircraft powered by 450 horsepower Liberty engines, each holding 465 US gallons of fuel, 30 gallons of oil, and 5 gallons of water for the cooling system.

It was planned to start the event at Seattle, Washington, where the aircraft would be equipped with floats at the Sand Point Naval Air Station after being delivered from Santa Monica, California. The four aircraft, christened Seattle, Chicago, New Orleans, and Boston, finally took off on April 6, 1924, and flew for eight hours and ten minutes non-stop for 650 miles to Prince Rupert. While flying up the inside passage in poor weather, two of the aircraft came close to colliding with a coastal steamer. However, all arrived safely with the exception of

Three of the four Douglas World Cruisers of U.S. Air Service moored in Prince Rupert Harbour, April 6, 1924. P.R. Archives

Godfrey was met by Lieutenant Earl McLeod, who had arrived earlier by train. McLeod would be the pilot on YDX for the summer and Godfrey returned to Vancouver by coastal steamer. McLeod wasted no time in setting up a base of operations at Seal Cove adjacent to the city downtown area. His selection of Seal Cove

the Seattle flown by Major Martin, which sustained damage to the float struts while landing in a snowstorm at Prince Rupert.

Repairs were undertaken locally by Prince Rupert workmen who were able to fabricate new Sitka spruce struts milled at a local mill. The City Fathers hosted the pilots and crewmen of the flight at a civic banquet. The four DWCs left on April 10, 1924, for Sitka, Alaska, the Aleutian Islands, Japan, India, Hungary, London, Iceland, and back to the Sand Point Naval Air Station in Seattle, Washington, after a flight of 175 days and 27,553 miles.

An interesting sidelight to the DWCs visit to Prince Rupert occurred when a local wag, only known to us as Jack, set himself up as an air service. However, he lacked an aircraft and seemed to rely heavily on bottled courage.

In 1924, the Jericho Beach Detachment again arrived at Seal Cove for the fishing season, with F/O Earl McLeod and Harold Davenport flying HS-2L, G-CYBB, and a second HS-2L, G-CYEB, flown by F/O A.H. Hull and crewman Norman Terry.

McLeod again visited the Queen Charlotte Islands during the summer and on his return to Prince Rupert had to make an emergency landing on Hecate Strait not far from Bonila Island.

McLeod explains the situation.

The problem was "due to a broken connecting rod that tore a circular hole, several inches in diameter, in

HS-2L Flying Boat G-CYEB at Port Edward. P.R. Archives

our crank case. Davenport was able to disconnect the connecting rod, place the piston in a safe position, and using the only material available to us, plugged the hole by soaking a quantity of cleaning cloths with shellac, using a kind of tourniquet to hold the improvised material in place. When the shellac hardened, the repair proved successful, and we completed our season's flying, on the remaining eleven cylinders, without trouble."

Earl McLeod was again in charge of operations at Prince Rupert in 1925 flying HS-2L G-CYGA, with F/O A.H. Hull flying HS-2L G-CYBU, as well as a third HS-2L for photographic operations, G-CYGM, flown by F/O A.L. Laurie. For some reason the RCAF detachment was unable to use Seal Cove that year and instead located their base at Casey Cove on Digby Island across Prince Rupert Harbour from the City.

The detachment was also assigned a fourth pilot, F/L F.J. Mawdesley, and later in the season the detachment was inspected by the RCAF Chief of Air Staff Group Captain J.S. Scott. The RCAF did not continue their Fisheries patrols at Prince Rupert beyond the 1925 fishing season. Instead that function was turned over to a private enterprise, Pacific Airways Ltd., operated by Major

Prince Rupert

Vickers Viking G-CAEB of the Dease Lake Mining Expedition, at Prince Rupert May 1925. P.R. Archives

In May 1925, an aircraft arrived at Prince Rupert by train. The Vickers Viking IV, G-CAEB, had been leased from Laurentide Air Services of Montreal by American mining interests known as the Dease Lake Mining Company. On their arrival at Prince Rupert, the aircraft was assembled and flown to Wrangell, Alaska, by the two pilots, Jack Caldwell and J. Scott Williams. At Wrangell they picked up mining engineers and equipment and flew up the Stikine River to Telegraph Creek, Dease Lake, and Laird River, where they spent the summer prospecting before returning to Wrangell, arriving back at Prince Rupert October 3, 1925.

In 1930, a local pilot, Desmond Murphy, incorporated Northern B.C. Airways Ltd. at the city, raising capital by selling $100 shares. One of these investors was Doctor R.G. Large, formerly of Bella Bella now practicing in Prince Rupert. Once enough capital was raised, Murphy purchased a float equipped 1929 de Haviland DH-60M Gipsy Moth, CF-AAB, from

Northern BC Airways de Havilland DH-60M CF-AAB, Spring 1931. P.R. Archives

D.R. Don MacLaren, a former Royal Flying Corp ace. Pacific Airways Ltd. was later acquired by Western Canada Airways, and this operation was eventually absorbed by Canadian Airways Ltd. These operations were based at Swanson Bay in Princess Royal Channel, 100 miles south of Prince Rupert.

the Yarrow Aircraft Corporation of Vancouver on February 28, 1931. The aircraft had previously been used on Provincial Forestry contracts at Nelson. Northern B.C. Airways established itself with a hangar, office, and workshop, on a barge on the waterfront of the city.

The aircraft later crashed while on a mercy flight to the Langara Island lighthouse. The pilot, Des Murphy, was not seriously injured. The wreckage was later sold June 26, 1933, to T. Jones of Vancouver.

On May 20, 1931, Northern B.C. Airways purchased a damaged Stinson SM-LFS Detroiter, CF-AMD serial #M-523, from Dominion Airways at Vancouver. The aircraft had crashed at Butedale after engine failure. There is no record of its repair and use at Prince Rupert. Des Murphy later joined the Department of Transport and became Superintendent of Air Services at Vancouver.

The propeller of Murphy's Gipsy Moth, CF-AAB, was later donated to the Prince Rupert City and Regional Archives, where it remains to this day.

Prince Rupert would host a unique around-the-world flight which arrived in the city August 18, 1932. The German registered twin-engine flying boat Dornier Wal D-2053 was flown by Captain Wolfgang Von Gronau, co-piloted by Ghert Von Roth, with Engineer Franz "Frankie" Hack, and Wireless Operator Fritz Albrecht.

Von Gronau had flown across the Atlantic Ocean twice before, in 1930 and 1931, from his

Northern BC Airways of Prince Rupert purchased this Stinson SM-IFS Detroiter CF-AMD, shown here at Vancouver. Attwood Collection

RCAF Vickers Vancouver #902 of No.4 (FB) Squadron at Seal Cove on detached duty from Jericho Beach during mid 1930's. P.R. Archives

base at List on the Island of Sylt near the Danish border. The flight of 1931 also used the same Dornier as on this 1932 around-the-world attempt, the aircraft being christened the Gronland-Wal (The Greenland Whale). They had arrived over the Labrador coast July 25 and proceeded westbound. By August 13, 1932, they arrived at the RCAF Station Cormorant Lake,

Prince Rupert

253

Dornier "Wal" D-2053 flown by Wolfgang Von Gronau at Prince Rupert on a Round-The-World flight. P.R. Archives

Manitoba, and on the 16th reached Lac La Biche, northeast of Edmonton, Alberta. Then on the 18th they flew direct to Prince Rupert where they remained until August 21, when they left for Juneau, Alaska, Japan, India, and then returning to Germany.

Von Gronau wrote of his experiences in his book "Weltflieger", which is very reminiscent of A Global Aviator 1926-47:

"The flight over the Rocky Mountains to Prince Rupert on the Pacific coast, was much easier than we had thought it would be. In just eight hours we covered the entire distance.

First there were dangerous, endless forests, then lakes - almost as big as a sea - and an occasional trapper's camp or a fishing cabin.

Coming up to the mountains we encountered a storm. We flew around it over land. The motors ran like clockwork. Then the mountains! There was no end to them. We flew from pass to pass, further and further toward the west. On our map was listed all the kinds of bears that lived in the mountains. In my mind I saw the terrifying grizzlies looking up at us. On the coast the visibility became bad. Flying at an altitude

of fifteen meters (50 feet) we glided into the protected bay at Prince Rupert, British Columbia.

No one came at first, it took quite a while before the representative of Shell Oil found us. We had barely tied up the "Whale" when the fog came down and enveloped everything with that notorious Alaskan weather - a foretaste of what awaited us in the next leg of the journey ahead.

On closer look, Prince Rupert turned out to be a friendly little city with a rich splendor of flowers, in odd contrast to the primeval forest which begins right behind the last houses. The residents were dependent on ship connections or the train which ran twice a week. On the whole they enjoy sufficient affluence. The streets are in good condition, and one sees elegantly dressed women and comfortable hotels. A large sawmill processes the inexhaustible wealth of the forest; and in the cold storage lie frozen some millions of kilograms of the blessings of the sea: salmon, halibut, and herring. For two dollars, a middle-sized bear skin could be had on the streets. We didn't let this offer escape us.

We had before us now that stretch that (Italian Minister for Air Transport) Balbo maintained would be impossible for an aircraft to fly. The warm, moist air of the peaceful ocean, driven by the prevailing westerly winds, collides against the rocky coast, is pushed upwards and condenses through cooling into haze, fog, or rain. Farther north, along the Aleutian chain of islands, it's even worse. There the warm water of the Pacific collides together with the cold water of the Bering Sea, and the residents reckon with two days in every month in which they can see the sun.

But we had to cross it. We intended to fly very cautiously and, when the visibility becomes too bad, to land and wait it out rather than run into a rock face.

Prince Rupert

At least that's what I had in mind. But that's easier said then done, for when we knew that our destination harbor was in the vicinity and we could reach it, we put ourselves, even so, from time to time into situations in which there was no turning back."

On July 5, 1933, a Bellanca CH-300, with American registration NC-403E, arrived over Prince Rupert in the mistaken belief that there was a landing field at the city. After circling the town for some time City officials cleared the main street believing that there was an emergency. However, the pilot decided to head for Terrace where he landed in a hay field. The aircraft had flown from New York and was searching for missing aviator Jimmy Mattern.

On October 14, 1937, W/C Cuff, the Commanding Officer RCAF Jericho Beach, wrote to the Senior Air Officer RCAF Headquarters Ottawa advising of his recommendations for the development of aerodromes and seaplane harbours for RCAF defensive use on the west coast.

W/C Cuff recommended to Ottawa that floating runways be developed at Prince Rupert and Bella Bella. In the reply to Cuff from his chief in Ottawa, it was stated that the National Research Council would undertake tests in this

RCAF Station Prince Rupert looking Northwest. RCAF PR-1130

Fleet 2 CF-ANM of the R.C. Church on its delivery flight to Prince Rupert, March 1938. Jasper Yellowhead Archives

regard. (see Bella Bella in ***Pacific Airways,*** the second book in this series, for details)

Prince Rupert

255

PRINCE RUPERT B.C. (Seaplane)

LOOKING SW

WEATHER
BROADCAST
Nil

METEOROLOGICAL
FACILITIES
Radio reporting station

GROUND FACILITIES	GENERAL INFORMATION	PILOTS NOTES
HANGARS Available **REPAIRS** Minor. **FUEL AND OIL** Gas: 80, 87 and 91, 98 octane Oil: Seasonal grades **MOORINGS** Unknown. **BEACHING** 2 ramps. Dock. **COMMUNICATIONS** Radio. Telephone. Teletype. Telegraph in town **TRANSPORTATION** **ACCOMMODATION** Available in town	**OPERATED BY** City of Prince Rupert **SEASONS USABLE** All year **REMARKS** Aircraft warned to keep 200' S.W. of the buoy on Prince Rupert Side. In Fern Passage maintain high rate of speed to counter currents. Customs port of entry and exit Customs house at Prince Rupert (2 miles)	

February 8, 1956

Prince Rupert

256

PRINCE RUPERT
(Seaplane) B.C.

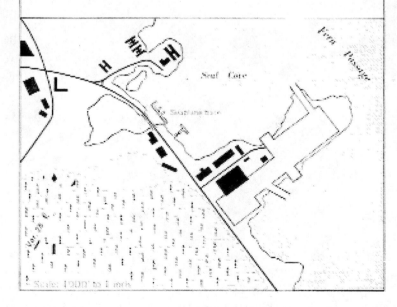

APPROACH PROCEDURE

1. Standard, Visual Flight Rules Approach.
2. Left Hand Circuit.

ELEVATION Sea Level

VARIATION 28° E. (1955)

POSITION

LAT. 54° 20' N.   LONG. 130° 17' W.
Immediately N.E. of city

AERONAUTICAL CHARTS

1:506,880 PRINCE RUPERT - STEWART
1:1,000,000 QUEEN CHARLOTTE ISLANDS 156
(US CHART)

ALIGHTING AREA

Prince Rupert Hbr.: 015° - 195° M: 5 miles
(opposite Seal Cove) 150° - 330° M: 2 miles

LIGHTING

OBSTRUCTIONS (ASL)

No shoals on reefs in alighting area. Rock
in Seal Cove marked with white buoy.
Floating logs and debris.

SEA CONDITIONS

Winter: Occasional 3' swell and decided
chop. Summer: comparatively calm,
considerable glassy water. S.E. winds
give rise to rougher water.
Depth: 120'. Tidal range: 26'
Tidal current: 3 knots
Break up: N.A. Freeze up: N.A.

RADIO DATA

	GUARDS	TRANS
CPA	2917	2917
	5461.5	5461.5

February 8, 1956

Prince Rupert

257

Q.C.A. Stranraer Flying Boat on the slide. CAI Archives

D.H. Rapide CF-BND's final landing, Digby Island July 29, 1949. J. Spillsbury

ered by a Kinner K-5 engine. The aircraft crashed June 6, 1938, on takeoff from Savory Lake, B.C. In 1939 Prince Rupert had the pleasure of another aircraft landing on wheels at the city. William Archibald, a retired Cominco mining manager at Trail, needed to see Cominco representative Mr. Dunn at the city. Archibald had been to Prince Rupert many times before, travelling by steamship from Vancouver. This time he had purchased a tide book and had flown in from Trail landing on the mud flats at low tide, then picking up Dunn and taking off again. Word of Archibald's transgression reached the Department of Transport, who in turn wrote to him demanding an explanation as to why they had not been informed that the aircraft had been mounted on floats. Several months later Archibald arrived at the DOT office in Vancouver to explain that he had landed on wheels.

With the coming of World War II, Prince Rupert's RCAF Station at Seal Cove grew one hundred fold. Number 9 (BR) Squadron was stationed there first with Blackburn Shark single engine seaplanes and later with Stranraer, Catalina, and Canso aircraft, the story of which is detailed in Jericho Beach And The West Coast Flying Boat Stations by this author.

On March 12, 1938, the Roman Catholic Episcopal Corporation of Prince Rupert acquired a 1930 Fleet Model 2, CF-ANM, on floats, pow-

QCA Stranraer "BYL" inflight before its disappearance Augusut 31, 1946.
J. Spillsbury

At the end of the war, the City of Prince Rupert became responsible for the seaplane facility at Seal Cove, and in March of 1946 a weekly scheduled flight was started by Queen Charlotte Airlines using Stranraer aircraft obtained surplus from the RCAF via the War Assets Disposal Corporation.

QCA's first two Stranraer's were CF-BYJ "Haida Queen" and CF-BYL "Skeena Queen". BYL was based at Prince Rupert's Seal Cove at the former RCAF Station and was christened there on July 23, 1946. The aircraft was painted black with yellow wings and was unofficially known as "the flying coffin".

On August 31, a call was received for a medivac flight to Stewart an hour after grounding time, but BYL's crew elected to go anyway as the weather was clear and the aircraft departed Prince Rupert at 7:07 p.m. The aircraft picked up a sick child at Stewart and was back over Prince Rupert at 8:50 p.m. However, as often happens on the north coast, a blanket of fog had enveloped the city and its harbour.

BYL's engines were heard overhead but it was not seen, and at 9:10 p.m. it was spotted

Remains of CF-BND, a de Havilland DH-89A Rapide of Q.C.A., that crashed at Digby IslandJuly 29, 1949. CW

by a timber cruiser at Work Inlet and again at Port Simpson seventeen miles northwest of Prince Rupert.

This was the last report of BYL's whereabouts. The pilot's body was later found and his watch had stopped at 9:23 p.m. The black Stranraer had probably struck either the water or a log and had broken up. Much later, parts of the aircraft were discovered after they became entangled in a fishing boat's gear.

At the beginning of 1947, Canadian Pacific Airlines began regular flights to the city using Canso aircraft, which also utilized Seal Cove.

The need for an airport at Prince Rupert was again emphasized when a light aircraft made a successful emergency landing on the ramp at Seal Cove. A feat that has been repeated many times. This author was scheduled to deliver a wheel-equipped Aeronca 7AC Champion, CF-HSR, to the city in mid-November 1954 when it was purchased from Vancouver operator Pacific Wings, but weather intervened and I left the aircraft at Smithers. In 1955 the Federal Government agreed to conduct a survey for the establishment of an airport at the city and selected a site on Digby Island, which was completed in August 1961.

The author has landed at Prince Rupert many times over the years, in float planes and amphibians at Seal Cove and wheel aircraft at Digby Island, including Mitsubishi MU-2F CF-AMP, Beech 80 "Queen Air" CF-FAB, "King Air" CF-MHJ, Aero Commander 680 CF-SNC, Turbo Commander 680T CF-FEO, and Jet Commander (Westwind) CF-FBC.

Prince Rupert's Digby Island Airfield looking North. CW

DH Gypsy six engine from Rapide CF-BND at Seal Cove 1998. CW

CPA Canso "A" CF-CRV was a frequent visitor to Seal Cove after 1947. CAI Archives

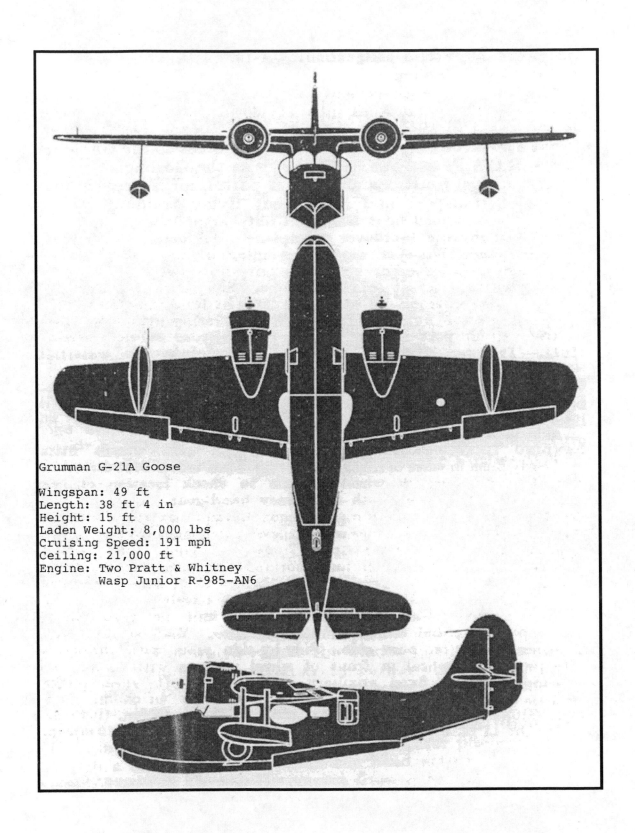

Grumman G-21A Goose

Wingspan: 49 ft
Length: 38 ft 4 in
Height: 15 ft
Laden Weight: 8,000 lbs
Cruising Speed: 191 mph
Ceiling: 21,000 ft
Engine: Two Pratt & Whitney
        Wasp Junior R-985-AN6

Stewart

During September 1923, Alaskan pilot Roy Franklin Jones landed his Curtiss MF flying boat christened "Northbird" at the head of the Portland Canal next to the twin cities of Hyder, Alaska, and Stewart, B.C.

Jones, who had started the first air service in southeast Alaska at Ketchikan in 1922, had a flair for the dramatic and announced his arrival by performing a chandelle followed by a prolonged slide-slip to his landing. This action cooled the cylinders on the down side of his 180 horsepowered Hispano-Suiza engine and warped the valves. Fortunately, a resourceful mechanic, Frank Wadman, was along on the flight and borrowed tools from the nearby Premier Mine and made a valve grinding compound from the glass of broken whiskey bottles mixed with oil. Two days later Jones, Wadman, and the two mining engineers who had chartered the flight were off to Ketchikan.

Friday, May 24, 1929: Grand Forks Gazette editorial reports that the City of Stewart is investigating a community airfield.

August 1929: Western Canada Airways opened a base at Stewart with a Junkers W-34 on floats,

Roy F. Jones flew Curtiss MF Flying Boat N-ABCS "Northbird" from Ketchikan to Hyder, Alaska, two miles from Stewart, in September 1922.
Jim Ruotsala Collection

CF-ABK, flown by Walter Gilbert who flew supplies to a mine on the Unuk River in Alaska. On September 10, 1929, Gilbert flew WCA's Boeing B-lE, CF-ABB, from Stewart to Burns Lake where he picked up the Cominco Mine Manager who had been mauled by a bear. Gilbert flew him to Vancouver.

Pioneer aviator Walter Gilbert tells of his time at Stewart in his book "Arctic Pilot":

"After the winter work at The Pas, I spent the summer between the Fisheries Patrol on the British Columbia coast and exploration and freighting to a

Stewart

263

new gold-bearing area on the Unak River in the mountains of Alaska.

The patrol was interesting work, but the Alaskan country and people meant more to me as the flights were bringing me nearer and nearer to the north.

To the west (of Stewart), the towering snow peaks of Alaska stand in seemingly unbroken array against the vivid blue of the sky. It is along the Canadian fringe of the ranges that great mineral discoveries may be made.

Prospects discovered in 1929 along the route we had just followed seemed to couple up remarkably well with those now under development on the Upper Taku River, 100 miles to the north.

Midway between, near the source of the Iskut and Unuk Rivers, prospectors, who years ago won their way up these streams, discovered valuable showings

Western Canada Airways based Junkers W-23 CF-ABK at Stewart during August 1929. PAC PA-88951

of copper and gold. Their very inaccessibility at that time made them seem so worthless that no precise record of their location was kept - only a tantalizing tale of the richness of the strikes.

Until the summer of 1929, lack of adequate transportation had paralyzed further opening up of the more remote parts of that country. Travel on foot entailed great hardship. There were few horse trails and their construction was very expensive. Game was not plentiful; the traveller could not economically "live off the country."

In July 1929, owing to the initiative of a few far-seeing business men of the Portland Canal district, air transportation came to this "Newest North." The arduous trip over the fifty-five miles of ice and rock into the valleys north of Bowser Lake, hitherto involving at least seventeen days of toil, could then be made in forty-five minutes. The exploratory trip into the Teigen Lakes, hitherto only a hoped-for possibility, occupied little over two hours. The old-timers, who for years had struggled to reach the "promised land" of those northern valleys, accepted the new form of transportation without a quibble.

Two of these old-timers, Tim Williams and C.H. Allen, had been prospecting for a mining company all the summer, and it was decided that I should take them with me as guides while I planned a route for future visits by air. We were to go into Treaty Creek where they had been working.

My guides took me by way of Meziadin and Bowser Lakes, as it was the route with which they were familiar. I shall never forget the sight of old Williams peering constantly over the side, his battered hat clutched

Walter Gilbert flew Boeing B-1E CF-ABB "Pintail" from Stewart to Burns Lake September 10, 1929. CAI Collection

in one hand, the slip-stream buffeting his straggling grey whiskers. His "There's one day!" and "There's another day!" as the miles of his many and weary previous journeys streamed past us, could not fail to impress me with an idea of what air transportation meant to these people.

The individual prospector was converted to the new order of things. All that was necessary now was an influx of men and capital behind him in his efforts

When we completed that pioneer trip we landed on a lake at the head of Treaty Creek. Some time later I heard that it was named "Gilbert Lake," and that little bit of news constituted one of my early flying thrills with the company."

On October 28, 1930, Alaska Washington Airways in Seattle dispatched pilot Robin Pat Renehan in Lockheed Vega NC-103W named the

Stewart

265

Two Jericho Beach based RCAF Fairchild FC-2W's, G-CYXN and YXQ, searched Portland Canal for missing aviator Pat Renehan November 1930. Attwood Coll.

Alaska Washington Airways Lockheed Vega NC-657E came up Portland Canal to Stewart in search of Pat Renehan, November 13, 1930. Crosson Coll.

in Grenville Channel, nothing else was known of the Vega's position.

A new search was started. Anscel Eckmann, Chief Pilot for Alaska Washington, left Seattle on November 3 searching south of Prince Rupert. Two RCAF Fairchilds FC-2Ws from Jericho Beach Air Station at Vancouver arrived at Prince Rupert on Tuesday, November 11, and met Eckmann there. The two Fairchilds began a search of the Portland Canal to Stewart following a report of wreckage. Flight Lieutenant L.E. Phinney and Flying Officer C.R. Dunlop found nothing and, in company of observers Sergeant A.H. Warner and Corporals W.C. Atwood and M. Squires, returned to Prince Rupert.

The logbook of Corporal William Cecil Atwood shows that he and F/O Dunlop flew Fairchild G-CYXQ on the search until November 28, when they returned to Comox Lake.

"Skagway" to help in the search for missing Canadian pilot Paddy Burke who was unreported in Junkers F-13 CF-AMX in the upper reaches of the Liard River.

Renahan, Frank Hatcher his mechanic, and prospector Sam Clerf failed to arrive at Prince Rupert and, other than a sighting by a fisherman

In response to a report of a body seen in the Portland Canal at Stewart, Anscel Eckmann flew his Company's Vega "Wrangel" NC-657E to Hyder, Alaska, which adjoins Stewart, B.C. Eckmann departed Ketchikan at 9:00 a.m. November 13, 1930, landing amid ice flows at the head of the canal. Here he was met by B.C. Provincial Police Sergeant

Pacific Airways Junkers F-13 CF-AMX was based at Stewart during Summer 1933. J. Ruotsala

Potterton, who informed the pilot that the body was a local man. Eckmann returned to Ketchikan at 5:00 p.m.

Canadian Airways based the Fokker Universal G-CAIZ, flown by Maurice McGregor, at Stewart during the Summer of 1934. W.C.A.M.

During the summer of 1933, a Pacific Airways Junkers F-13, CF-AMX, was based at Stewart serving the needs of Premier Gold Mines Ltd.

In mid-1934, a Canadian Airways 1928 Fokker Universal, G-CAIZ, powered by a Wright J-5 engine, arrived at Stewart flown by Maurice McGregor with engineer Bill Jacquot. AIZ was hauling supplies and equipment from either Stewart or Hyder into a mine at Tom MacKay Lake, a small lake at 4,000 feet elevation.

The following year William Archibald of the Consolidated Mining Company arrived at Stewart in a de Havilland DH-60 Moth on floats, later leaving for Ketchikan, Alaska.

Central B.C. Airways (CBCA) pilot Ayliffe "Pat" Carey arrived at Stewart at the end of July 1946 with an ex-RCAF Norseman and began work for Tommy McKay on an exploration project behind the Franklin Glacier.

Stewart

267

Junkers ATF after landing at mine, 1953. Dan McIvor

ATF heading inland to glacier, 1953. Dan McIvor

DHC-2 Beaver CF-GYO taking off at Stewart for mine, 1953. Dan McIvor

Beaver "GYO" at mine site above Stewart, 1953. Dan McIvor

On August 26, 1953, an RCAF Norseman MkV on floats, coded GB-M, from Whitehorse landed at the head of the Portland Canal at Stewart, tying up to the Imperial Oil fuel dock. GB-M was participating in a search for an Aeronca Sedan missing on a flight from Atlin to Stewart two days earlier.

Stewart became the supply point for the Granduc Copper Mine about 25 miles north of the town, but the mine was inaccessible except by air and a landing strip was built on top of a 3,000 foot high glacier.

In 1953, Dan McIvor, working for CBCA, began a series of flights in Junkers 33/34 and de Havilland Beavers. McIvor recalled landing at the mine strip and discovering that it was covered with 10 feet of powder snow, requiring him to get

RCAF Norseman GB-M arrived at Stewart from Whitehorse to search for a missing Aeronca Sedan August 26, 1953. Al Hampshire

out his snowshoes and tramp back and forth to compact the snow enough to allow a takeoff.

Soon CBCA became P.W.A. (Pacific Western Airlines) and began flying even larger aircraft into the mine, first DC-3's and later the Curtiss C-46, after considerable improvement to the strip, but still a "hairy" operation.

The two C-46's, CF-HYH and HYI, had been leased by PWA from the Flying Tigers in the USA and had been used on Dew Line operations starting in 1955 with Captains Sheldon Luck and Bert Sechrist. The author flew in both these aircraft while employed with PWA in the Arctic.

CF-MAI was a 1937 Fairchild 82A that Granduc Mines purchased from Associated Air Taxi in Vancouver on November 30, 1954, to support their mining operations near Stewart. On July 28, 1956, the aircraft was air dropping supplies at the Salmon Glacier near the mine when it was caught in a severe downdraft of air, lost control, and crashed into the glacier itself.

PWA Junkers W-34 CF-ATF loading at Stewart for flight to glacier, 1953.
Dan McIvor

The author has landed at Stewart, B.C. many times. On June 23, 1980 in Block Brothers Beechcraft A-90 "King Air" CF-MHJ (**M**ike Guteman, Chief Pilot, **H**enry Block, **J**esus).

Starting August 5, 1987 I made many visits to Stewart in CF-AMP, a Mitsubishi Mu-2B owned by A.L.C. Airlift for whom I was chief pilot.

My last visit to Stewart by air occurred December 21, 1990 in C-GVBO, a Piper Pa-3IT Cheyenne.

CF-HYI, a Curtiss C-46, operated by PWA into the glacier strip behind Stewart in 1961. CW

Pilot Andrew Weicht fuels MU2 from drums at Stewart 1989. CW

Modern air photo of Stewart/Hyder, looking North. CW

GROUND FACILITIES

ELEVATION - 24'

POSITION
LAT. 55º56'N.   LONG. 129º59'W.
Adjacent to town

OPERATED BY
Village of Stewart

REMARKS
Snow compaction in winter

RUNWAYS
DIRT AND GRAVEL

OBSTRUCTIONS (ASL)
Mountains to 8500' in area

Landing area at Stewart 1953. CW

References

A Thousand Shall Fall: Murray Peden; Stoddart Publishing Co.
Aeronca C-2: Jay P. Spenser; Smithsonian Press
Air Board: F.H. Hitchers; National Museum of Man, Ottawa
Airbourne Gottschalk: Ash International
Airbourne From Edmonton: E.L. Miles; Ryerson Press
Alaska Bush Pilots: Archie Satterfield, 1969; Superior Publishing, Seattle
Alaska Flying Expedition, The: Stan Cohen; Pictorial Histories Publishing Co.
Alaskan Aviation History Volume1,2: Robert W. Stevens, 1990; Polynas Press, Des Moines
Aleutian Warriors, The: John Haile Cloe, 1990; Anchorage Chapter, Air force Pictorial Histories
                                        Association & Publishing Co.
And I Shall Fly: Z. Lewis Leigh; Canav Books
Arctic Pilot: W.E. Gilbert & Kathleen Shackleton; Thomas Nelson & Sons
Artic War Birds: Steven E. Mills, 1971; Superior Publishing Company, Seattle
Aviation in Canada: Larry Milberry, 1979; McGraw-Hill Ryerson
Barnstorming to Bush Flying: Peter Corley-Smith, 1989; Sono Nis Press
BC Aviator, The Flight of the Polar Bear; July/August 1992
Behind the Story: Ted Barris; MacMillan Canada
Boeing, An Aircraft Album Number 4: Kenneth Munson & Gordon Swanborough, 1972
Bush Flying to Blind Flying: Peter Corley-Smith; Sono Nis Press
Bush Pilots, The: J.A. Foster; McLelland & Stewart Inc.
Bush Pilots, The: Time-Life Books, 1983; Alexander, Virginia
Bush Pilot with a Brief-case: Ronald A. Keith; Doubleday
Bush to Boardroom: Duncan D. McLaren; Watson & Dwyer Limited
C.A.P. 384, 2nd edition: 1945; RCAF Department of National Defence for Air
Canada Air Pilot : 1955; Surveys and Mapping Branch, Dept. of Mines & Technical Surveys; Ottawa
Canada's Aviation Hall of Fame: 1974; Oil City Press, Calgary
Canada's Aviation Pioneers: Alice Gibson Sutherland. 1978; McGraw-Hill Ryerson
Canada's Flying Heritage: Frank H. Ellis, 1954; University of Toronto Press
Canada's National Aviation Museum: K.M.Molson, 1988; National Museum of Science and Technology
Canada's War in the Air: Leslie Roberts, 1942; Alvah M. Beatty Publications
Canadian Aeronautics: G.A. Fuller/ J.A. Griffin/K.M. Molson, 1983; Canadian Aviation Historical Society
Canadian Aircraft Since 1909: K.M. Molson & H.A. Taylor, 1982; Canada's Wings Inc., Sittsville, Ontario
Canadian Airmen of the First World War: S.F. Wise. 1980; University of Toronto Press
Canadian Civil Aircraft Register (1920-1945): John R. Ellis
Canadian Flying Services Emblems and Insignia 1914-1984: Bill Hampson; published by author
Canadian Military Aircraft Serials and Photographs 1920-1968: J.A. Griffin, 1969;Canadian War Museum

Canadian Pacific Airlines: D.M. Bain, 1987; Kishorn Publications, Calgary
Challenge of the Skies, The: Michael Hartley; Puckrins House
Creation of a National Air Force, The: W.A.B. Douglas, 1986; University of Toronto Press
DeHavilland Aircraft since 1909: A.J. Jackson, 1987; Naval Institute Press
DeHavilland Canada Story: Fred Hotson; Canav Books
December 1941 America's First 25 Days at War: Donald J. Young, 1992; Pictorial Histories Publishing Co.
Double Cross: Shirley Render; Douglas & McIntyre Ltd
Early Flying in British Columbia, in Retrospect: Earl MacLeod, 1972
Ernie Boffa: Florence Whyard; Alaska NW Publishing
Established Landing Fields and Seaplane Bases: 1936, Shell Oil Company

more references

Flight Deck: George Lothian; McGraw-Hill Ryerson Ltd

Flying North, The:Jean Potter; Ballantine Books

Flying Off the Pavement: Link Grindle; Lasenda Publishers

Flying the Alaska Highway: Transport Canada

Flying the Mail: Time-Life Books, 1982; Alexander, Virginia

Forgotten War, The, Volume 1,2,3,4: Stan Cohen; Pictorial Histories Publishing

Fokker Commercial Aircraft: Fokker Aircraft, 1994; Amsterdam-Zuidoost, Holland

Fort Nelson Story, The: Gerry Young; self published

Frank Barr: Dermot Cole; Alaska NW Publishing Co.

General Dynamics Aircraft: John Wegg, 1990; Naval Institute Press

Harvard the North American Trainers in Canada: David Fletcher

History of Canadian Airports: T.M. McGrath, 1992; Transport Canada, Lugus Publications, Ottawa

In Canadian Skies: Frank H. Ellis, 1959;Ryerson Press

In the Shadow of Eagles: Bilberg & Reardon; Alaska NW Books

It Seems Like Only Yesterday: Phillip Smith; McClelland & Stewart Inc.

Janes All the World's Aircraft: C.G. Grey, 1919; Sampson Low & Marston

Janes All the World's Aircraft: C.G. Grey, 1927; Sampson Low & Marston & Co. Ltd.

Janes All the World's Aircraft: C.G. Grey & Leonard Bridgman, 1938; Sampson Low & Marston Co. Ltd.

Janes All the World's Aircraft: Leonard Bridgman,1935, 1941, 1944 ; MacMillan Company

Janes Encyclopedia of Aviation: Michael Taylor, 1980; Portland House

Japan's World War II Balloon Bomb Attacks on North America; R.C. Mikesh, 1973; Smithsonian Institution Press

Jericho Beach and the West Coast Flying Boat Stations: Chris Weicht; MCW Enterprises

Magnificent Distances, The: Dennis Duffy & carol Crane, 1980; British Columbia Provincial Archives

Marine Atlas Volume 2, Port Hardy to Skagway: Frank Morris & W.R. Heath, 1959; Bayless Enterprises

Number 120 Bomber Reconnaissance Squadron: A.J.D. Angus (recollections)

On Track: Skylark Aviation

Outlaw Pilot: James F. Anderson; Writer's Den

Pedigree of Champions – Boeing Since 1916: The Boeing Company

Pilots of the Panhandle: Jim Ruotsala, 1997; Seadome Press, Juneau, Alaska

Pilots to Presidents: Peter Corley-Smith; Sono Nis Prss

Pioneer Bush Pilot: Ira Harkley; University of Washington Press

Pioneering Aviation in the West: Lloyd Bungey, 1992; Hancock House

Plan, The: James N. Williams; Canadian Wings Inc.

Recovery of a Secret Weapon, The: Ray E. Woolston (recollections)

Royal Canadian Air Force at War 1939-1945: Larry Milberry and Hugh Halliday, 1990; CANAV Books

Royal Canadian Air Force Squadrons and Aircraft: S Kostenuk & J. Griffin, 1977; Historical Publication 14, Canadian War Museum, National Museum of Man, Ottawa; Samuel Stevens Hakkert & Co., Toronto & Sarasota

Seaplanes and Flying Boats, An illustrated History of: Maurice Allward; Dorset Press

Seaplanes and Flying Boats, The Illustrated History of: Louis S. Casey & John Batchelor; Phoebus Publishing Co. Ltd.

Silent Seige III: Bert Webber

Sixty Years, the RCAF and CF Air Command 1924-1984: Larry Milberry, 1984; CANAV Books

Sky Riders: Patricia A. Myers; Fifth House Ltd

Snowbird Decades, The: William Paul Ferguson, 1979; Butterworth and Co.

Sourdough Sky: Steven E. Mills Jr., 1970; Bonanza Books, New York

Spirit of the Yukon: June Lunny; Caitlin Press

There shall be Wings: Leslie Roberts, 1959; Clarke Irwin & Co.

Thousand Mile War, The: Brian Garfield, 1969; Bantam Books
Travel Air: Bruce Bissonette, 1996; Aviation Publishing Inc., Destin, Florida
Uncharted Skies: Walter Henry; Reidmore
Up in the Air, 1924-1938, Mary M. Worthylake; self-published, Woodburn, Oregon
Walking on Air: Ted Beaudoin; Paramount House Publishing
Warplanes to Alaska: Blake W. Smith; Hancock House
Washington State Pilots Guide, Washington Division of Aeronautics
Where Eagles Flew: Barb Lawrence & Judy Robb
Wings Across Time: David Collins; Griffin House
Wings for Victory: Spencer Dunmore; McLelland & Stewart Inc.
Wings Over Calgary: Bruce W. Gowans; Historical Society of Alberta
Wings Over Lethbridge: Bruce W. Gowans; Historical Society of Alberta
Wings Over the West: John Condit; Harbour Publishing
Wings Over Washington: David G. Gordon; Museum of Flight
Wingwalkers: Peter Pigott: Harbour Publishing

Periodicals

B.C. Aviator, Sept/Oct, The Flight of the Polar Bear: Jack Schofield, 1992
Canadian Aviation Historical Society Journal: Winter 2002

Index

Index of Aircraft

Index of Aircraft cont.

Military Unit Index

About the Author

Chris Weicht the son of an R.A.F. Officer and former journalist was born at London, England in 1935. In 1948 he immigrated to Vancouver, B.C. with his parents.

In 1949 he joined an Air Cadet Squadron and rose through the ranks to Warrant Officer. In 1952 he was presented his wings on completion of a flight scholarship. In 1953 he enlisted in the R.C.A.F. at Jericho Beach, later serving at R.C.A.F Station Comox.

In 1956 Chris was hired by Pacific Western Airlines and served on D.E.W. Line operations in the North West Territories.

A vision problem caused Chris to leave aviation in 1960, but he utilized this time to advance his education and four years later he was hired in a management position with and oil company. Chris was advised to apply in the United States for an F.A.A. licence. This application was successful and he immediately obtained employment as a pilot flying on U.S. Forest Service operations.

In 1967 he was successful in an appeal to reinstate his Canadian medical and was hired as base manager at Dawson Creek, B.C. on a contract for the B.C. Forest Service. Chris returned to the B.C. coast in 1971 as a pilot for Air West Airlines, and in 1978 he became Chief Pilot for a corporate aviation department.

In 1980 he became an instructor for an Air Cadet Squadron at Abbotsford, B.C. and in 1982 he was promoted to Captain and became the Commanding Officer. In 1983 he founded a flight scholarship program that eventually gave sixty-five teens an Ultra Light Pilot licence.

In 1984 an economic slowdown resulted in the closure of the flight department that employed Christopher and he subsequently was hired as Chief Pilot and Operations Manager for a First Nations airline operating Navajo, Beech 99 and D.C.-3 aircraft. In 1987 he joined Airlift Canada as Chief Pilot IFR and flew charters throughout North America.

In 1991 Chris returned to support the Air Cadet movement, serving for three summers at C.F.B. Penhold, Alberta as a tow plane officer pilot on the cadet glider program.

At this time Chris became aware of plans to permanently close the military base at Jericho Beach in Vancouver. Chris contacted the Chief of Staff B.C. District with respect to writing a history of the long-

More about the Author

standing military presence at Jericho Beach. Captain Christopher Weicht was appointed Special Projects Officer and dispatched to Ottawa to carry out preliminary research. Chris received substantial support from both Air Command and Land Forces Western Region.

In 1997 Jericho Beach and the West Coast Flying Boat Stations was published and was an instant success with over 5,000 copies printed. In 1999 Air Command honored Chris by appointing him Associate Air Force Historian.

In 1995 at age sixty Chris allowed his instrument flight rating to lapse but took a position in the Queen Charlotte Islands flying a deHavilland Beaver in support of logging activities. In 2002 at age 67 he retired from commercial aviation with over 17,000 hours of flight time.

On September 27, 2002 he celebrated the 50th anniversary of his first solo by a flight above the Coast Mountains.

Ordering Information for

North by Northwest

_____ Copies of *North by Northwest*
@ **$41.95 each**   _____
plus **$7.00 for shipping**   _____

and/or

_____ Copies of *Jericho Beach and the*
West Coast Flying Boat Stations
@ **$39.95 each**   _____
plus **$7.00 for shipping**   _____

Total   _____

_____ Have my books signed by Chris Weicht
Please make cheque or money order (no credit cards) payable to:

Creekside Publications
846 Joe Road, RR #26
Roberts Creek, BC
Canada V0N 2W6

Name_____

Street_____

City_____Province/State_____

Postal Code/Zip_____Country_____

Telephone _____Fax_____email address_____